Also by Sonja Southwell
(jointly with Ian Southwell)

Safely Led to Serve: A Joint Biography
Published by Balboa Press; Bloomington, IN47403, USA; 2017.
www.balboapress.com.au

A SAFE ARRIVAL

SONJA SOUTHWELL

BALBOA.
PRESS

A DIVISION OF HAY HOUSE

Contents

Foreword ix
Preface.. xiii
Acknowledgements xv
Illustration Acknowledgements.. xix

Chapter 1   Ryer's early life..1
Chapter 2   Jo's background 18
Chapter 3   Time for decisions 33
Chapter 4   Netherlands East Indies before the war 43
Chapter 5   Malang and De Wijk.................................54
Chapter 6   Solo and Banyu Biru 86
Chapter 7   Freedom gained, lost, regained.............. 121
Chapter 8   Ryer in Tarakan 138
Chapter 9   Ryer in Borneo 159
Chapter 10   After Liberation: In Australia and Holland 177
Chapter 11   Indonesia after WWII 1946–1949 199
Chapter 12   Indonesia after Independence 1950–1953.................221
Chapter 13   A safe arrival 235
Chapter 14   The onward journey...............................248

Endnotes..263
Glossary of Terms and Abbreviations.............................277
Bibliography 283
    Published works 283
    Unpublished works..286

Foreword

Give sorrow words;
The grief that does not speak
Knits up the o'er wrought heart
And bids it break.

That truth, as old as mankind, was written down in the early 17th century by William Shakespeare.

Another well-meant piece of advice, given to me by my beloved high school biology teacher, Roelof Horrëus de Haas (with whom I had kept in contact) in the early 1980s: 'Joost, if you don't write it down, it has never happened...'

Both statements are so appropriate in this case.

What a wonderful job Sonja has done in writing *A Safe Arrival*. This is a precious little monument for all those inmates of the Japanese concentration camps in Indonesia during WWII. A monument for those who died, and for those who survived but did not let themselves be walked all over as if they were dead and buried.

And even more a monument for all those brave Salvation Army members who were so important in daily camp life. They became our 'secret army'. In general they were modest but most effective. These 'servants' did their marvellous and difficult job, kept smiling, held several important positions, and spread their consoling and optimistic messages day after day, month after month, year after year. The Salvation Army was already operating among all those living in Indonesia before the war and never let us down during those dark years after the Japanese invasion.

Since I was an inmate of Banyu Biru 10 months before the Van Kralingen family arrived, I found so many recognisable stories in her book. Banyu Biru 10 was, in my opinion, one of the worst camps after the infamous Tjideng camp in Batavia.

The high walls of Banyu Biru 10 were so threatening for those who spent all those years behind them. It even influenced the Japanese military and Javanese guards who had 'to look after us'. They were cruel, untrustworthy, calculating, and manifested any bad habit you can think of. But all those mothers and children who were prisoners there stood their ground. Those who died lie buried together at Kalibanteng cemetery in Semarang. One of these was little three-year-old Letje Lopez Cardozo who, I think, was the first victim to die in Banyu Biru 10 on 25 May 1944. She was our little neighbour in Block III, ward 15.

My family and 400 other mothers and children were so fortunate to be able and allowed to leave this hell and reach Banyu Biru 11, 500 metres south of Banyu Biru 10, with unhindered sight of Mount Baldhead. Its picture (see page 112), taken in 1986, brought me to Sonja who had the same good memories about him.

Thank you Sonja for all your effort to find me in the Netherlands! Your book is a gift, especially because it is written in English. As far as I know it is the first to give English-speaking people all over the world such a detailed and heart-warming story of you and your family.

Joost van Bodegom
Beetsterzwaag, Friesland, The Netherlands, 26 November 2017

Joost van Bodegom was born in 1936. A former prisoner of Galoehan, Banyu Biru 10 and 11; camp announcer in Banyu Biru 11, he was evacuated from Banyu Biru 11, 26 November 1945. He was Chairman of the 'Remembrance Foundation on 15 August 1945' (The Netherlands) from September 2005 until September 2010.

'God has not promised us a calm journey, but a safe arrival.'

Preface

For as many years as I can remember since World War II, my parents had a plaque on the wall of their living room. It depicted a ship on a stormy sea, with the words, in Dutch, *'God heeft ons geen kalme reis beloofd, maar wel een behouden aankomst.'* The meaning: 'God has not promised us a calm journey, but a safe arrival.' Eventually the plaque came to me, and now adorns my office wall.

Knowing what my parents, sister and I experienced during those war years and subsequently, I cannot help but think how appropriate that message is. My parents experienced many storms from their early lives in the Netherlands through to the period in the Netherlands East Indies, internment and separation during the war, repatriation to Australia, time in Holland, and a return to Indonesia before finally settling in Australia. They were confident that God was with them, guiding and protecting.

For many years I felt that this story needed to be told, especially as I listened to my father in the 1960s and secured his debriefing report plus related data from the Netherlands Institute of War Documentation in 2004–2005. The demands of busy appointments around the world as a Salvation Army officer myself, made it impossible for me to do so until the last 10 years.

This book has been very much a family project. I am particularly grateful to our eldest daughter, Sharon, for recording and then transcribing so much of the material in the early chapters of this book. She has also carefully reviewed the changes I have made and added many helpful suggestions, rationalising the multiple references and particularly collaborating for the final presentation. Her husband, Greg Restall, has provided clarifying maps of Java and Borneo. Our second daughter, Jenni, made most helpful suggestions for the back cover and advertising content. Third daughter Cathy with her family, have also contributed toward production. Stephanie Elkington, our granddaughter, has used her skills in photography and graphic design to modernise the image of the original plaque for the cover of this book. My sister, Joan Stolk, who participated in many of the events outlined, has checked the contents to the best of her ability. Ian, my husband and a constant source of encouragement, has assisted in editing many drafts of the script and compiling a glossary of terms which appears at the back of this volume. Other resource persons and organisations are acknowledged separately.

My prayer is that this book will encourage and inspire readers to trust God's guidance and protection in their own lives so that they, too, may experience *a safe arrival*.

Sonja Southwell, Lieut-Colonel
Melbourne, Australia; February 2018

Acknowledgements

As well as the support of family members as mentioned in the preface, I am grateful to a number of other people and organisations that have assisted my research and supported the development of this book.

I want to acknowledge Lindsay Cox, the Territorial Archivist at The Salvation Army Australia Southern Territory Archives and Museum in Melbourne. Lindsay and his team, including Major Donna Bryan, Dorothy Skewes and George Ellis, provided copies of my parents' officer career cards together with photographs and articles about their service from the Australian editions of *The War Cry*.

Tara Knower, the Assistant Archivist, and Ruth Macdonald, the Acting Archivist, from the International Heritage Centre, William Booth College in the United Kingdom and Republic of Ireland Territory, kindly provided me with the obituary and other career details of Commissioner Charles Durman who was most significant in welcoming our family to Australia to work among Dutch migrants.

I am grateful to The General of The Salvation Army for permission to reproduce copyright material of The Salvation Army.

The staff at the Netherland Instituut voor Oorlogsdocumentatie (NIOD, Netherlands Institute of War Documentation) led by René Kruis, Coordinator of Research, were so helpful during visits my husband and I made in 2004 and 2005. They provided maps, photographs and diagrams of Banyu Biru 10 POW camp, and to my great surprise, my father's debriefing report after his evacuation from

Borneo to Australia in 1945. René van Heijningen of NIOD has also been an ongoing support through internet contact.

I am particularly grateful to a number of readers who have reviewed the material and made helpful comments, including Howard Dick, economic historian and internationally known Indonesia specialist, who took time from his work as Professorial Fellow at the University of Melbourne to look over the manuscript.

Similarly, Commissioner John H. Clinch who served as an International Secretary for South Pacific and East Asia and as Territorial Commander in Australia Southern Territory, read the manuscript in detail. John and his wife, Beth Clinch, were soldiers of the Fairfield Corps and accepted candidates for officership when our family arrived in Australia in 1953 and were inspired by the stories my parents told of their adventures in Indonesia.

Commissioner Hans van Vliet, currently the Territorial Commander for The Salvation Army in the Netherlands, Czech Republic and Slovakia Territory, made time amid his busy schedule to read through and comment on the manuscript.

Joost van Bodegom, photographer and historian from the Netherlands, also read and reviewed the manuscript thoroughly. He suggested a number of modifications from his experiences as a prisoner of war in Java, before supplying the wonderful foreword to this book. We shared so many experiences in common.

Most recently, Mr Tim Gellel, Head, Australian Army History Unit at the Australian War Memorial in Canberra has indicated official approval for me to insert a significant page from the War Diary of the 2/31st Battalion in this book.

I am deeply grateful to my friend, Dawn Volz, of Ringwood Corps and the Literary Department of The Salvation Army in Australia, who undertook extensive reviews of the manuscript, and checked the final proofs.

Similarly, I am grateful to the publishing consultants, the content evaluator, designers and other members of the team at Balboa Press for their patience with the material, resulting in the production of an attractive volume.

Sonja Southwell, Lieut-Colonel
Melbourne, Australia; February 2018

Illustration Acknowledgements

Cover Photograph and Design:

© *A Safe Arrival* inspired by wall-plaque design (1930s): Stephanie Elkington (2017)

Author Photograph (back cover and page 289):

© 2006 Photography courtesy of Tony Isbitt, Bromley, Kent, UK, used by his permission (December 2017)

Other Photographs:

Most were taken by the author's relatives, friends and colleagues. Others are part of the author's personal collection with known sources for specific photos noted as follows:

Photo of wall plaque in author's office (see page xii) by Ian Southwell.

Sketch map of Java showing the most significant places in this story, (see page 110) © Greg Restall 2017, son-in-law of the author, used with his permission.

Sketch map of Borneo showing the most significant locations mentioned in Chapters 8 and 9 (see page 114) © Greg Restall 2017, son-in-law of the author, used with his permission.

The view of Gunung Boctak (Mount Baldhead) in the foothills of Mount Telomoyo, near Banyu Biru (often written Banjoebiroe in documents) 10 POW Camp, which the author remembers (see page 112). Photograph taken by Joost van Bodegom, 1986, and used with his permission.

An aerial view of Banyu Biru 10 POW Camp (see page 112) comes from Fotoarchief ML-KNIL, 28 January 1945 and taken from Van Dulm, J.; Krijgsveld, W.J.; Legemaate, H.J.; Liesker, H.A.M.; Weijers, G.; and Braches, E.: *Geïllustreerde Atlas van de Japanse Kampen in Nederlands-Indië 1942–1945*, Asia Maior, Purmerend, 2000, p. 150. (Material supplied to author by the Netherlands Institute of War Documentation in 2004–05. According to the Netherlands Chamber of Commerce, Asia Maior in the Netherlands ceased operating in July 2017.

The threatening, yet ultimately protective, walls of Banyu Biru 10 (BB10) as at 1986 (see page 113). Photograph taken by Joost van Bodegom, 1986, and used with his permission.

The copy of the page from the Australian War Memorial, War Diaries, 2 /31st Battalion, https://www.awm.gov.au/collection/U56074 https://www.awm.gov.au/collection/C1368285 (see page 116) used with permission of the Commonwealth of Australia.

Jo (extreme left) and Ryer (extreme right in adult group) with Dutch immigrants to Australia who participated in a Salvation Army Congress meeting in the Melbourne Exhibition Building in 1954 (see page 119). Taken from *The War Cry* (Australia) August 1954, used with permission of the Territorial Archives and Museum (November 2017).

Jo (left front) and her wartime colleague and companion, Mrs Brigadier Marie Luitjes (right front), at a 1969 reunion of those who trained as Salvation Army officers together in Holland in 1930 (see page 120). Taken by Foto Muis, Velp, Hooldstradt 220, The Netherlands, in 1969. (According to the Netherlands Chamber of Commerce, Foto Muis ceased operating in 2002.)

CHAPTER 1

Ryer's early life

Ryer Leendert van Kralingen, my father, was born on 17 November 1904 to Arie and Jacoba van Kralingen in the town of Vlaardingen, the Netherlands. His first name was variously spelt Rijer, Rey and Ryer. Rijer Leendert van Kralingen was the name registered at birth and used on his marriage certificate. In this book I have used 'Ryer', the name by which he was eventually known in The Salvation Army in Australia. At home my mother usually called him 'Rey', pronounced 'Ray' in English.

Grandfather Arie van Kralingen was born in the town of Spijkenisse in 1861, in the province of Zeeland. It was here in about 1773 that the name Ryer van Kralingen began to appear in church baptismal registers.

Arie married Margarietha 't Hart[a] on an unknown date. Sadly, Margarietha died in 1885, not long after giving birth to a daughter, Abra.

At the age of 25 years, Arie married again, this time to Jacoba Vermaas, on 11 August 1887. The bride was 21 years of age. For reasons unknown, the young couple left home and family to make their new home in the fishing village of Vlaardingen. Could it be that Arie, who was a carpenter like his father and brothers, was looking for better work prospects in a village where a large part of the population was employed by the fishing trade? Jacoba bore Arie 17 children; Ryer was her second youngest child.

---

[a] Short for *Het Hart* (or The Hart)

A difficult start

The Van Kralingen family register reflects that a number of children from this second marriage died before their first birthday. Infant mortality was high and there were many illnesses that could be fatal for small children, alongside the ever-present risk of childhood accidents. One child ran in front of a horse and cart and was killed, for instance. Of Jacoba's 17 children perhaps fewer than eight lived to become adults. Cootje, named after Jacoba, was born after Ryer. He was most protective of her when she grew up. The deaths of various siblings at birth and early childhood caused a significant age gap between Ryer and his older siblings.

Ryer was four months old when his half-sister, Abra, married at age 20. When he was still a child, his older brothers lived in a man's world, working and already looking for marriage partners. It was not uncommon then for boys in large families to commence work before the end of primary school. The gap of 10 or more years between Ryer and his older brothers and sisters may well have been the reason he did not fit into their company or forge a sense of belonging to his older siblings. There were other contributors as well. He was a sensitive, quiet child; perhaps his withdrawal was his response to the harsh voice and hard hands of his father. Quite early he was the focus of criticisms such as, 'He is utterly useless for the life of a carpenter.' And such a criticism could only sting because his father, Arie, was an excellent carpenter and expected his sons to join him in his trade. At least two other brothers had done so already and were working with him.

Unfortunately for Ryer, Arie was right. Throughout his life, Ryer struggled with all woodwork and anything mechanical. I remember that he had a wonderful array of tools in his shed, and he knew the use of each tool, but he could not hit a nail straight in the wall. My mother was desperate sometimes. If he was going to knock a nail into something, he might use six nails where one was required, and none of them went in straight. Nor could he start the lawn mower. I still recall Mum standing by the kitchen window on a Saturday, grass cutting day, watching the scene outside, hands on her face: 'Please God help him get the thing started!' Anxious moments would pass as he tinkered with the starter, face tense, before a moment of relief when the mower rumbled and sprang to life as the engine engaged. Mum would sigh with relief and followed that with a prayer, 'Oh, thank you, Lord. Now keep it going till he has finished!'

Being different in this way as a child may not only have alienated him from the men in the family but would have been a personal humiliation. It was perhaps due to a sensitive disposition and the tension in the home that Ryer suffered with indigestion and stomach pains. The potions and powders prescribed by the local doctor did little to relieve his discomfort. One effect of this was that he missed a lot of schooling and opportunities for formal education, although he was alert and quick to learn. His frequent illnesses drew comments from his brothers such as, 'Is Mother's boy staying home again?' They were many years older than him, of course, so these comments affected him deeply and were one more source of tension. As he grew older he also resented these remarks and they caused him to withdraw from family gatherings. The doctor told his mother that he had stomach ulcers. This was the most obvious diagnosis and there was probably some truth to it, but I suspect that there was more going on. When I look at his childhood, I can see he lived on the edge of his nerves, already introverted but becoming increasingly withdrawn, and this was affecting his health.

Hopeful seeds

In Ryer's story, as is often the case in our places of pain, it was alongside these difficulties that other more hopeful seeds were planted.

I can imagine Jacoba's concern for this child. She was at an age where she thought she wouldn't have any more children. He was precious; another boy at a time when that mattered. And this lad was different. He had a different temperament to the others. He was a 'loner' and sensitive to criticism. Even as a little boy, when there were arguments with his brothers or when his father became angry, he would leave and hide. With Arie's fiery temper and a household of teenagers, there were frequently raised and angry voices in the home. At times like this Jacoba drew the young ones aside into her domain, the kitchen or the parlour. And it was there that she began to engage Ryer within the household when he was not well and could not go to school. Like a proper Dutch housewife she showed him how to care for linoleum floors, clean windows and the daily task of peeling potatoes—an important staple food of the Dutch family. Of course, there were always boots and shoes to be cleaned on Saturday so the family would look their Sunday-best when attending the local Reformed Church. During those early years at home, through her actions, his mother laid foundations of compassion and caring for all things vulnerable.

It was also in his early teenage years that Ryer found himself drawn to the shipyards and the waterfront at Vlaardingen, on the north bank of the New Maas / New Waterway River where it meets the Old Maas or Meuse, which rises in France and travels through Belgium and Holland before flowing into the North Sea at Vlaardingen. Vlaardingen remains Holland's traditional herring town and it had the largest herring fleet in Holland. There is an abundance of herring in the North Sea and boats from Vlaardingen don't have far to go to gather the 'silver from the sea', as herring is called.

In Ryer's early teens, especially on days when his father and brothers were at home and he felt the pressure of their jibes, he would put on his jacket and cap, and regardless of the weather, head out. He would walk towards the shipyards. The attraction of the boats and the distant sound of the waves and the taste of salt on his lips were part of his life yet never lost their attraction. I imagine that sometimes his walk became a run to the harbour, to escape the tension of home. He described to me later how on these occasions he would watch the men mend nets. He had gotten to know some of the ships, their names and some of the men aboard. It was a small community. He watched them at work and listened to their banter. He could never get enough of seeing this scene as he walked from one ship to the other. There was a strong smell of tar and, as always, a breeze came across the water and he could smell the sea. Ryer breathed in great gulps of fresh air, enjoying the endless horizon. Where would it end? It was here he dreamed about distant horizons, listening to the sound of waves coming in and out—in and out, where the waters of the harbour met the open sea. The sea stretched on and on in the distance. There were shadows of islands. Maybe they were where his grandfather had lived. Perhaps they were in Zeeland. Imagine sailing out to Belgium and France and to the United Kingdom, places the seamen took their ships every year.

November made its presence felt each year through icy winds and ominous grey skies, reminders that winter was not far way. It was also the start of the herring fishing season. The old harbour in Vlaardingen was a frequent beehive of activity for some weeks as men prepared vessels and equipment for their journeys. Some of the crew would expect to be away from home for up to three months. Much of their time would be on the unpredictable waters of the North Sea and along the east and south coasts of England and Belgium. In the month he turned 15, Ryer was at the waterfront to see the herring fleet sail off. He knew some of the men and their families. People gathered near the waterfront to farewell their loved ones: husbands, fathers, brothers and sweethearts. People were rugged up in heavy coats and shawls. Others had earmuffs and knitted beanies as a protection against the cold wind.

Ryer's frequent escapes to the waterfront, the sea and its distant horizon shaped his still unformed and unnamed hopes for his future. It was on one of these occasions that it occurred to him how different he was from his older siblings. He wanted to do something else and it was not carpentry. 'I want to get out; I want to do what these men are doing, fishing and seeing the world!' He knew little of the dangers but he did know that he wanted to get away. How do you express that when you are 15 years of age?

The fishing industry shaped much of the life of Vlaardingen, including the employment opportunities for men who stayed on land. In the 19th century, the fleets would go out to the North Sea during the three coldest months in the year to keep their catch cold before the days of refrigeration. Early in the 20th century there were changes in the types of boats and equipment for catching fish that enabled boats to be out fishing for longer periods. This was a gradual process though and many fishermen were still with companies that went out for only three months. This meant that they had time on their hands and no income out of season. Town and provincial governments recognised this and felt the need to provide employment so that men were able to stay in the area. One such initiative was the Hollandia Factory, which included many different industries such as carpentry, cheese-making and sugar beet refining. The factory provided seasonal employment for fishermen, who could be absorbed back into roles when they returned from the ships. The factory also provided a place for young men to commence a trade.

So, when Ryer was 15 he began work at the Hollandia Factory. His father and brothers were already there as carpenters. Much to his father's disapproval, Ryer was employed in the sugar refinery on the top floor. Apparently, the refinery needed to be at that elevation because the liquid sugar extract needed to fall a distance as part of the cooling and crystallising process.

It was here at the Hollandia Factory that Ryer van Kralingen met Jan van Kapel. In some ways they were very different men, but underneath those differences there were commonalities that drew them together. One more obvious difference was their religious backgrounds. Ryer and his family attended the Reformed Church, but that was the extent of their commitment. Ryer had no understanding or belief at this stage. By contrast, Jan attended the newly established Salvation Army regularly. He was a deep thinker, whose father in particular had given him a strong foundation of Christian faith. Jan was the eldest in a family of five children; his father died at the age of 39 when Jan was 14. Ryer was the youngest son of a large family, but he felt isolated. Both of them were introverts and able to be alone, but each was lonely for male company of the sort they did not have, with someone their own age. They both carried burdens. Jan was the carer of his family, after his father died. As a teenager, to make ends meet, he had odd jobs such as selling kerosene. People did not have gas laid on then in their homes. Instead, they used kerosene burners of various sizes, buying the fuel from people who sold it on the street or door to door. While Ryer's early burden was that of isolation, he was also the child who looked after his parents when the older siblings had left home. They were born in the same year, Jan in February and Ryer in November, and being the two youngest men in a factory of adult male employees it may have felt quite natural for them to become company for each other. From that beginning they forged a friendship that lasted a lifetime.

On 2 February 1971, a day after Ryer died, Jan, my mother's eldest brother, wrote to her. 'You know, Jo, I knew him a lot earlier than you, because of our joint employment in the sugar refinery in the Hollandia Factory. I saw again that thin figure, in a striped jumper and blue trousers, racing down the stairs, calling, "Refinery!" thereby indicating to those employed by the different machines what product was coming down and at what stage the sugar was. And this will probably not make much sense to those who have never been in a refinery.'[1]

In a letter to me on 13 June 1971, Jan mentioned how Ryer looked 'bone thin and sharp-nosed'. I have never known him to look sharp-nosed, but I can imagine why he was so thin in his face and body: he was so wound up in himself and still suffering stomach problems that he looked undernourished, all arms and legs. Adding more to that picture of those early days when he and Ryer were such close friends, Jan continued:

> Both of us worked at the sugar refinery, Hollandia. Your father was set to work in the cooking vessels department, a boiling hot area, and I was in the smithy. I often had to go to your father's department for repairs. I can still see him running, an almost emaciated figure with striped jumper, short sleeves, blue trousers and a sweating face, calling down the stairs 'Refinery!'—or a word used for partially

rcfincd raw brown sugar. One thing will seem strange to you, so here's the explanation. As I mentioned before, your father worked in 'the cooking pans', in the very tropical attic of the factory. I mean the sixth floor. On that floor were huge kettles or cooking pans which extracted the sugar from its source, sugar beet, at high temperatures and a vacuum process, and turned it into syrup. The product at end of this process was then conveyed downwards with the aforementioned shout, which was your father's job. I already mentioned he did not have an ounce of fat on his body, because of the unbelievable temperatures. In those days your grandfather, Arie van Kralingen, was also there as chief carpenter, small in stature, with a bearded face and a pair of eyes…!! In short, an appearance to cause children to escape into bed, all the more since he was very short tempered. So much so that I once saw the head of the factory flee before the axe of the chief carpenter. I can tell you many more funny things, but I'll run out of paper. [2]

The turning point

In the year Ryer started work at the factory Jacoba sensed that his condition was getting worse. He struggled with diarrhoea and vomiting. Today we might say that he was under stress, and that he felt rejected, a no-hoper. These were certainly ideas about himself that he carried all his life in many ways. Today we might even say that this young man was depressed. That was not a term Jacoba knew though, or that her doctor might have used. Anxious for his health and future and sensing an increasing restlessness in Ryer, she decided to visit the family doctor alone. Arie was at work so she could go without anyone knowing.

A bright ray of sunshine found its way through the small kitchen window and began its unhurried journey across the wall. The ray of light jumped across a line-up of spoons and ladles hanging above the kitchen range, like fingers on a keyboard, and beamed its warm glow onto a large enamel pot on the stove and onto the work bench.

A small, silent miracle was taking place—it was spring! But this small spring wonder passed unnoticed by the young man who was washing the kitchen floor, his final chore for the day. After putting away the cleaning cloths and bucket, he stepped back into the kitchen and found it transformed by the sunlight. His face lit up—the sky was blue, no clouds in sight! After the weeks of grey skies, rain, snow and fog and cold winds, spring had come! Sunshine! This was worth a celebration.

He remembered his mother's words as she left to see the doctor, 'When you've finished your chores, Ryer, leave the house and enjoy the sunshine and fresh air. See you for dinner tonight. Bye.'

Yes, he would! A quick mental check: range cleaned and ashes removed, ready to be lit. Done! Floor cleaned and polished. Done! Potatoes, peeled and on the stove. Done! Finished! Yes, now was the time to go.

He picked up his jacket, cap and scarf in the passageway on his way out into the cobbled street. A soft, southerly wind was blowing warm air from the Mediterranean. Enthusiastic housewives had strung their washing lines across the narrow street; large white sheets billowed between the houses like sails on a ship.

He breathed in the fresh air. Off to the waterfront to see if there were any sailing ships. He walked hands in pockets. Blue sky and sunshine had brought people out of their homes. Some he recognised. He nodded and touched his cap as he passed by. His steps quickened. At the end of the road was the Fish Market, always a beehive of activity. If you wanted to make an arrangement to meet a friend it would be, 'See you at the Fish Market'. It was one of Ryer's favourite places.

But Ryer's most favourite place was the centre of the town of Vlaardingen, situated on the west side of the old harbour with its great variety of boats docked along the harbour wall. Breathing deeply, he caught a whiff of the salty sea air. Ryer never grew tired of watching fishermen at work on their boats.

Meanwhile, Jacoba walked to Dr Jensen's waiting room. She had known him for many years. How long? It was difficult to remember.

He seemed to have always been there. He was now quite elderly and like a trusted friend. There wasn't much that he didn't know about the household. Sometimes she had just sat with him and talked, and felt better when she left the surgery.

And again today, she felt a need to talk about her youngest son, Ryer. He would be 16 by the end of the year. He was so thin, so pale, and his constant stomach problems made it difficult for him to eat much food. The stomach powders didn't help him either. He didn't mix easily with other people. He was quiet, withdrawn. He had started at the Hollandia Factory but his condition had not improved. She worried. Dr Jensen did not appear to be too busy. She was ushered into his room and sat down.

Having heard snippets of this story from Ryer, I imagine the discussion between his mother and Dr Jensen may have been as follows.

'And what can I do for you, Jacoba?' he asked in his calm and gentle way. Just looking at her face, he knew what the problem would be.

'Well, Doctor, I'm here again for Ryer, of course. Spring is here and he is really not much better. Restless would be a word to describe him.'

Dr Jensen looked at Ryer's medical record. It was a big bundle of record cards. Many of his complaints were repeats of the same thing. Stomach troubles! Endless potions and powders hadn't really worked very well, and he noted that this year, in November, he would be 16 years of age. He wondered if today would be the day when he would have to tell her and perhaps suggest a drastic change. He could think of no alternative route.

Jacoba looked at him expectantly. 'You know,' she said, 'it's not that he's weak. While he's been at home so often, he's been a tremendous help to me. He's strong, he can lift things. He does the floors for me without any complaint. He does them better than I do. He's so thorough. You should see him peel potatoes. At the speed of lightning, he can do them now.'

Dr Jensen smiled, 'Well, when you had 17 children that would have been useful, wouldn't it? It would take a long time to peel potatoes for that many.' They laughed. It was good to see her laugh.

'It's not that he can't do things but that he does not want to be a carpenter,' she said. 'He wants to go to sea. I can understand that. He thinks differently about things.'

'Jacoba, unless we try something else, and it is just a trial, I think you need to understand that Ryer...I can't see him getting old bones... Do you understand what I'm saying by that?'

'You mean, he won't have a long life?'

'Not if he stays the way he is. I agree with you. He should be working with other men. He should be engaged in activity. So, I'm going to suggest something. You may want to talk it over with Arie. I think he should take the drastic step of going to sea with the fishing fleet. It's not unusual for them to take a teenager. Not at all! There are lots of chores on the ships to be done while they learn the trade of being a fisherman. I believe the sea air, the lifestyle...it's tough, but I think he could do it, don't you?'

'You mean, to leave home and work with those tough, strong men?'

'Yes, as you say, he's not weak, and you could try three...six months. Give it a trial. Why not? Talk it over with Arie. Perhaps he needs to hear from you that Ryer does not want to be a carpenter and that here's another option. How about it?'

She nodded slowly, the possibility forming in her mind. 'Yes, yes, you may have something there. I'll speak to Arie tonight and I think he'll know a way through. And if he accepts it, I'll talk to Ryer. Thank you,' she said. 'Yes, thank you. We can try that.'

Dr Jensen was a perceptive man. He knew the story behind the story. And his perceptions of Ryer's condition proved to be correct, although he did not verbalise this to Jacoba. Somehow, he sensed that she understood what he was trying to convey. Dr Jensen knew the crew master; he was known as a tough but compassionate man. I wonder if he had a visit from the doctor that evening.

Jacoba left Dr Jensen that day with a lighter step than she'd had for a long time. She walked home, believing that a change was coming in the right direction.

That evening Jacoba and Arie sat together when she gave him the doctor's report. Arie was quiet for some time, staring into space. Jacoba watched her husband's face; his silence surprised her. Ryer was an important son to him, but he was different, and this family found it hard to tolerate difference. 'The fleet goes out in November and he would barely be 16 years then,' she said.

He nodded his head slowly, 'I know!'

She tried to interpret the look in his eyes. Was it pain, fear...? 'I will see the crew master tomorrow and discuss the matter with him. He may have a solution...a vacancy. Don't say anything to Ryer about it or about your visit to the doctor: plenty of time for that later.' Jacoba nodded her head. Tomorrow was going to be a long day!

When Ryer came home the next day his father called him into the family room. Knowing his father, Ryer was immediately on guard, but on this occasion his fears were proven wrong. Arie said, 'You know son, we are concerned about you. Is there something else you want to do with your life? You like to be at the shipyard, with the boats; are you more interested in something like that? Would you like to go to sea?' Ryer couldn't believe it. Before he could say anything, Arie added, 'If you want to, I can arrange it for you.'

That clinched it. He needed to return to the factory for a time, but in the year Ryer turned 16, he went out with the herring fleet.

This is how Dad described it to me many years later. He could see that his mother would have made the suggestion, but what moved Dad most was that his father 'listened and was concerned'. To him, perhaps, it was a small indication that Arie did care about him. 'Perhaps all his abuse to me was to get me going in the direction he hoped for me. He didn't understand that people are different.' Arie had probably thought he could teach Ryer his profession of carpentry, but that for some inexplicable reason he wasn't interested. Why wasn't he interested? Because Ryer was actually unsuited to it! Although Arie himself was from a large family, and every child was different in their own way, it seems it was only on this day that Arie grasped this and saw a way forward. In those days, as long as you had work, whatever it was, that was what mattered.

Going to sea

Life changed for Ryer. He was taken on as a deckhand, to help with the cleaning. This was the way young men entered the trade. He was teased, of course, for being young and skinny, but the captain of the boat knew why he was there; he was a good man and he kept an eye out for Ryer. He knew that the young men who were starting out needed extra care; seafaring was an extremely tough life. Ryer had to work; there was little time to think and even less to be sick. You either ate or didn't; that was up to you, but you were in the herring business and you had to work. He was in the company of men and it made a man of him.

He made good. Ryer may have been a shy and withdrawn child, but this did not hold him back in this new life. Here he slowly came into his own. He had learnt about language and humour at home. Years later, when he got together with the Van Kralingen brothers, in particular, they shared a great sense of humour, and very clever word play with the idioms of the Dutch language and the way it varies from province to province. Another layer of word play was added when he went to sea. I recall him talking with great humour and much laughter about the diversity of provincial Dutch idioms and the play on words he learned as he visited different islands as a seaman. This capacity for humour he developed on the boats would later stand him in good stead in his work with military personnel, where he proved himself to be a man who could get along well with men.

In addition to a capacity for humour, though, Ryer also discovered a capacity for violence, fuelled by years of compressed rage. There were some incidents where he let fly, even after he had been at sea a while and had become one of the crew. It was not unusual for men to disagree with each other or for tensions to arise. One particular person questioned how Ryer was accepted on board at such a young age. 'What are you doing here? I don't know about this boy. Aren't you supposed to be home with Mother?' These comments reminded Ryer of what his brothers used to say to him at home. The man kept it up with the occasional barb of this sort until one day in anger Ryer summoned all his strength and grabbed him by his trousers and shirt and dropped him overboard. The moment he released the man he realised what he had done.

No-one could swim. Ryer couldn't swim either. There was an immediate uproar: 'Man overboard!' The whole crew was alerted. The captain arrived and Ryer confessed, 'Yes, I threw him overboard.' It could have ended in disaster. Instead, the captain told Ryer, 'Go to my room!'

A lifebuoy was thrown overboard and the man was quickly pulled out of the cold water and taken care of.

The captain was aware the man had been goading Ryer, the young lad, for some time. All that the captain said to Ryer was that he had to learn to control his anger or he might never be on a boat again. 'It's been dealt with; apologise, and then it's over.' So Ryer found the man and apologised, and that cleared the air. The captain was in control; he kept an eye on the young ones. Ryer never learned what the captain said to the other man, but he was never provoked in that manner again. The man involved was not on the ship the next journey.

This was an important 'growing up' experience; it was one Dad told me to illustrate how some of that long pent-up anger came out.

The return

There was a distinct difference in Ryer when he came home after his first trip away. His health problems were gone. He had put on weight. The tension was gone. He had a sense of worth. When he came home for his breaks he lived at home, but no longer under pressure from his father or brothers. He was saddened, however, to learn Dr Jensen had died six weeks after his departure.

Ryer was a carer; foundations of care were probably demonstrated by Jacoba his mother, but caring came naturally to Ryer; it was a gift.

In those days, people lived hard lives and in their 50s his parents were elderly. So, when Ryer was home he supported them by doing the things Jacoba had taught him, the household tasks that none of the other brothers did. Ryer told me, 'I'd leave home at 6:00am in the morning for the factory; by that time I'd done all the floors in the kitchen, peeled the potatoes for the day, and got all the food ready on the stove.' He didn't do the cooking, but he did the heavy work and left things ready for his mother.

So, for some years he had a steady income at the factory and at sea. Then later, as the ships and fisheries arrangements changed with refrigeration on the ships for the catch, he began to do longer trips away and throughout the year. Of course, these longer stints away from home meant he was away for longer periods from his aging parents. Fortunately, the Van Kralingen family lived in Vlaardingen, so there were people around to offer help when needed. Even then, fishermen did not spend 12 months away. They probably had times at home while another crew went out. This would have been particularly important for the married men with families. It is possible that during those periods at home Ryer returned for shorter periods to the factory. Whatever the balance of his employment, his Salvation Army record states that when he entered training to become a Salvation Army officer his profession was 'full-time fisherman'.

Meanwhile, Ryer continued to develop a sense of self. He enjoyed the camaraderie between fishermen and was known as a good worker. His health problems were behind him. He discovered the joys of being free. Ryer journeyed with the fishing crew along the eastern coast of England across the Channel and to Belgium. On the journeys to the coastal townships of Europe and England, he was introduced to the world of entertainment and learned to smoke and drink beer. He was also a favourite with the girls on the dance floor. The life of a seaman was tough and demanding, but he enjoyed the freedom of the journey across the seas.

The Salvation Army

Over these years, Ryer's friendship with Jan van Kapel continued. It seems that a very significant bond of friendship had been formed. When Ryer was in town they met regularly. And when they got together, Ryer would tell of his adventures and Jan would marvel at the change in his friend.

It was Jan who eventually invited Ryer to The Salvation Army. One weekend when Ryer was short of something else to do, Jan suggested he come with him to The Salvation Army, a newly commenced church. Jan described the Sunday night service as quite hilarious and a lot of entertainment. 'Most of the fellows here in Vlaardingen go there on Sunday evenings. There is no other entertainment in town on the Sunday.' So somewhat reluctantly Ryer attended the night service and it gradually became a regular part of his life. There was something there that drew him back every Sunday.

I think that at first Ryer was overwhelmed by the experience. The Salvation Army was very new at that time, having commenced in Vlaardingen in 1906, and it was most unlike the traditional services of the Dutch Reformed Church. In addition to that, Ryer had no contact with any other Christian fellowship. He knew the basics. He would have been baptised as an infant and received teachings of the Christian faith at his church as a teenager. Yet rarely a word about church or faith was spoken in his home or in conversation.

By comparison, Jan understood everything that was going on. He had been brought up in The Salvation Army. He also attended the meetings to support his brother Geer (Gerard) who was a fine musician and became the choirmaster or songster leader at the age of 17. People knew Jan as the son of Hermanus van Kapel, who had a leading part in the early Salvation Army in the Vlaardingen Corps, corps being the Salvation Army word for a church or congregation. Despite this background, Jan never talked about his family connections to Ryer or anyone else, and didn't really want people to think he was 'religious'.

Meanwhile, Ryer kept attending Sunday services with Jan, and over the months he listened and started to pay more attention to the meaning in the novelty. Something changed in him that he could not describe. He was also aware that there was a question for him behind all this activity. It was not uncommon towards the end of the service for someone to come and tap him on the shoulder, and ask, 'How are you doing, Ryer? Where do you stand in your life with God?' In The Salvation Army this practice is called 'fishing'. These were questions he had not been asked before, and he talked to Jan about them. Jan knew the way, but at that stage had closed himself to it.

There were other things Ryer noticed as well. There was music. It was very different from the church music he knew and the hymns were sung in a different way. There was a band of musicians and a choir with great singers. Among them, his attention was caught on several occasions by a young woman singer who often sang alone.

One evening he nudged Jan and asked, 'Who is that? She's a great singer.'

Jan turned to him with a blank expression; he was quiet for a moment and said, 'Her name is Johanna van Kapel.'

This time it was Ryer's turn to be quiet. 'Kapel?' He looked at Jan who nodded his head and smiled. Ryer said, 'You mean…?'

'Yes, I mean she is my sister,' was Jan's reply.

'I didn't know. You didn't tell me!' said Ryer.

Jan replied, 'You didn't ask me.' And that was the end of the conversation.

Ryer was taken aback by Jan's reply. He had known Jan since they were teenagers and had been attending The Salvation Army for over a year. Up till that point though, their friendship had not involved their families. In that moment, Ryer realised just how little they knew about each other's families. But suddenly it all made sense to Ryer. Jan's family had a significant connection to The Salvation Army. Geer, Jan's brother, was the leader of the choir or songsters and Johanna was one of the songsters.

CHAPTER 2

Jo's background

Much of my knowledge of the Van Kapel family is based on an essay by my late uncle Jan van Kapel (1904–1985), written in connection with the 75th anniversary of The Salvation Army Vlaardingen Corps, 7 June 1906–1981, which I have translated. My maternal grandfather, Hermanus (Herman) van Kapel, was born on 17 October 1878 in the village of Heenvliet on Voorne and Putten, previously two islands subsequently joined through land reclamation, in the province of Zeeland.

There are a few things we know about the background of Hermanus. My uncle Jan writes that the father of Hermanus, also called 'Jan', was a farm worker, and that he and his wife, Marijke, were 'hardworking' farmers during the last quarter of the 19th century.

> They had never heard of religion and to my understanding remained disinterested in later life despite efforts of my father, Hermanus! Their belief was they did no harm to anyone, so therefore, 'What more could our dear Lord desire of a person?'[3]

If they were not too familiar with the Christian faith, we might assume that neither was their eldest son, Hermanus. In his early twenties, according to Jan, Hermanus made the decision to leave home. Fitting all his earthly possessions including his precious clarinet in his rucksack, he took a ferry and crossed the water channels of Zeeland expecting to find a better life across the water in Vlaardingen.

Hermanus had no relations in Vlaardingen but we know he was soon involved in a small music group. He played the clarinet at marketplaces, and was popular on the dance floor, but none of these activities provided sufficient income for a living. Hermanus was a tall, good-looking young man and he quickly made friends who provided him work on a small tugboat named *Zeeland*, which provided services for herring ships and sail luggers by guiding them from the channel known as The Waterweg or 'Waterway' into the open sea. 'On Sundays, the tugboat was frequently moored close to the Vishal [fish market], awaiting requests for assistance from incoming fishermen.'

> On a beautiful quiet Sunday afternoon, [Hermanus] picked up his clarinet, and soon its melodious tones wafted on the breeze along the nearly deserted Queen Wilhelmina Harbour. By chance a casual walker, Mr Guillard, musician and conductor of several music groups in Vlaardingen including the Orchestral Band, 'De Schutterij', heard the sound and sensed something good... The lone walker's sensitive ear was caught by the mellow tones of a clarinet. Sensing something special, he made his way towards the boat from which the sound came. A conversation took place that afternoon with the young clarinet player during which Mr Guillard offered [Hermanus] a place in his music group and promised to contact him for further discussions. [Hermanus's] immediate reaction was: 'I'm a member of the fishing fleet and am not a resident here. It is a pity, but impossible!' But [Mr Guillard] knew what to do. He promised to arrange employment for [Hermanus] in Vlaardingen at the soon to be opened sugar refinery. [4]

Mr Guillard was sponsored in his musical activities by Mr M. Hummelinck, manager of the Hollandia Dairy Factories and the new sugar refinery in Vlaardingen.

It seemed that Hermanus's decision to come to Vlaardingen had changed his life. Not only had he made friends during the last few months but—if he was willing to be part of a music group—there would be employment for him in the new factory. Could things get any better?[5]

Everything appeared to fall into place for Hermanus. For some time, he had been seeing a lovely young woman from Vlaardingen called Petronella Klos. The young couple were married in Vlaardingen on 27 May 1903. It was a happy marriage. Their first two children were Jan, a son, born on 20 February 1904, and my mother Johanna (Jo), born on 23 March 1909. Three other children followed. There was always music in the home and Petronella was a clever seamstress and housekeeper.

Hermanus became a valued member of Mr Guillard's orchestra; playing his clarinet helped him improve his musical skills. Many concerts took place and, not infrequently, there were awards and first prizes to take home for the group and for Hermanus personally.[6]

During the summer months of June 1906, an unexpected event changed the course of this young family's life. Petronella's mother, Grandmother Johanna Klos, visited the village market and her attention was caught by a public notice which read:

> *The Salvation Army has invaded Holland and*
> *will declare War in the village hall tonight.*

Now, Grandmother Johanna Klos was a strong, God-fearing woman. She turned to her neighbour and said: 'How about it? Let's go and hear what they have to say!' And that evening in 1906, in the heartland of the Dutch Reformed Church, The Salvation Army was born in the town of Vlaardingen. My great-grandmother, Johanna Klos, was one of its first converts and founding members. Her strong, indomitable spirit entered right into the joyous expressions of this new Christian movement.

Petronella was soon invited by her mother to attend an evening service of that 'New Army' that everyone was talking about in Vlaardingen. Later that night, on her return home, a surprised Hermanus asked: 'Where have you been?' After satisfying his curiosity, he commented: 'I wouldn't advise you to go again, I have heard some strange stories about it.' To which Petronella responded, 'Have you attended? No? Well, you should also go. Only then can you pass judgment—not now!'

The following night Hermanus attended the meeting. On his return home that evening Petronella asked him: 'And was the "clutter" better than expected?' Hermanus had used that word during an earlier conversation in which he repeated some derogatory opinions he had heard regarding this 'New Army'. He was quiet and did not enter into a discussion; he was still thinking about that evening's experience. Not long afterwards Hermanus came to the mercy seat to make his commitment to Christ. The mercy seat is a bench provided as a place where people attending a Salvation Army service can pray, seeking salvation or sanctification, or making a special consecration to God's will and service. In most halls, the mercy seat is the focal point, usually situated between the platform and the seats of the congregation. God touched Hermanus's life in a wonderful way. He became a man of grace and led many to the Lord. Like many early-day Salvationists, he later wore his Salvation Army uniform every day.[7]

During the early days of the corps there was a recurring need for a music ensemble and a suitable leader. Brother Johannes van Rij, a factory worker, and brother Gog, a cooper (barrel-maker), would beat the big corps drum. Brother Van Aken was given the smaller drum in anticipation of one day establishing a corps band. When a person wanted to make a commitment to God during an open-air meeting, the drum was placed on its side and became the mercy seat, a place where individuals could kneel and ask God to forgive their sins. Sometimes when the corps had financial needs the drum was put on its flat side for a 'drum collection' of a free-will offering. It was these men, the corps drummers, Brothers Van Rij and Van Aken, who earnestly prayed for a suitable leader, and God answered their prayers. After his conversion, Hermanus became a regular attendee at corps activities. He joined the musicians and was soon accepted as their leader. It did not take long before a group of enthusiastic musicians with a variety of instruments came together and decided on a fixed evening for rehearsals. Their ultimate desire was to provide musical support in the meetings.

Sunday was generally considered a non-work day. It was a day to attend church, meditate and read your Bible. Factories and public houses were all closed. Prior to refrigeration facilities for fishing vessels, many fishermen and other workers would be home on Sundays. For this reason, among others, the early years of the corps were difficult because the public regarded the Army's meetings generally as a type of entertainment, like a circus. Young men with nothing better to do on a Sunday evening discovered a wonderful place for entertainment at the 'New Army'. The evening or evangelistic meetings in particular were often the prime target for young hooligans. Disturbances and restoration of order occurred frequently. When friendly requests and reminders appeared fruitless, and the troublemakers refused to leave the hall, some corps members acted as 'riot police' at the door and would take drastic measures to restore order. Often young offenders entrenched themselves against the back wall on low benches. The chaos was complete when the adjacent seats were also torn down. Thanks to burly and energetic Johannes van Rij, the offenders usually found themselves swiftly outside the door and removed from view. In later years when Hermanus sensed trouble brewing, he would quietly move to the back of the hall and seat himself between known culprits. His calm, quiet presence and the popularity that he enjoyed amongst those young men, was often enough to settle them.[8]

On summer evenings, rehearsals often took place at the Van Kapel home. Many musicians were still unfamiliar with notation. As Jan, the eldest son, commented many years later, 'The initial unarticulated sounds they drew from their instruments had to be released and converted into melodious and pleasing sounds.' Hermanus proved to be the right person to help that process. In fact, he was so pleased with the progress being made by the musicians that he gave up the orchestra and devoted his time to the ministry with The Salvation Army. His former activities with the orchestra had developed his skills as a musician, especially as a soloist.

As my uncle Jan wrote, however, 'a path seemingly paved with roses also has thorns'.

> The director of the sugar refinery and patron of the orchestra, Mr Hummelinck, was not pleased. The orchestra was not playing as well as before. He called on the conductor for an explanation. Hermanus was considered the chief culprit because he had resigned from the orchestra to concentrate on his work with The Salvation Army. As an employee of the refinery Hermanus was instructed to appear at the headquarters of the company. Mr Hummelinck left Hermanus in no doubt about his dissatisfaction over his retirement from the orchestra. He reminded Hermanus that his current employment was on the condition that he would use his music qualifications and skills to enhance the performance of the orchestra. In short, his job at the Hollandia Factory and his musicianship in the orchestra were indivisible. If he did not return to the orchestra it would cost him his job. The choice was his.

Hermanus responded that he could perfectly understand the view of the company's most senior director and sponsor; however, something in his life had changed. He had given himself now and for the future to what he considered only the best and highest ideal, namely to the service of God and The Salvation Army, even if this meant he lost his job.

Mr Hummelinck's response was very different to the one Hermanus expected. The director stood up and said: 'Give me five (shake hands on this)! You're a good man; if you had caved in I would have considered it a weak solution.'[9]

From that time onwards Hermanus would always personally seek support from Mr Hummelinck to assist tuberculosis patients in the district who the Army was trying to help with milk, eggs and butter. These items were sometimes made available free of charge when the Hollandia shops were still in business and were highly recommended to combat the disease. Hermanus had begun to search out areas of the town where people lived in dire situations: no work, no income, and no food on the table. People were sick and often lived in squalor. Hermanus prayed with people he visited. He tried to get food for families and milk for the children. He became a familiar face in the township. Petronella was concerned when he arrived home after those visits and his clothes had an unpleasant odour. She would send him to the washroom before he touched anything in the kitchen, or the food.

Band rehearsals at the Van Kapel home were often noisy and boisterous, but the neighbours never really complained. The years 1908–1910 saw a significant growth in the number of musicians in the corps, and supplies of music and instruments were needed to keep pace with the growth. Hermanus made an approach to a Mr Hanke, a Rotterdam supplier. Jan remembers him as an Old Testament-like figure, a musician with a lion's mane and a beard. Whoever covered the cost of the instruments is a mystery. Neither The Salvation Army Corps nor Hermanus would have had the financial wherewithal to pay for the new instruments nor would any of the musicians. Hermanus, however, knew the supplier. Could it have been that Mr Hanke, the Rotterdam supplier, provided this support?

Jan recalled the occasion when the new instruments arrived:

> Imagine the excitement when eventually a large delivery came from England. Crates with the treasure trove stood in the house. An evening was arranged for the proposed players to collect their particular instruments. It was a winter's day, and Hermanus and Petronella received their guests in the 'drawing room'. A big coke-fuelled heater provided a pleasant temperature. On top of it, approximately 1.40 m above the floor, stood a large filter coffee pot.

> Then came the unwrapping of the parcels and a Saint Nicholas atmosphere was palpable. A number of large instruments including a trombone, a euphonium and some other brass instruments were unpacked. Brother L. van

Oeveren was first to take possession of his trombone and in the ensuing excitement he forgot where he was. With cries of joy and excitement he embraced the new instrument. Because tones of jubilation from the instrument require moving the slide, suddenly, in his hands, the instrument extended about 20 to 30 cm in length and collided with the aforementioned coffee pot. The contents spilled on to the beautiful carpet. At that point, the visitors came 'down to earth' and decided it was time go home—to the great relief of Petronella.[10]

Family life

My mother told me stories of family life. Family was obviously important to both Hermanus and Petronella. Grace was said before and after meals and Hermanus read Bible stories to the children. It was not unusual on winter evenings for neighbourhood children to come in and sit on the floor to listen to him. They would sing 'Army' songs. In the evenings, the family would sit at the table and sometimes play a board game or they would all be quiet, reading their own book. In the winter months, there would be an open fire to warm the room. Petronella would often be sewing or knitting stockings or teaching Jo how to mend socks. Jo recalled that there was usually something to nibble at the table such as peanuts or some sweets. When it was bedtime the little ones would hold onto their father's trousers as he climbed up the stairs to the loft where he would put them to bed. There was a hug and prayer for each one before they were tucked in for the night.

Corps life

Summer provided opportunity for the corps to commence outdoor activities in the community. Open-air meetings increased the attendances of the indoor services significantly. These activities were also commenced in West Nieuwland on the property of a livery stable. The most favourite outing of all was a united field day with all The Salvation Army corps in that area on a Whit Monday at the

Woodlands Heaths. This area was kindly made available by the landlord of the 'Nimmerdor' Estate.

My uncle Jan was a young boy at that time, about 10–12 years of age. He recalled the highlight of the united fellowship with all the other corps in this beautiful nature resort was the visit of the Army's Founder, General William Booth. He recalled clearly that 'I saw the General that day... This remains an enduring memory for me—an open carriage drawn by two white horses, with two coachmen in livery all made possible by the landlord; and in the open carriage, the striking figure of the General.'

The way Jan describes all that took place on that Whit Monday is quite remarkable. He continued:

> Most of those attending needed to return that night by train, filled with pipe or cigarette smoke, to Rotterdam and then walk the rest of the way home accompanied by marching music; these were really special events. Things like that did not happen in everyday life. Holidays were usually spent at home; everyone made their own entertainment. The Army brought a new dimension to life.[11]

Jan recalls one corps excursion to a united Army event in the Province of Zeeland across the River Maas:

> On one occasion a weather depression caused a wild storm during the night. By morning, the rain was easing but the wind was so strong that tree branches covered the ground on shore. However, the hired boat arrived through the turbulent waters of the Nieuwe Maas (river) with a large number of Schiedam Corps comrades already on board to which Vlaardingen added its numbers onto the heaving ship. In the 1920s everyone was responsible for their own safety.
>
> The boat was fully laden with people; a few leaky overhead canvases covered the deck and the crowded cabin. Despite

the rain and wind and the turbulent waters it did not take long before the lovely 'Army' songs about sailing to the Christians' home in heaven echoed across the waters:

We are out on the ocean sailing;
Homeward bound we sweetly glide.
We are out on the ocean sailing;
To a home beyond the tide.

All the storms will soon be over,
Then we'll anchor in the harbour;
We are out on the ocean sailing,
To a home beyond the tide.[12]

Another favourite was: 'A little ship was on the sea, it was a pretty sight'. Jan continued:

Those were appropriate songs on a day out when the weather was delightful; but when they crossed the stretch of water where the River Maas connected to the North Sea, the waves became turbulent and the singing quietened down. Real danger existed that the boat would capsize if anyone panicked or moved unexpectedly to retrieve a hat that might have been blown away by the wind. Fortunately, everyone followed the captain's orders and the ship would successfully be brought to land at Den Brielle.[b] A large but empty auctioneer's building was hired. Very quickly a meeting was organised for the citizens from Den Brielle who listened with great interest. They did not have the enjoyment of music and song every day.

Reading Jan's lively stories about the adventures he experienced as a teenager in the 'pioneer days' of the Vlaardingen Corps, I sense a homesickness for the early days of the 'Army', the Van Kapel family experienced. He expressed this well in his essay, *'Such was the*

---

[b] Den Brielle is a town on the joined islands of Voorne and Putten.

flexibility and sheer enthusiasm of Salvationists in the Netherlands in those days' [author's emphasis].

A warrior goes 'Home'

Hermanus was much involved with the poor and families of the unemployed. He did not hesitate to pray with the sick and the dying, leading many to the Lord. He became a well-known person in the community for his care and was recognised by his uniform as a member of The Salvation Army.

People understood little about infectious diseases. It was in a slum area where Hermanus visited a man who was unwell and disturbed. A few days later Hermanus became ill—and then progressively worse. Infectious diseases such as cholera, typhoid and influenza often swept through Europe within a matter of weeks, taking thousands of lives.

I believe Hermanus would have spoken to his eldest son, Jan, while he was able to do so. 'I am so proud of you! You will be the "man" in the family. Continue to follow Jesus. Support your mother. She will have another baby in June. Be a good example to Jo and your brothers, Gerard and Cor.'

Despite her age, Johanna Klos, better known as Opoe, old Dutch for grandmother, was not a person to be ignored. She lived in Steijnstraat just opposite her daughter Petronella. I assume that from the day Hermanus became ill she made herself available to support her daughter, Petronella, and her four frightened children who watched their loving, energetic father/husband die within a matter of a few days. The family stood around the bed. Hermanus's voice became slower and softer. 'Goodbye... Goodbye... Goodbye.' The Lord called Hermanus van Kapel 'Home' on 4 March 1918. He was only 39 years.

It did not take long for the news of Hermanus's death to stir the citizens of Vlaardingen. Cross-street washing-lines were removed and shops closed for the day. Workers were free to attend the funeral and were told their wages would not be reduced for time lost. People who had never attended The Salvation Army quietly entered the corps building. When seating proved to be insufficient, people stood or leaned against the walls throughout the funeral service. At the end of the service the congregation stood as the coffin was carried out and placed in the hearse drawn by a couple of horses. Silently grieving men and women stood weeping outside their homes on Steijnstraat as they watched the hearse pass by.

> There'll be no sorrow in God's tomorrow,
> There'll be no sadness, doubt or fears;
> There'll be no sorrow in God's tomorrow,
> For he will wipe away all tears.[13]

Jan, the eldest son, was 14 on 20 February; he was the boy-image of his father. Jo turned nine on 23 March; Gerard (Geer) turned eight in July and Cornelis (Cor) was six on 11 March, a week after his father's 'promotion to Glory', the Army's description of the death of Salvationists. Would they ever forget hearing him say, 'Goodbye... Goodbye...'?

Life without Hermanus

Life changed completely in the happy van Kapel household. Laughter, happy songs and bedtime stories were lost in a teary silence of unspoken grief. But life went on. Jo and Geer returned to school. Fourteen-year-old Jan had a job—selling kerosene for household kerosene cookers, from door to door. Little Cor was still too young for school and stayed home with Mother. Petronella was a strong woman, like her mother; both she and Hermanus had dreams of giving their children a good education. As a skilled seamstress, she also wanted to see her children well dressed. Mother Johanna Klos had trained her well. But now, as a widow without an income and another baby expected in the next couple of months, she must have wondered, 'Oh God, how am I going to manage?'

Opoe Johanna Klos (1853–1931) was the quiet presence and

mentor for her daughter when the children were at school. She supported Petronella in many practical ways as well. Not only did she serve as a midwife in the community, she was also available to wash the bodies of the dead at their homes before their transfer to the mortuary. These roles provided her with some financial support. When unable to pay in cash for her services, people would give her goods or clothing.

During the later months of pregnancy, it was not uncommon for women to avoid public places. It was a sign of modesty. As a result, Petronella did not attend many of the Vlaardingen Corps meetings. But God bless Opoe Johanna Klos! Every Sunday she took the children to the Sunday services at The Salvation Army. I think that continued contact consolidated the spiritual foundations for each of those children—especially for the older ones.

On 8 June 1918, baby Marijke was born and Opoe Klos was there to look after mother and the baby.

I recall my mother, telling me that folk would come and ask for a new lining for heavy winter coats. Inevitably this required removing the existing lining first. When Jo was a little older her mother taught her how to do this without damaging the garment. It took Jo many hours the first time, but her mother was patient and would compliment her. Over a period of time, Jo also learned how to do 'invisible' (small) stitching when doing hems. This allowed Petronella to concentrate on sewing.

Life had its amusing moments. It still made Jo laugh when she recalled a particular incident: A road worker knocked on the door one day with one leather boot on his foot and the other boot in his hand; it had a tear in the upper calf section of the boot. He wondered if Petronella could mend the tear. She looked at it and began to laugh, saying she would try and do her best. It was only a small manual Singer machine but 'her best' showed how deft she was. Using the same needle, she placed the boot in position and turned the handle of the machine and it brought the torn ends together and fixed the boot. Jo remembered this incident because both the man and her mother laughed spontaneously at the successful result—it was a happy moment, like a celebration. Petronella refused a payment: 'A successful result and a good laugh covered the cost!'

She was a proud woman, determined her children would not look poverty-stricken. As my mother later recalled, 'We were the best dressed children in the street because mother was most particular about our appearance.'

Petronella was a petite and attractive woman, but she grieved deeply for Hermanus. When her children married and left home, she began to wear black clothing and continued to do so for the rest of her life.

Jo van Kapel

As mentioned above, Jo turned nine years the month her father died. As the only girl in the family she wanted to help her mother. Petronella was busy with household chores and her sewing. Much of the responsibility of looking after six-year-old Cor—still too young for primary school for which the entry age was seven in Holland at that time—fell on the shoulders of Jo when she was home. Jo loved this quiet little boy, and he reciprocated by calling her 'Yoey', a name that stuck. Years later, in a 1946 letter, Cor recalled how grateful he was to Jo for the way she had looked after him. Jo, young as she was at that time, became the 'mother figure' for Cor. Little did she realise then how the skills and experiences of childhood and early teens laid foundations she could build on in later life.

Aside from all the changes within family life, Jo also attended the local primary school. Hermanus and Petronella had wanted their children to have a good education and it shows something about the strength and determination of Petronella that she managed to have each of her children complete primary school and other levels of education as well. In Jo's case, Petronella sent her to a local 'finishing school'. The students had to be in uniform, including aprons. Girls were taught 'refinement of speech'. Jo was taught cooking, ironing and housekeeping, all the things she did at home. By the age of 14, she was bored. Many of her friends had already commenced work and were getting a small wage. Jo was still dependent on her mother. She decided to leave school, and found a job. When Jo eventually informed her mother that she was employed it was too late for Petronella to reverse Jo's decision.

Jo was a regular member of The Salvation Army. She was attractive, contemporary photographs suggest, full of energy, and had a lot of friends. The time came when she made a confession of faith and asked Jesus into her heart and life to be her Lord and Saviour. It was not long before she became a uniform-wearing Salvation Army soldier. Grandmother Klos would have been delighted. She was a great encourager to Jo and her other siblings in this regard. Jo's brother Geer had the musical gifting of his father. He joined the band at a young age and played a cornet. At the age of 17 he was given the position of bandmaster. Vlaardingen Corps had a big band and some may have considered Geer too young to take up this responsibility, but he had the needed skills and musical ability. Later, he also became the songster leader. Jo became a member of the choir or songsters. She had a lovely contralto voice and occasionally sang a solo. She was also active in the young people's corps of Vlaardingen Corps and was an enthusiastic 'corps cadet', the term for a young Salvationist who is being trained for leadership.

By comparison, Jan, Jo's brother, attended the Army regularly but to my knowledge never became a uniform-wearing soldier. As mentioned in Chapter One, it was during his time of working at the Hollandia factory that he became a friend to Ryer van Kralingen. They were two young men who were isolated from their siblings for different reasons. They had totally different lives and responsibilities and one came from a strong Christian background while the other one was much more nominal. Despite these differences, attending the Sunday evening services together became routine, and without knowing the family connection and unbeknown to Jan, Ryer had noticed and become attracted to Jo. Little wonder. Jo was the sort of person who made friends. She had a good voice, sang in the songsters, was involved in other corps activities and was a most attractive young woman.

CHAPTER 3

Time for decisions

Having introduced the Van Kapel family and their involvement in The Salvation Army Vlaardingen Corps, let us return to Ryer's story.

A radical change

Jan van Kapel had invited Ryer to attend the Sunday evening worship services at The Salvation Army. As mentioned in Chapter Two, for the youth of the town who had nothing better to do on a Sunday evening these services were regarded as entertainment. Jan was a regular because it was his church and he enjoyed it. For Ryer, it was the first time in many years that he had been to a place of worship. After initially being overwhelmed he was captivated by what happened there and he continued to attend.

The day came though when, during the sermon, Ryer became very serious. Much of what he had heard on other Sundays had made an impact, but on this occasion it was different. The Bible message had been preached and people were being encouraged to make a commitment to Christ. As I have previously mentioned, after the sermon some senior leaders of the corps would quietly move among the congregation and tap people on the shoulder asking, 'Should this be the time for you to step forward and make a commitment?' The usually noisy back row was subdued. Then Ryer got up and went to the mercy seat in a very determined way, and Jan said that he watched: 'When Ryer got up from the mercy seat, he seemed a totally different person. His face had changed. And when he sat down next to me, I knew I had "lost" a friend. It would never be the same again. And I wondered what was going to happen to him.'[14]

From Jan's correspondence to my mother we know a little of what happened immediately after this decision. In Chapter One, I quoted from Jan's letter on 2 February 1971, the day after Ryer had died, 'You know Jo...I knew him a lot earlier than you, because of our joint employment in the sugar refinery, Hollandia.' Then he added, 'And also from the beginning of his career...his involvement with The Salvation Army. From the moment that he kneeled at the mercy seat a radical turnaround took place in his life. The following day Ryer went on his way to break all association with amusement clubs. He met Cor Horsder, machinist at Hollandia, a chap who had little time for God or church, and told him what had taken place in his life the night before and the things he was about to do. Horsder immediately extended his hand and said, "Ryer, my boy, you have my heartfelt congratulations." He similarly visited the local public house, where he went every evening for a drink before going home. He spoke to the publican there who said, "Ryer, I heard the good news. I wish I had the strength to do the same." He also emptied his pockets and took out all his cigarettes. What surprised me was that nobody seemed to make fun of it. People could see that his life had changed and would never be the same again.'[15]

My mother recalled that when Ryer became converted he had this tremendous hunger to read everything he could get his hands on, something he had done very little of earlier in his life due to years of illness. He began to 'devour' anything that he could read about The Salvation Army, and about Christian beliefs and teaching. At first, he dived into whatever he could borrow from others that might stimulate his thinking. Ryer had this rush of energy to prepare himself because he knew clearly from the moment he got up from the mercy seat that he had to become a Salvation Army officer. This is the term for a member of The Salvation Army who has been trained for leadership and who is recognised as a minister of religion. My mother told me she remembered Ryer saying, 'I know I have to go to College. I have to become an officer. This is the work I have to do.'

I look back at Ryer's experiences as a teenager, and wonder whether all those years of escaping to the waterfront to look out at the sea, followed by many years as a professional seaman for the herring fishing industry in the North Sea, laid a foundation for these next steps. He was an adventurous young man who was so open to new horizons. This was evident very early in his officership. Is it possible that these early experiences eventually contributed to his sense of a call to work overseas?

Whatever the factors behind Ryer's commitment, he was so certain of his calling to officership it seemed natural for him to take the first step of membership of The Salvation Army, becoming a soldier or lay member. He was then accepted into the band and given a foundation in music. He also tried his voice in the songsters. He had always loved singing and it was a special feature of worship in The Salvation Army. Being in the songsters helped him to learn Christian hymns and songs and to become familiar with the new songs that were being written at that time by Salvationist musicians.

Family responses

Arie van Kralingen appears to have accepted Ryer's involvement with The Salvation Army without comment, and this is not as surprising as it might seem. Four of Ryer's older siblings, two brothers, Arie and Leenderd, and two sisters, Greta and Treijn, each one older than him, became Salvationists. I remember meeting them as a seven-year-old in Holland during our family's visit in 1947. At that time, they were all married and were Salvationists, as were some of their spouses. I have no record as to how and when they joined the Army. In itself, this extent of involvement in one family indicates something of the impact that The Salvation Army had in Vlaardingen; it was so totally different from the traditional church in those days and captured a great deal of attention.

In time, Ryer also developed a friendship with Jo van Kapel, the talented singer he admired in the songsters. One of Ryer's sisters, perhaps a bit of a gossiper, mentioned to her father Arie, 'It seems that Ryer is having friendship with the daughter of Hermanus.' I don't know what response she anticipated, but it wasn't what she expected. Arie apparently said, 'Any daughter or son of Hermanus van Kapel is good enough for me and for my children', and that was the end of the conversation. My guess is that, like many people of his generation, Arie had known Hermanus and had attended his funeral.

Ryer was preparing himself for entry to The Salvation Army Training College. When not on duty with the fishing trade and still living at home, he would usually wear his soldier's uniform. On one occasion, there was a knock on the door. An elderly gentleman introduced himself as the Reverend Van Kralingen, Ryer's uncle. Ryer had never heard of him, but invited him in. The visitor said, 'I've come to see you,' and Ryer thought, 'Oh, well, why not?' It was probably Sunday, because Ryer was home from work. Arie wasn't home, though.

The visitor continued, 'I've heard a lot of things about what you're doing these days and I'm here because I'm very concerned about your soul.'

'Oh? No-one was ever worried about my soul before I went to The Salvation Army,' said Ryer.

And the Reverend explained, 'Yes, well, uh, you have left the mother church. The teachings of these people are not correct and very confusing.'

At this point, Ryer stood up. He wasn't going to have any of this nonsense. He replied, 'But I've never been better. I found "salvation" and I know I am saved!'

'But,' his guest continued, 'nobody can be sure of that. That's incorrect. Only God decides that.'

And Ryer said, 'I know it. I know it here,' pointing to his heart, 'and my family can tell you that. And I would say again, you never showed concern when I stopped coming to the church. I didn't even know I had an uncle who was a minister!' Still standing, Ryer gestured toward the door and said, 'Why don't you leave?'

Ryer no longer feared his father and later that day confronted him, suspecting that Arie knew of the visit. Arie just smirked. Perhaps he was glad his son had dealt with this visit. The rest of the family was not concerned about Ryer's decision.

The 'mother church' was, of course, the Dutch Reformed Church, similar in doctrine to the Presbyterian Church. The theological issue at stake here was that the Dutch Reformed Church believed in the conversion of people by God's election, not by personal choice and decision, as did The Salvation Army and many other evangelical churches, especially of the Wesleyan tradition. The idea of election is based on what the Apostle Paul writes on the topic, although the evangelical churches would argue that his intention has been misunderstood. According to the doctrine of election, you can never be certain you have been saved. Such a doctrine readily led to either an anxious sense that salvation might be associated with good works—a sort of bribery of God—or to a sense of discouragement. It was because the church offered no certainty that many young people left. Ryer had been brought up in this tradition, and understood it. This added to the significance of his witness, 'I'm saved', on this occasion. He was expressing a distinct belief and conviction that salvation could be accepted by faith and assured, because Christ died for us. Ryer's ability to offer this testimony says something about the strength of his conviction at this time.

Training and early officership

In those days, it was a pretty quick transition to the officer Training College. Ryer applied for College and he was accepted. He was 23 when he made his commitment to Christ and 25 when he went to officer Training College in September 1929. He was a little older than many of the cadets and he entered college on the condition that Jo, who was now his fiancée, would be accepted for the next session. This in itself stretched the rules at that time, as cadets had not previously been allowed to be engaged when they entered College. It was perhaps for this reason that when he was interviewed for a place at the College he was told he had to take off his engagement ring. The

Salvation Army in Holland was very conservative, and strict with its officers. In response, Ryer replied, 'No, no. I won't. This is a promise that I have made.' And he would not be swayed.

Fortunately for Ryer and Jo, The Salvation Army in Holland at that time had a Danish Chief Secretary, Colonel Theodor Westergaard, who was a broad thinker. When he heard Ryer, he responded, 'Well we can start something new, can't we? That's accepted.'

Ryer entered the Training College in September 1929. The age of the majority of cadets in the early sessions ranged from 18 to 30 years of age. Only single people were accepted and the actual duration of in-training was less than a year. When Ryer left home to enter the Training College, Jo van Kapel remained active in the Vlaardingen Corps. She entered the Training College in 1930.

There were many things for Ryer to focus on when he entered training. His education had been so limited. In College, he absorbed everything that came to him and anything he could find to read. When I think about the extent of officer training today, including the entry requirements, the resources available, the depth of content and the formal assessments, it is amazing what these early-day officers achieved. Whatever their training involved, I think it was sheer enthusiasm based on their commitment to the service of the Lord that sent them out. When they were commissioned, their Bible was the only study book they had. How blessed we are today with the availability of the Bible in many translations and versions together with in-depth commentaries and theology textbooks.

At his commissioning on June 1930, Ryer was appointed to the Army's 'Gospel Ship' together with a group of other officers. He was made the captain of the boat. The group would live on the Gospel Ship. They then commenced their journey through the canals and waterways of Friesland conducting evangelistic meetings for adults, and Bible-related activities for children. Ryer was delighted with the appointment and it suited him to a tee. During the summer, they moved from one village to another. The boat was big enough to allow small groups of people on board for worship, to hear the Gospel message and sing familiar hymns. Many houseboats were permanently anchored along the canals; it was for these people that the ministry of God's love was particularly relevant. For some the nearest church was more than a walking distance from home. Ryer did not hesitate to make 'pastoral visits' to the people in houseboats. When people learned he had been a seaman on the North Sea herring fleet, he was warmly welcomed.

Ryer's next journey was a brief two-month appointment to Scheveningen, known for its beautiful beach and holiday resorts. From mid-August to the end of October 1931 Ryer conducted short 'beach evangelism' outreach with a small group of Salvationists. Each of the 15-minute meetings included two accompanied vocal items, a Bible reading, a five-minute comment and a prayer. They would then move on to another section of the beach and repeat the open-air meeting.

After this brief but enjoyable interlude, Ryer was appointed in October 1931 to Spijkenisse to open a new corps. I see it as a strategic and well thought through appointment. This was the area his parents had come from and Ryer was familiar with the area. This was the first outreach into the province of Zeeland. The Salvation Army did not have a presence there nor did it have the financial resources to support Ryer. In addition to having robust health, it was also recognised that Ryer had the capacities needed for this sort of pioneering work. He was particularly good at getting along with men, and this was one more appointment near the sea that would allow him to use his knowledge of fishing and seafaring in his ministry. So, The Salvation Army's Territorial Headquarters (THQ) gave him a Salvation Army flag and the public transport fare to get there. That was it. Ryer was indeed an adventurer. He knew the Lord would lead the way and he was excited about the challenge.

It is likely that Ryer travelled via Vlaardingen to see his father. Arie was still alive. He had initially been doubtful about Ryer becoming an officer, but he could see the change in Ryer's character and by this time he was also pleased at what his son had achieved. To make this appointment to Spijkenisse easier, Arie gave Ryer a guilder.

Now, a guilder was a lot of money in those days, and Dad told me that even the thought of this gift felt like a 'triumph' of recognition by his father. It was also a considerable financial help, Ryer's own income being very meagre. Junior officers lived on whatever they received in collections during their appointments.

Ryer went to Spijkenisse with an assistant officer. He found accommodation for them both and quickly located a suitable place for fellowship and worship. My parents visited the corps when they were in Holland in 1946–47 and were given a warm welcome; there were elderly soldiers who were Ryer's first converts. The Salvation Army was still doing well in Spijkenisse. It was a particular delight for Ryer to see that the corps record books had preserved the memory that he and his assistant commenced the work there. Under their leadership the new corps progressed. The congregation was happy with the two energetic officers and made sure they were well looked after.

In the meantime, Jo van Kapel commenced her officer training in September 1930. She was commissioned in June 1931 and her first appointment was to the town of Kampen. I have no record of a second appointment prior to her marriage.

Marriage

By late 1932, Spijkenisse Corps was progressing and Ryer felt it was time for Jo and him to be married. During the early years of The Salvation Army, leadership required that officers marry officers. Ryer was 28 and he wanted to be married. He made his request to the Chief Secretary of the day who was pleased to give his consent. By that time Jo had been commissioned for two years.

Ryer was still in his appointment at Spijkenisse. The happy couple were married on a freezing cold day. The wedding took place in Vlaardingen on 18 January 1933, just across the water from Spijkenisse. Jo's mother, Petronella van Kapel, and Jo's three brothers, Jan, Geer and Cor, and sister Marijke (Rie) attended the service, as did Ryer's Father, Arie, and his brothers and sisters.

By tradition, Salvation Army weddings in those days were very serious occasions. Salvationist-couples came in their Salvation Army uniforms and the bride wore her bonnet; flowers had their appropriate places in discreet locations, and the wedding ceremony itself happened during a full Salvation Army meeting, open to the public. The bride and groom spoke, probably giving testimonies, and there was a sermon and an appeal for people to commit to Christ. However strange this style of service may seem now, both families were familiar with it. It was a large celebration and a memorable event for the families and the corps members.

Ryer and Johanna began married life in Spijkenisse and were transferred to Vlissingen in July 1933. Joan was born there in the February 1934. Mum recalled that one morning when she woke up the temperature was so low that her blanket had frozen to the wall. She had to pull the blankets off the wall and there were bits of fluff left behind. She remembered that those freezing temperatures in the winters made it a challenge to keep a baby warm.

Perhaps for these reasons among others, Mum was glad to think about going to somewhere like the Netherlands East Indies (NEI) where it was so much warmer. After their appointment together in Vlissingen, their final appointment in Holland was to the corps in Wageningen, in April 1935. It was not unusual for appointments to be so short, but perhaps this was a holding appointment until their departure overseas.

Ryer and Jo returned to Vlaardingen for their farewell meeting. Writing about the event to Jo, her brother Jan recalled a song from the service entitled, 'Where He Leads Me I Will Follow'. 'I can still remember that,' he said. 'Many years later I went to the remembrance service for Ryer in Vlaardingen and they closed the service with that chorus and the memories all came back to me like a flood. I remembered that Sunday night when Ryer went to the mercy-seat and God changed his life forever.'[16]

Even now this moves me, both in what Jan's words say about the commitment of my parents and about his spiritual sensitivity. He may not have called himself an active Salvationist, but after all those years this was how he wrote of these memories.

> *Where he leads me I will follow,*
> *Where he leads me I will follow,*
> *Where he leads me I will follow,*
> *I'll go with Him, with Him,*
> *All the way.*[17]

CHAPTER 4

Netherlands East Indies before the war

In the 1930s overseas travel was often a long holiday by sea. On April 1935, Jo with Ryer and baby Joan were booked on the SS *Christiaan Huijgens*, a regular passenger-carrier to the Netherlands East Indies (NEI) via the Mediterranean Sea and through the Suez Canal. It was a long, slow journey for the passengers and it provided a gradual introduction to the tropical climate.

On arrival in Batavia (the pre-independence name of Jakarta), Ryer and Jo were very surprised to learn they were not receiving a corps appointment. During their interview in Holland they had indicated their desire to work with the local people, but this was not to happen.

Holland had a large colonial military force in the country at that time. England would have had something similar in India, Singapore and Malaysia. Life for the colonial soldier was often lonely, with little wholesome entertainment. For many it was their first experience of leaving their home country (Holland) and living in military barracks for three years. Just a few came with their families. As a result, military personnel were vulnerable to all the temptations you might imagine, including alcohol abuse and sexual immorality. This in turn adversely shaped the local economy and communities, creating a demand for bars and brothels, and facilitating the spread of sexually transmitted diseases. Therefore, in an effort both to care for military personnel and to manage the effects on the local population, the

Dutch government subsidised churches to develop large rest homes where military personnel on their days off could have a relaxed time away from their barracks. All such Salvation Army military homes in Indonesia were called 'The Open Door'.

When I think of it retrospectively, I can see the hand of God in my parents' appointments to these homes. When Dad was a young lad, a law in Holland required a certain percentage of boys in the family be released for military training. In large families there was no need for all boys to be called up. As Ryer was the youngest boy, his name never came up and neither did those of his brothers. In this respect both he and Mum were totally unprepared. This notwithstanding, God knew my parents, their abilities and capabilities, though these were yet to be proven. Mum came from a family of boys and was a natural leader, even in her corps. This wasn't a surprise. She was the eldest daughter of a widowed mother and she had helped run that family. Of course, in the 1930s, often very little credit or consideration was given to the capacity of women. Having been a professional seaman for almost eight years, Ryer knew how to work with men. Very few officers were academically trained at this time, but Dad's gifts in this area would have been recognised. They were both practical people. All of their early formation and training soon found expression in their work.

The first Open Door military home to which Ryer and Jo were appointed was centrally located in Solo (Surakarta) (see map of Java page 110). Many of these military rest homes were situated near barracks or an airfield, and this was the case in Solo. As an aside here, these homes were open to all members of the defence service. Mum and Dad worked with a wide range of service personnel over the years, and I recall them speaking about how the armed services differed in their cultures, and also how they learnt to effectively bring them together.

Although most of the money for these homes came from the government, the churches also contributed some funding and were free to choose how to establish the centre and what they offered. From my post-war memories of the rest home we lived in, I can imagine something of what these homes must have been like before the war. In retrospect, facilities were very basic indeed. They lacked many of the domestic luxuries we take for granted now. Even radios were very rare. A telegraph system, for example, was the main way of sending messages. Radio was used, but largely for news broadcasts. The homes had a telephone, but that was considered very modern. The government subsidised cigarettes and these were provided, despite The Salvation Army's general stance in this regard. After the war the Army did not give out cigarettes. Army centres did not provide alcohol, but tea and coffee were available 24 hours a day. There was no air conditioning in those days—it didn't exist. We did have fans and large open verandahs, however, and these helped the air to circulate and provide some cooling. The homes offered shared rooms, but that did not matter; they were away from the barracks. I recall also that besides providing accommodation and facilities for military personnel, Dad always made sure he had a couple of small rooms set aside for chaplains who may have been travelling or who needed a rest. A laundry service was available and there were good meals. A bell would ring so the men knew it was time for a meal, and there was always a prayer before the meal commenced. Our parents ate with 'the boys', as the military personnel were called. In my memory from after the war, we always sat in the same room and ate the same food. There were local staff employed for cleaning and cooking, and the government also provided certain food items and subsidised others. This was particularly important after the war when supplies were extremely limited.

All Salvation Army military homes had a worship centre with a regular congregation, and services were conducted on Sunday. In effect, a small corps or spiritual community was associated with each of the homes. This meant that part of Ryer's work was to pastor his congregation and to be available for the military personnel needing someone to speak to privately—away from the barracks.

Mum would look after the home. She had a good sense of humour and knew how to get on with military personnel. I remember, in Jakarta after the war she was called 'Mum' or 'Mother' by some of the younger servicemen in particular. These were qualities she had learnt earlier, of course, before the war, as she cared for these men and provided a home for them. Together, Ryer and Jo were available for them, day and night. The extent of their commitment was evident later on, in particular, when times were dangerous, before, during and after the war.

Ryer and Jo quickly learnt about the network of church and Salvation Army homes spread across Java. The term 'The Red Shield Services' was first used in Canada as a way of speaking about the social and other support services provided to military personnel when The Salvation Army joined in with the military during the Second World War. In effect though, and without that name, the military homes in Indonesia were the beginnings of the Red Shield services there.

After two years in Solo, Ryer and Jo were sent to a very active corps in Surabaya on the north coast of Java. There was no Open Door Military Home in Surabaya; however, my parents had met a number of military personnel in their previous appointments and many of the soldiers attended the Sunday meetings. Surabaya had large military barracks in the city itself. There was also considerable movement between barracks, with personnel moving from the coast to central locations and back. While air force personnel sometimes departed by plane, most other military personnel eventually needed to come to the coast to ship out. This meant that Ryer and Jo developed many links with military personnel they had first met in Solo and their other appointments. The corps itself had a large indigenous and mixed-race congregation and Ryer and Jo enjoyed the work. I think, though, that it was their work with the military that most helped them understand what was going on in the country politically. It certainly opened their eyes to the needs of military personnel.

After just over a year in Surabaya, in July 1937, my parents were appointed for one year as corps officers of the Batavia I Corps. 'Corps officer' is The Salvation Army term for the minister of the local Salvation Army congregation or church. It was a small corps and the congregation was a mixture of Indo-Europeans and Chinese people who met in rented premises. My parents enjoyed that little corps and the friendly congregation. Joan was a little girl of three-and-a-half years.

My father regularly visited the local men's prison in that district. He discovered that a number of the men were professional robbers. They were mostly unemployed, had no steady income and had families needing to be fed. Stealing was their way of surviving. The men came from different backgrounds—farmers or city people—but they had no work. Sadly, it was common for these men to use their young sons to help them with robberies. At night when they wanted to break into a house, the little boy was pushed through the usually open small toilet window. He then walked to the front door, unlocked and opened it. Few people locked their doors on the inside. If caught, these children would go to jail with their parents. They would grow up in an environment of stealing instead of attending school because their desperate parents needed an income.

On one visit to the prison Ryer sat with a man and engaged him in conversation. His little boy sat next to him. The man told Ryer, 'I don't want to be like this. I don't want my son to grow up like this. He needs to go to school. I want him to have an education and all he gets from me is a bad example. He's getting too big. He can't get through small windows any more.' The man pleaded with Ryer to take the boy home with him, time and time again. 'Please take him. You can look after him. You'll do better with him.'

Ryer said, 'I can't do that; he's your child, your boy. I can't just take a child like that!'

'Yes, you can. Just put him in a home!' was the father's reply.

This went on for several weeks. Eventually, Ryer spoke with the management at the prison. 'I could probably find a suitable home for this young lad. What is the legality of taking a child like that and how can we do this?'

The man in charge said: 'Oh yes, if he gives you permission then you can to do that. There's no problem. Take him. He will be better off.'

The boy was about school age. Ryer took the lad's hand and walked him out of the prison to his bicycle. He lifted him onto the passenger seat and cycled home. Jo must have been quite surprised to see Ryer walking with the young boy, who in turn must have wondered what was going on. My parents did not know what to do; it was all so unexpected. He was fed, and my mother dressed him in clean clothes. All this had been observed by our elderly live-in cook, a lovely woman called Kokkie, the common name for the cook. She asked Dad to let her talk with the boy. She soon discovered the village he came from and assured Dad that she would look after him.

'It's all right. I'll keep an eye on him and then later on I can take him to the village where my family is and we can look after him there.' It seemed a very a simple arrangement and the boy was happy to be with Kokkie.

During the short period he was with us he commenced school. Joan was not quite four years old at the time. Eventually Kokkie took the boy home to familiar surroundings, and he attended the village school. My parents were pleased with how things worked out for this young lad in such a caring way. They saw it as a happy ending for him and a hope for his future. For them it was the end of an unusual episode.

The capital city, Batavia, had a large port where all the ships from Europe arrived and departed. That meant Ryer was responsible for farewelling officers or greeting new ones—often helping the newcomers go on their way to The Salvation Army's THQ in Bandung in West Java. The Palace of the Dutch Governor-General for the Netherlands East Indies (NEI) was situated in Batavia. The city had a large commercial centre. It was also where the greatest proportion of military personnel was located. This gave Ryer, in particular, insights into what was happening in the country.

Twelve months later, in 1938, Dad and Mum were sent to Rembang on the north coast of East Java. Joan remembers, 'It was where I was cured of my bronchitis. Our house was situated so close to the sea that only coconut plantations separated the two. The doctor advised Mum to make me plunge into the sea as soon as I was awake in the morning and have me breathe in the sea air for a while. This was done, and although we were there only eight months I was forever cured of my bronchitis. As I recall, Rembang was the shortest appointment Mum and Dad ever had.'

From Rembang, Ryer and Jo were appointed to the Jogya military home in April 1939. Yogyakarta is now spelt with a 'Y', whereas previously it was spelt with 'J', and it is still called 'Jogya' for short. My birth certificate records I was born in the Province of Yogyakarta. I was actually not born in the capital city itself, which has the same name, but somewhere nearby. My parents were there just long enough to be settled and for my birth in November 1939.

One wonders when The Salvation Army leadership in Bandung concluded how superbly suited Adjutants Ryer and Jo van Kralingen were for a Christian ministry with the defence forces. Under their leadership, the Open Door Clubhouses they managed were constantly filled with visitors. In August 1940, my parents were appointed to the military home in Malang, 44 km south of Surabaya. This was a large home strategically located for both military and navy personnel with occasional visits from members of the air force. Surabaya contained a naval base and multiple oil refineries. The two cities were connected by road and railway. The Army's Open Door was situated on the main road between two social extremities: the back wall of the local jail on the right, and the residence of the Regent or local governor and his family on the left. The facility was a typical colonial-style residence with a large front verandah and garden. It was a home-away-from-home for the men who used its facilities on their 'rest days'. The back of the house had a wide U-shaped covered verandah with multiple rooms. This allowed for kitchen and other domestic requirements as well as accommodation for employees and visitors, such as military chaplains. Adjoining the building was a Salvation Army worship centre.

Joan recalled how on one occasion Ryer said: 'There is nothing worse than having navy and military personnel together in the home.' But he spoke their language rather than with Bible readings or prayer before they went to bed. They were invited to Sunday morning meetings, which were held in the adjacent building. 'If any of you are churchgoers, there is a service this morning and you are more than welcome to attend,' he would say. His unspoken philosophy was: 'There is little I can do other than be there for them and provide a word in season when we are having a conversation.'

A number of the men who visited the Open Door Clubhouse in Malang were based in Surabaya where some attended the local Salvation Army corps. Others remembered Ryer and Jo from when they were the managers of the Open Door in Solo and Yogyakarta.

Daily contact with members of the defence forces who lived with the expectation of conflict alerted Ryer and Jo to the imminence of war. My parents became politically aware in ways that would not have occurred if they had only been corps officers. Both sensed tension among the men as they sat around the radio with their coffee listening to news of Japan's latest moves. A major military assault was expected. It was only a question of when.

In retrospect, it was clear that the Japanese military had carefully planned invasion routes via the north of Sulawesi, to the oil-rich areas of Tarakan and Borneo, and to Java and Bali. Dutch defence forces had already been deployed to the east coast of Borneo, to places such as Tarakan and Balikpapan. It was expected that these would be targeted by the Japanese.

As B. Hackett points out,

> On 26 July 1941, in an attempt to halt Japanese aggression in China, American President Franklin Roosevelt issued an executive order which embargoed all oil exports to Japan in August 1941. The Dutch joined the embargo. As a result Japan lost 93 per cent of its oil supply. Japan's reserves included only about a year and a half's oil.[18]

So, Malang was the place where Ryer and Jo began to wonder, 'Will this be our last appointment? What will happen?'

An unexpected request

Late in August 1941, Commissioner Arend C. Beekhuis, the Territorial Commander (TC) of The Salvation Army in the Netherlands East Indies, based in Bandung, was asked by the Netherlands East Indies (NEI) Government for 'a suitable Welfare Officer and Chaplain for the 7th Battalion Infantry (NEI), including Artillery & Engineers (Professionals) for Tarakan for a period of six months. Urgent!' The position of welfare officer included the refurbishment of the Open Door Military Clubhouse. Recreational facilities on the island were limited and the morale of the men was low.

Salvation Army leadership understood the urgency of this request implied war was imminent. The gravity of the political situation added weight to the request. The choice for this appointment was a sensitive one—it meant separating a married couple with two young children, namely Adjutants Ryer and Johanna van Kralingen, situated in Malang, East Java. They had a small family, whereas some of the other officers who may have been appointed had huge families. They had done well in their appointments and they had wide experience across a whole range of military hostels and services.

Recounting this turning point in a post-war essay, Jo wrote:

> Major William Palstra, the Social Services Secretary, sent
> by Commissioner Arend Beekhuis, visited us in Malang at
> the end of August 1941 to ask us whether we were willing
> to each have a separate appointment for six months.
> Dad (Ryer), [would be] chaplain for all the military and
> the military home in Tarakan, with an assistant officer
> promoted earlier from cadet to probationary-lieutenant.
> I too would be given a cadet promoted to officer rank to
> assist me.[19]

Major Palstra explained that the government's request for Tarakan was 'ostensibly' for six months. Cadet-Lieutenant Estafanus Simatupang would be appointed to assist Ryer with the added responsibilities for the local corps.[20] Jo would remain in Malang to manage The Open Door military home and support the corps officer with the pastoral responsibilities and prison work of the corps. Probationary-Lieutenant Johanna Nelwan would be her assistant.

Ryer was familiar with welfare work and refurbishing military homes, but he knew instinctively, however, that to be a chaplain for military personnel would become the most significant aspect of his ministry. Under this appointment and at government request, Ryer would be appointed as a civilian chaplain for the military. If they agreed to the request, Ryer's departure date from Semarang to Tarakan would be on 16 September. Ensign Derek Ramaker would accompany Ryer on the journey to Tarakan with the newly commissioned Lieut. Simatupang.

At the end of what had been a long discussion, the Major drew the conversation to a close by committing Jo and Ryer to the Lord in prayer. After the Major had left, Jo and Ryer sat in silence for some time. I imagine the conversation would have gone something like this: 'Is this really what we should be doing?' The question seemed to hang in the air. Sitting on the edge of his seat, Ryer leaned towards Jo and reminded her how wonderfully the Lord had led them thus far and that he would continue to do so! Ryer asked Jo how she felt about it. She looked at his face, with tears, but nodded her head in agreement. They both understood the reason for the request and the urgency of the matter. Tarakan had to be defended. They also realised that their separation could stretch well past six months. Jo would be alone in Malang where there was much military activity at the time. However, numbers would rapidly diminish as troops were called up for frontline war service. Then, holding hands, and in the privacy of their own room, they knelt beside the bed as they committed themselves the Lord, trusting him for the future.

Jo's immediate thought then was of their two children. 'How are we going to tell Joan about you going away? She'll miss you and you won't be here for her eighth birthday in February. Sonja will be 22 months when you leave, too small to understand what is happening.' Joan was 'Daddy's girl'. Ryer took her everywhere on his bicycle, read her stories, put her to bed—all the things he had missed in his own childhood. 'Let's leave that for tomorrow. I'll need time to think about that,' he said. And that is what he did! The following day father and daughter spent some special time together as Ryer explained that he would be away for six months. After some teary moments, he produced a surprise: a six-month calendar he had made—from 14 September 1941 to 13 March 1942—to hang up in her room. 'Every night before you go to bed you cross out one day. Do you think you can do that? Pray for Mummy and Daddy as we do for you and Sonja,' he said.

Word of Ryer's departure for Tarakan spread rapidly. Men came to shake his hand and wish him well. He was touched by their kindness.

On the day of his departure Ryer's last memory would be of Jo and the children waving him goodbye. Ryer left Malang on 13 September 1941 for Semarang where he boarded a ferry for Tarakan.

In retrospect, I believe this change of appointment was divinely timed. God's hand was on their decision—it was the right one. As will be outlined in later chapters, Ryer and Jo's ministries extended far beyond the island of Tarakan and the city of Malang, to places unexpected as the war progressed.

CHAPTER 5

Malang and De Wijk

New responsibilities

Jo continued the management of the military home in Malang. The Japanese did not enter the city until 10 March 1942. During the intervening months, life changed dramatically for her. Overnight she became counsellor, guide, chaplain and mother to countless young men who came to see her at odd times of the day or night. She was only 33 years of age.

The Open Door Military Clubhouse had a number of trusted and loyal employees. Jo loved these behind-the-scenes workers. Her daily routine involved an early morning visit to the kitchen for a discussion with the small, grey-haired cook, to confirm the number of guests for the main meal (rice table). Aside from the delicious soups and rice dishes she prepared each day, Kokkie knew the art of making crisps and delectable nibbles for special afternoon teas. The laundry and ironing women were next—they worked as a team with the women who cleaned rooms and cupboards and washed endless floors. And then there was the gardener who, aside from trimming bushes and grass, chased spiders and removed their webs from external walls and verandah ceilings. He was also the handyman who could repair anything! He knew how to whitewash the external walls of the building. In a hidden corner of the garden he grew some tobacco plants—which Jo was not supposed to know about!—and rolled his own cigarettes from the dried leaves. Jo knew all the staff by name and kept an eye on their health and wellbeing. They respected her as the *Nonya* or Lady of the house and protected her and the children.

Prior to Ryer's departure, Jo arranged a time to sit with Min. He was the senior employee and fulfilled a number of roles within the clubhouse. He knew many of the military visitors and to them he appeared as the 'front of house' waiter. But he was also the unofficial supervisor of the 'back of house' and a great support to Jo. She informed him that another officer would come to support her. Min had promised Ryer that he would look after the Nonya in his absence and he took this responsibility seriously.

On 7 December 1941, the world was shaken by the news that Japanese planes had attacked the United States Naval Base at Pearl Harbor, in Hawaii. The bombing killed more than 2,300 Americans. This attack forced the Unites States into World War II. It was only to be expected that the following day, 8 December, the Netherlands declared war on Japan. This meant that the Netherlands East Indies (NEI) was also at war with Japan. Initially, the declaration of war on Japan by the NEI confirmed what the military and many people already expected. For some time, Navy personnel continued to visit The Open Door but gradually numbers declined as men were called up for duty. Some grieved for their families in Holland. Jo took time to listen to them with sympathy. With Ryer now in Tarakan, she understood the grief of separation.

It was just a couple of weeks into 1942 when the newly appointed assistant officer, Lieutenant Johanna Nelwan, arrived in Malang following her commissioning as a Salvation Army officer. Jo was delighted and gave the young woman a warm welcome. In her essay Jo remarks, 'She settled in quickly at both The Open Door and with her corps activities and she carried her responsibilities in an excellent way. I could just leave her to whatever task she was given, she did it well.' Jo also knew the officer-parents of the Lieutenant. For Jo, the arrival of the young officer meant companionship—another woman with whom to converse.

In writing about Johanna Nelwan, I had a sudden sense of déjà vu related to a memory of 1988. My husband Ian and I visited Indonesia and spent a few days in the city of Bandung visiting some very elderly friends in The Salvation Army retirement village. It was a Sunday morning and Ian and I were standing outside the worship centre greeting the people as they entered the building. A tall, retired woman officer came to me and, speaking in Dutch, said: 'My name is Major Johanna Nelwan. Please give my greetings to your mother. My first appointment was with her in Malang. She was so good to me.' When I shared this story with my mother some weeks later, she was deeply moved by the message and her mind was instantly flooded with memories.

The military home was well known in Malang. It was not unusual for local friends and business associates to visit The Open Door in the evenings for some relaxation around the billiard table. Others would sit in the lounge room with a cup of coffee or a cool drink while discussing business. Alcohol was not permitted in the military homes. Following Ryer's departure to Tarakan, Jo became increasingly aware of people expressing their concern about Japanese influence in local business and property matters. Many small shops in cities and villages were owned by Japanese who had lived in NEI for many years. They were courteous and part of the business scene in most towns. Many lived in rural villages and spoke both Dutch and the local language. They also had strong influences on village structures and rural life.

Jo wrote of this time:

> We knew there was war from the beginning, but where we lived we had not heard any shooting or fighting. We did hear a bomb explosion in the centre square in front of the governor's residence. We saw the soil spurting up metres and metres into the air—was it a mistake? Were these accidents? Were they intended—considering where they took place—but no explanation was given.[21]

The pilot's story

Now, Malang was also situated quite close to the south coast of Java, but a good distance from the larger provincial cities in Central Java. It was built on a low mountain plateau with one main road and a railway line north to Surabaya. Reconnaissance flights by small planes took place along the south coast of Java and along some main highways. Because the town was in a somewhat isolated area, planes had little competition for airspace and the nearby airport was ideal for training pilots. I distinctly remember one story told by Jo of a young pilot who came to see her in a state of real distress. For the second time his plane had come down, with his parachute opening to ensure he had a safe landing. He was on a reconnaissance flight over land and he came out alive. This time, however, his plane had been shot down; it was his first encounter with war and he was so fearful. Jo saw and heard his distressed voice and guided him towards the privacy of a quiet room, at the same time signalling Min for a cup of coffee. Jo sat opposite the young man and encouraged him to tell her his story.

'Ma'am, I've come through twice alive, but I know the next time I won't, and I am so scared. What am I going to do?'

Jo nodded her head and noticed his nervous hand movements. She encouraged him to relax by taking some deep breaths—slowly—and encouraged him to drink some coffee. Jo reassured him that he was in a in a safe place and gradually he calmed down. Eventually, Jo asked him what he feared most.

'I am afraid of death. I am not ready to die,' was his answer.

This would not be the last time Jo was confronted by such an honest fear of death. Jo reminded him that they were in a time of war and what he described was going to happen to others. The important thing for a Christian believer was that death is not the end. 'God loves us all. He loves you too. He has promised that those who love him will see him. God is trustworthy. You can depend on him. He is with you, even in dark days,' she said. Calmly Jo outlined John 3:16–17, 'God loved the world so much that he gave his only Son, that everyone who has faith in him may not die but have eternal life. It was not to judge the world that God send his Son into the world, but that through him the world might be saved.'[22] She guided him through the steps of salvation including repentance and faith to accept Jesus as Lord of his life. 'If he calls you home, he will be there to receive you.' Jo encouraged him to talk with God at any time. She then prayed with him. Sometime later the young pilot left quietly, now calm in his spirit.

These were hard times for Jo but God was with her! Perhaps, if Ryer had been there, she would have left it to him to speak with the young man, but times were different now. Dark days of uncertainty were ahead. War was on the doorstep. Every Christian had to be ready to speak out. She was grateful to God for using her to guide one who was lost and full of fear to a place of refuge where he found peace in the love of Jesus.

With the declaration of war in December 1941 all Royal Netherlands Indies Army (Koningkrijk Nederlands Indiës Leger—KNIL) and naval personnel who had families living in Malang were called up for active war service. Within a matter of days, all these soldiers or sailors were deployed for the defence of the NEI, leaving their wives and families in Malang. Writing about the departure of the troops from Malang in her post-war essay, Jo reflected:

> This may well have been the reason for the sudden influx of women—mainly wives and children of the KNIL personnel—their frightened women and children came to seek refuge with us fearful of what the Japanese would do to them. So, they packed their bags, took their children and landed unannounced on the doorstep of The Open Door demanding accommodation; 12 women and 12 children. They remained with us until early March 1943 when we were transferred to De Wijk. Throughout that time there was never a word of gratitude or 'thank you' from these women. Yet they expected the servants to do their washing, ironing, clean their rooms and even look after their children![23]

Within days of their arrival, Min, the senior employee, asked to see Jo about the 'women'. Jo was disturbed by the attitude of the women towards the staff. She noted what Min said and promised something would be done about it. Jo decided to have a regular morning tea with the women. A day and time was arranged. Jo spoke with the women and her suggestions were well received. Peace was restored—temporarily.

Despite the attitude and behaviour of these seemingly ungrateful women, Jo reached out to them pastorally. She invited them to attend the Sunday services, and the women's weekly home league activities. The children were invited to attend Sunday school, along with Joan and me. The opportunity for their children to attend Sunday school was well accepted by the women. There was also a Brownie Club for those of Joan's age, seven to 10 years. Jo also commenced a sewing group for the women and a Bible reading/study group. Eventually most of the women were involved in some aspect of the activities offered them. Jo also encouraged the women to teach their children to read and write by teaching them the alphabet.

Recalling this period many years later, I remember her saying: 'I found it easier to work with 100 men than with a dozen women!' Joan and I were highly amused by this statement. The idea of a women's liberation movement was still a long way off. I wonder how my mother would have responded to the idea.

11 January 1942

The situation was tense. It was Sunday morning, 11 January. Some soldiers were sitting on the verandah with their coffee listening to the news. Jo was returning from the Sunday morning service in the adjacent corps building, with Joan and me. The radio was loud. As she stepped on to the verandah she heard and listened to the news broadcast:

> Japan made its first air attacks on the Netherlands East Indies in two areas: The island of Tarakan, where the military destroyed all the oil installations during the week in

expectation of an invasion. A second air attack was directed
on the town of Manado on the island of Celebes.

Air attacks on the island of Tarakan and the town of Manado, in
North Celebes, were Japan's rallying war cry against the NEI. The
broadcaster's loud voice was turned down. The men looked at Jo in
silence. Then one voice spoke for all. 'We're sorry you had to hear
that Mrs Van Kralingen.' Jo nodded and expressed her thanks for
their sensitivity. I believe my mother would have expressed her strong
faith in a God who was present in Malang and in Tarakan together
with all those men, including Ryer.

Leaving the children to play in their own room, Jo walked through
to her private quarters and kneeling at her bedside poured out her
grief to the God who never slumbers and who is always available.

> *All your anxiety, all your care,*
> *Bring to the mercy seat, leave it there,*
> *Never a burden he cannot bear,*
> *Never a friend like Jesus.*[24]

During the days immediately following the air attack on Tarakan,
Jo's mind was in turmoil. She experienced grief, loneliness and a sense
of isolation. Her thoughts were constantly with Ryer: 'O God, protect
him.' The corps officer and members of the corps supported Jo with
prayer. Friends from the local community came to inquire. Following
the events of the last two weeks an unwelcome but recurring thought
overwhelmed her: war was now a reality. It was only a matter of
when. Ryer would not return to Java as anticipated.

That evening as she settled the children for the night, Joan brought
out the calendar Ryer had made for her to tick off another day closer
to his return home to Malang. They went through the evening ritual
of 'crossing out' and Joan's earnest prayer, 'Please look after Daddy
and keep him safe.' Jo knew that during the next two months left on
the calendar Joan would have her ninth birthday in mid-February.

Jo's prayer, undoubtedly would have been, 'Give me the right words to prepare her for the delay of Ryer's return home.'

The declaration of war prompted The Salvation Army THQ in Bandung to close its accounts before capitulation and to distribute its social funds and salaries to its various institutions through the bank. Before the bank collapsed, Jo managed to withdraw all the money in The Salvation Army's account for Malang and kept the balance under lock and key in a safe.

Looking after The Open Door accounts was not Jo's favourite task. As she sat down at the Ryer's desk, everything in the office reminded Jo of him; nothing was out of place. Book spines were clearly labelled and placed in date order in a locked cupboard. The keys to desk and cupboard were clearly labelled. Even the pencils in the jar on the desk were sharpened and inviting her to 'get on with it!'

Laughter from the billiard room filtered through the half open door. In her mind, she could see Ryer there...a moment of quiet concentration...all eyes watching silently as the cue aligned with the ball... Jo followed the scene in her mind. She waited for the moment of cue-to-ball contact...click...yes! The game is on its way! She smiled at the memory. How often had she watched this non-verbal game? It required disciplined concentration and a steady hand. It cleared the mind of other distractions. Jo sighed. 'A cup of coffee would be a good start.' Jo was an organised person. Life had to go on, including the accounts.

God's amazing provision

> *God moves in a mysterious way,*
> *His wonders to perform;*
> *He plants his footsteps in the sea,*
> *And rides upon the storm.*[25]

God certainly moved in a mysterious way to provide amazingly for two of his women followers. He knew they would need each other to ride with him 'upon the storm' of circumstances—including the war. They had two important foundation stones in common: God's call to become Salvation Army officers, and the one-year live-in training session of 1930–31 they shared at The Salvation Army Officer Training College in Holland.

In those early years of the Army in the Netherlands, there were large numbers of cadets in training sessions. On arrival at the Training College, cadets were placed into small groups or brigades for class teaching purposes and outdoor training activities. Cadets usually remained in their assigned brigade till the day they were commissioned. Men and women were trained separately in those days. Opportunities to mingle with cadets from other brigades were limited to monthly spiritual days, united prayer meetings or large public events. Jo van Kapel and Marie Luitjes were assigned to different brigades and were virtual 'strangers' to each other. Later, both women married, Marie to Tjerk Luitjes and Jo to Ryer van Kralingen. Their paths separated, yet both couples eventually met each other in the NEI.

When asked, Jo admitted she knew Marie from a distance like many other cadets in her session. She recalled, however, vague comments such as her being 'a tomboy' and having 'a strange accent and big hands'. Marie had a broad provincial accent at that time and was not always easy to understand. As an officer she had proved to be a hard worker with a good mind. Jo was aware that Marie and Tjerk had been through much grief following the sudden death of their beautiful little girl a couple of years earlier when they lived in Ambon. Tjerk was the Army's Property Secretary and, together with his wife and their little son, Jantje, the family lived in a Salvation Army compound in Batavia. This gave Tjerk ready access to ships when he visited Army properties on distant islands; sometimes he was away for many weeks. Despite having good neighbours, Marie was a lonely person.

It was mid-afternoon in the first week of March 1942, the hottest time of the day. The children were having their afternoon nap. The institute's two dogs were stretched out on the cool stone floor near Jo who was resting on the couch in the sitting room. The workers had their own places for their resting mats—in rooms or the shade on the back verandah's cool floor. Min was on a mat in his workroom where he brewed his coffee and kept the biscuits, but not too far from the front door, which was closed at this time of the day. It was time for an afternoon rest. All was quiet, but not for long.

A loud knocking on the front door broke the silence of the rest period. The dogs responded instantly, barking furiously at the strange voices. Jo sat up and knew Min was already at the door. She wondered at the sound of another voice and then recognised the face. 'Marie! Marie Luitjes! What are you and Jantje doing here all the way from Batavia? Come in, you both look exhausted!' Jo took Marie's case and directed them both to the sitting room to some comfortable chairs.

'What brings you here, and where is Tjerk?' Jo asked.

'Tjerk is in Ambon to direct the building of a new hall and an officer's quarters, and I don't expect him back now because the Japs have invaded Java and are in control of the harbours,' Marie replied. 'Don't ask me why we are here. All I can say is that God sent us here. He guided us on the journey.'

Jo realised there was much more to Marie's story. She suggested they take time to enjoy the refreshments Min brought in while a room was prepared for them. Once the children were in bed, after the evening meal, Marie continued to tell Jo her amazing story.

> For some time now I became aware of a Voice, 'Go to Van Kapel'.[c] As time went by it became increasingly more urgent, *'Go to Van Kapel!'* It was there every day, it would not leave me. I was told to go to you—it was urgent! I knew Ryer had gone to Tarakan and you were here by yourself. I tried to ignore the Voice, but it was persistent. After I had bought the ticket and stepped into the train it felt as if a great weight was lifted from my shoulders; I knew I had done the right thing![26]

Jo was glued to her seat and listened with amazement. She had

---

[c] In the early training days, cadets were addressed by their surname, hence 'Van Kapel'.

no memory of ever having such a long conversation with Marie, who continued:

> We heard about the attack on Tarakan on 11 January and on Manado. In Batavia the expectation was that the Japs would continue to move further south and take Java. And they have. Late February Japanese troops landed on Java's most northern point, closing off the Bantam Bay [the sea channel between Java and Sumatra].

Marie went on:

> When I heard the last train to East Java was going the following day I knew it was time to go to Malang! All the electricity would be switched off, including trains, after that. I packed my bags, and informed the people on the compound where I was going and my reason for doing so. When I got to the station it seemed as if the whole city of Batavia was trying to escape to East Java. People were fighting their way to a ticket window. There were no queues. It was a case of who had the longest arm to reach the window with their ticket money. Imagine little me! They didn't see me... I had Jantje hanging on my skirt, my case in my left hand and money in my right. There were no other women, only men. What could I do? The train was soon to depart. I said to God, 'If you want me on this train then you will need to help me!' A tall, well-built Arab was standing in front of me; he was at least twice my height. He was getting impatient, the person in front of him had difficulties getting his money out—the crowd was pushing and shouting from all sides. I took a leap onto the Arab's back and stretched my right hand, with the correct money for two seats, to the man in the ticket box. He was so startled that he took the money without checking the amount, and gave me the two tickets. I remembered to say: *'Terima kasih'* [thank you] as I slipped off the Arab's back. I slung my bag around my neck, grabbed Jantje with my left hand and the luggage with my other hand and we ran to the carriage. We were the first people in the compartment, and

there were two seats, one for Jantje and one for me. Well,
God left me in no doubt; He got me here. He also helped me
get the tickets. And the best thing was that my heart was at
peace. The Voice stopped.[27]

Jo listened to the Marie's story with utter amazement. Silently she
wondered: 'Is this really the same woman I remember from training
days?' She couldn't help but laugh at Marie's story about the Arab
and admired her courage.

'You are an amazing woman, Marie. I could never have done that!'
Jo's sincere words of praise and admiration of Marie's courageous
actions laid the foundation of a lasting bond of friendship with Marie.

Facing reality: finances, furniture and sales

That same evening Jo, knowing Marie and her husband, Tjerk,
had previously managed an Open Door Clubhouse, asked Marie
what she deemed to be her special strength in management. The
answer was brief and to the point. 'I am a businesswoman and in our
appointments, I always looked after the accounts.'

Jo looked at Marie and began to laugh! 'Well, I know why the
Lord sent you here!'

It did not take long for Jo to discover that Marie was an astute
businesswoman. During the few hours she had been in the clubhouse,
Marie assessed its finances, the number of staff and the 'all take no
give' free lodgers.

The following morning the two women sat down to discuss
business. Firstly, Marie applauded Jo for withdrawing all the money
before the banks collapsed. 'We live in difficult times and must pull
together! This means making some difficult decisions.' They needed
to consider staff reductions, but that could wait for later.

Marie commenced the discussion with a property assessment.
She confirmed that, while the building known as The Open Door was
rented by The Salvation Army, all the furniture was the property of
The Salvation Army. She then suggested that Jo check the furniture

inventory and bring it up-to-date if required. This would include entertainment equipment and furniture, such as the billiard and table tennis tables, chairs, bed frames and cupboards. These would be valuable on the black market and should be considered for sale while the public arena for trade was still open for business.

Marie also touched on the need for helpers with wagons and oxen, men with four-wheeled carts, and additional people from the market who wanted a day job to earn some money. As Jo listened to Marie she realised what a godsend she was and how timely her arrival. 'Thank you, Lord.'

Later that day, when the doors were closed and everyone had settled for the night Jo sat in the sitting room adjacent to her bedroom. It was her end-of-the-day time with the Lord. She took time to muse over the events of that day. I wonder if it went something like this: 'Lord, I was lonely and you sent me Johanna Nelwan. She is a lovely young woman and she is doing well with pastoral work in the corps. I've been concerned about the financial administration of the Home. And then you called Marie! I know you sent her and I am so grateful you did. Help us to make a good team. I was rather judgmental about her because she is "different". Please forgive me for this.'

The following day the two women went to the market. Marie took her time as she walked around and observed the variety of goods for sale and quite naturally engaged in conversation with the stall owners. She asked the right questions and, in turn, was asked what she wanted to trade. Her cautious mention of a 'variety of furniture' and possibly a 'billiard table' drew an instant response of interest from Chinese businessmen. Jo was the silent observer. She was amazed at the ease with which Marie engaged in conversation with the stall owners; she even made them laugh. They obviously recognised Marie as one of 'them' and were happy to advise her on market sale procedures in Malang for large furniture. By the time they went home Marie had the names of potential buyers who were open for business.

In the meantime, Jo completed the revised inventory. Rooms previously used to accommodate military personnel became storage rooms. She knew that moving furniture for the purpose of sale would unsettle Min and the other employees. It was time to alert him to the financial emergency they were facing. Jo called him in and explained that The Open Door was no longer receiving financial support from either the NEI government or from The Salvation Army. Using simple language, she explained the need for money to provide food sufficient for many people! Jo pointed out that some workers would have to be sent home because there was no money to pay them. Similarly, the Army would be selling all the furniture before the 'Nippon' closed the *pasar*, the open-air market. Nippon was the word then commonly used for the Japanese by Europeans and Indonesians. 'We do not know how long we will be here. We must sell our goods now!' She said. 'Early tomorrow morning Adjutant Marie and I will go to the market; Lieut. Nelwan will be in charge. Please look after her. We will come back with many carts. You may be needed to help carry furniture.'

Early on the day of the big sale as the first rays of the sun lit the sky, Marie shocked Jo by appearing in black trousers! 'Yes,' said Marie before Jo could say a word, 'I know you are shocked, but this is me, and this job cannot be properly done in a white uniform dress. So, let's get going!'

They cycled to the market to hire men with two-wheeled wagons pulled by oxen to transport furniture. Quite an entourage arrived at The Open Door a few hours later. The largest and heaviest load was the billiard table. Jo's eyes suddenly filled with tears as she saw it being covered with old blankets to protect it from being damaged on the journey. It had been at the hub of the entertainment activities of the clubhouse. Memories of Ryer and his 'boys', as he called them, flooded her mind. It was like saying 'goodbye' to an old friend. With her hand on her face she watched as it was wheeled out of the building. Momentarily she seemed frozen to the ground. A gentle touch on her arm and Marie's unexpected quiet voice brought Jo back to reality. 'How about some *koppie tubruk* for the workers, and ourselves, before we all return to the market with the goods? I think they'll appreciate a cup. I'll get Min to give you a hand.' And she was gone. *Koppie tubruk* is strong coffee made with unfiltered ground coffee.

All saleable furniture from the billiard table to bed frames, cupboards and rattan chairs were piled on oxcarts and sold on the market. Their departure left the clubhouse looking empty and deprived of character.

I can only imagine it, but at the end of what must have been an exhausting day Jo and Marie were in the sitting room with their feet up. Both women were delighted with the financial outcome of their sale. The amount of money received was beyond their expectations. The workers who helped with transporting the goods were all paid correct wages in cash on the spot, and Marie had arranged receipts for the payments to be signed. 'Marie, you are an amazing woman; you thought of everything, even the little receipt books. I am sure that some of the workers did not know what a receipt book is.'

Marie laughed! 'Well, they learned something new today. However, tomorrow I will lock myself up in the office not to be interrupted except for some refreshments, to count all the money again and set up a system to keep us afloat for as long as possible. Now I am going to bed.'

The coming of war

Sometime during February 1942, the electricity was switched off in Malang, East Java, depriving its citizens of radio, telephone connections and lighting. No accurate date for 'lights out' on Java could be found. Possibly this took place before the first air attack on Surabaya on 3 February 1942.

Writing about the situation in West Java, Salvation Army historian, Lieut-Colonel Melattie Brouwer, recorded later:

> The Japanese landed in Java on 28th February, 1942. Eight days later, Batavia was taken by the Japanese and declared 'open city', all lights went on. After heavy fighting on the mountains and air raids on Bandung and its airfield, this town, too, capitulated. On the 9th March Bandung was entered. [28]

Immediate restrictions were placed on church and government positions; these came under investigation from the day the Japanese entered. In the case of Malang, the Japanese entered on 10 March 1942.

In Malang, printing presses were closed and newspapers ceased to be published. This meant that Malang was now cut off from all national news, including contact with Surabaya. The Japanese, however, appeared to maintain a comprehensive communication system on Java and beyond.

Surabaya was considered the most important city on the island of Java during World War II. Situated on the north coast of East Java, it housed the main Dutch naval base in the NEI. Its facilities included a well-placed harbour, an oil refinery and underground fuel tanks, submarine and seaplane bases, radio communication and numerous other facilities. Its refineries were connected by many kilometres of pipelines through which the Bataafse Petroleum Maatschappij (BPM, or Batavian Oil Company, a subsidiary of the Royal Dutch Shell)—later called the Shell Oil Company—distributed crude oil to numerous coastal and inland refineries, and refined oil to towns in Central Java. Due to the restrictions of electricity and communications mentioned above, the first Japanese air strike on Surabaya on 3 February 1942 passed unnoticed by the rest of Java. The Imperial Japanese Navy (IJN) took over the control of the extensive former Royal Dutch Shell Company in Java. Following the destruction of the oilfields in Tarakan and Balikpapan, Surabaya became the main refuelling harbour for the Japanese fleet.

Again, due to restrictions in communications, the general population was unaware that a disastrous battle was about to take place in the usually calm waters of the Java Sea.

> The Battle of the Java Sea occurred on February 27, 1942, and was an early naval engagement of World War II in the Pacific. In early 1942, with the Japanese rapidly advancing south through the Dutch East Indies, the Allies attempted to mount a defense [sic] of Java in an effort to hold the Malay Barrier. Concentrating under the unified command known as American-British-Dutch-Australian (ABDA)

Command, Allied naval units were divided between bases at Tandjong Priok (Batavia) in the west and Surabaya in the east.[29]

Most civilians in Java, with the exception of the Dutch military and political leaders, were unaware of this major sea battle off the coast of Java in which 2,300 sailors of the Allied forces lost their lives.

Night visitors

One of the stories from Jo's post-war essays comes from this period:

> One dark moonless night during the first week of March 1942, a military truck came into our front yard, very quietly. There was a knocking at the door and 15 to 20 men came in under cover with a camouflage light. The first thing the men said was, 'Do not be afraid. We all belong to the Navy, but there is no Navy anymore. We were commanded to destroy everything in Surabaya that belonged to the Navy. This included all the ships, all the weapons and all the buildings, leaving no possibility for ships to enter. Even the storage buildings were destroyed.'
>
> Looking at the partially covered faces I caught a glimpse of who they were and eventually recognised each one of the men. I cannot describe what the men looked like... they were in a state of shock...they were not themselves. They were strangely dressed—not in uniform. 'Can we stay here please? We have enough food with us, plenty of tins and we have enough money.' What could I do? It was late, all I could say was, 'Yes, you all need food and rest but first of all you need a hot cup of coffee, then you'll all want to *mandie*.'

Jo provided them with towels and soap for a mandie or bath and took them to The Salvation Army hall just a few metres to the left of the residence, where they remained for the night. She noted the truck was parked where it was not visible from the road. These men had been here before and they knew what they were doing. Jo continued:

> The following day I transferred them to where we used to lodge our military and navy personnel. I told the women and children to stay away from there. The men were not themselves; they had gone through a nightmare. But I pleaded with...

Jo's hand-written essay stops abruptly at this point, mid-sentence, and was never completed. Something must have distracted her and she forgot to continue the story. All we can assume is that these men disappeared the following night as quietly as they arrived. They had driven through the night after the destruction of Navy equipment in Surabaya to Malang for a temporary safe haven. Jo did add a small retrospective addendum to this incident:

> It was only when the leader of the group spoke that it dawned on me that *we did not know* 'it was all over for us'. In Malang we knew nothing about this; radio connections were cut and printing presses no longer functioned...

The Japanese entered Java in three stages; the most important was West Java, the seat of government, defence and commerce. Hackett continues his account of the surrender of Java as follows:

> At 0900, 8 March 1942 the Commanding Officer-in-Charge (C-in-C) of the Allied forces, Dutch Lt General Hein Ter Poorten announced the surrender of the Royal Netherlands Indies Army in Java. That afternoon, Governor, Sir Dr. A.W.L. Tjarda Van Starkenborgh Stachouwer and Ter Poorten met the C-in-C of the Japanese forces Lt General Hitoshi Imamura at Kalidjati, Java, and agreed to capitulate... The next day the commander of Dutch Forces in East Java also surrendered.[30]

Following this surrender, East Java came under the control of the Japanese Navy and on 10 March 1942 they entered Malang. The piercing sound of sirens became an almost daily routine. The reasons given were vague. Perhaps they were warning of an air attack: 'Find a safe place. Get under cover!' Writing about this period, Jo said:

> The first weeks after the Japanese took control of the country we were able to visit Dutch military prisoners. We also had three Salvation Army officers there [amongst the prisoners], Adjutant Gladpootjes and Captains Wiersema and Sprokkereef. What could I give them? I hired three Indonesian men, each to carry a bag on their head, with a mattress and a pillow. Would the Japanese allow that? Each pillow was wrapped around in a striped tropical blanket with safety pins. Mrs Luitjes (or Auntie Marie) and her son Jantje and I carried bags with fruit, food and six bath towels. We managed to get all that to our friends. Once more the camp was opened, but that was the last time. In the meantime we still tried to get permission from the Japs to bring in articles for personal use, soap, toothpaste and toothbrushes, underwear and sandals...'

Jo was brought up in the in the days of 'aggressive Salvationism'. Not for her a lukewarm, half-hearted expression of faith. Jo's summary of this period was, 'It would take too much time to write down all that happened during those days. We, in Malang, were able to do our work as Salvation Army officers and wear our uniforms until the 16 March 1943. The Open Door Military Clubhouse remained open until early 1943.'

Christmas 1942 – New Year 1943

The clocks did not stop and the sun continued to rise every day—life continued. As my mother recounted:

> It was December and Christmas was not far away. Ladies from the Red Cross were also preparing for that. One Red Cross lady and I decided to request an interview with the Japanese Commander in his office. The Christmas

appeal for the [neighbouring] prison was an annual event, except this year it required the consent of the Japanese commander. We were both nervous and were aware of what could happen to us. I was in my uniform. Initially we were questioned about the reason for our visit. We spoke in Dutch. The fellow went, and then came back with the reply: 'Come back next week!' We went outside and looked at each other. 'We are still free, he did not keep us there and he did not say: "No"!'

We were back the following week with the same uncertainties, same request: 'We would like to bring in some food and clothing and daily necessities to the prisoners.' We waited a full hour. This time the man in charge came, and gave us each a five-pound tin with butter! We could not believe our eyes, and again... 'Come back next week!' Time had run out. We were now in the week of Christmas. Christmas joy for the prisoners was fading.

As we walked out of the building onto the road a deep sense of urgency stirred within me...there is another way...a Higher Command! I stood still and turned to my companion. She looked at me, surprised:

'What is it?' she asked.

'Do you believe in the power of prayer?'

She smiled, nodding her head, 'Yes, yes I do!'

'Good,' I replied. 'We have a week. Let's pray every day and ask your friends to support you, I will do the same.' This was faith multiplied and hope reborn.

The week following Christmas, the Commander said: 'Yes! Bring in all you have in one day!' We had three days to get ourselves organised. But he said something more! 'All that comes in must come in with the stamp of the Bala Keselamatan (The Salvation Army), no Red Cross!' I found that not only terrible for the lovely Red Cross lady with me, but the Red Cross had plenty of money and the Bala Keselamatan had very little.

News of the delay for the Christmas appeal this year went through the town like wildfire. Everyone knew about it. Goods began to arrive almost from the moment I walked into the house. I began to place goods on the floor against walls of the billiard room. Clothing and linen found a place on a table until we could stack no higher. There were many practical gifts aside from clothing, blankets and toiletries—gifts too many to mention. They covered all aspects of daily needs and beyond.

Early on the second morning people again began to arrive with fresh food: tins with cakes, biscuits—lots of eats and again daily necessities. People's kindness and generosity was overwhelming. We began to clear the next room—more the shape of a passage. People came throughout the day. A sense of unease rose within me as the unending stream of generous people continued to bring their gifts. How could we possibly manage to transport all this in the time available? The prison may have been next door, but the entrance was on the other side of the building at the end of the street. There were no cars, only bicycles. Fear overwhelmed my joy as I surveyed the mountain of goods, tinned food, cakes, cutlery, crockery and clothing. We did not have cardboard boxes to pack things and tomorrow was a few hours away. How would we cope? My thoughts became an unspoken prayer, 'Oh Lord, you answered our prayers beyond our expectations, but how do we get all of this from here to there, in one day?' My fear was greater than my joy.

By seven o'clock the last visitors had gone home. It was New Year's Eve, 31 December 1942, and all was quiet. It was a dark night. I closed the door. And suddenly I felt so alone!

I was startled by a knock on the front door, 'Is there anybody home?' Major Uilings, an older Army officer, came in with his bicycle looking very tired. He was really a sick man. I looked at him and thought, 'I'll never forget that face.' He had come from Kesilir (an area east of Malang) where he regularly visited an agricultural farm for men without employment. He would spend hours cycling to this camp from Surabaya to hear their stories and to be their friend. Nothing was too much for him.

Major Uilings made occasional visits from Surabaya to visit Kesilir and then usually stayed with us for the night before returning home on his bicycle. The major's appearance concerned me; he was so frail and obviously very tired. He looked around in amazement at the parcels of food and clothing and asked: 'What's this here?' I told him and explained that I was tired too and shared my fears with him as to how I was going to get it all out the next morning. His face changed all of a sudden. 'Have you got a meal and a drink for me, and an Aspirin?' When he finished all that, he said: 'I am going to bed now. Call me at 5.00am and I'll go to the market and hire as many men with carts and oxen as I can muster to come here tomorrow. We'll get it all out into the prison camp in one day.'

I awoke on New Year's Day. True to his word the major was up before dawn. After a quick breakfast, he took his bike and went to the market, returning an hour later with an entourage of every available transport an eastern market could provide. On his return, Uilings gave me an armful of flowers and said: 'Give that to the Commander in the prison for his New Year. He'll like that!' The march started: 18 carts with drivers, oxen pulling large, two-wheeled wagons with their drivers and Uilings and I on our bikes at the head of the march. I did not know Uilings' mind but, shame on me, I felt like a conqueror while at the same time thanking God for answered prayer. Why had I been anxious? God's time is always on time![31]

Intimidation

Civilian life continued fairly quietly for some months after the Japanese came in. But then began the almost daily visits of representatives from the Japanese Military Command. They were polite but invasive. They questioned and they made demands. Jo explained to the Japanese visitors that people with S's on their collar did not involve themselves in worldly pursuits because they were servants of God. And God protected her. She learned very early to look the aggressor in the eye and never allowed herself to be stared down. She learned diversionary tactics, made endless cups of coffee, played table tennis with them or board games. She made every effort to keep the Japs away from the terrified women at the back of the building, who did not understand that she was actually trying to protect them. They misunderstood the reasons Jo kept the Japanese in the front of the building. The Japanese were aware she was protecting at least 10 to 12 wives whose husbands were members of KNIL who had recently been called up for military service. Jo was not to be compromised—The Open Door was dedicated to the glory of God and his service alone—not for worldly entertainment or forced prostitution.

It was quite obvious Ryer was no longer in Malang. The Commandant in charge would sometimes visit with a group, or with a minor officer. On several occasions he invited Jo to go out with him for a meal. Politely and tactfully she reminded him that she was a married woman. On a couple of occasions, she noted him walk past the house to catch her attention. Jo simply did not 'see' him and continued what she was doing. But she took caution as her guide and refrained from sitting on the verandah.

Not long afterwards, Jo received a summons from the Japanese commander. He wanted to see her. Jo wondered what in the world he wanted to see her about. She felt most uneasy regarding this request. 'I am coming to support you,' said Marie. 'Lieut. Nelwan is quite capable to look after the place for a morning with Min's support. We now have very few visitors and the military has gone.' The three women met together in earnest prayer to God for Jo's protection before Marie and Jo departed.

There were people everywhere when they arrived at the building. Jo and Marie were given a seat. They waited for an hour before Jo was taken to the office of the Japanese commander. Marie was refused entry and returned to her seat outside. Uncertain of what to expect,

Jo entered his room, but was left in no doubt of the commander's intentions; there was no desk or seat for Jo. He sat on a bench covered with a narrow pallet, similar to what the house boy used for his afternoon nap. With a narrow cane he tapped his hand. Not a word was spoken. Jo kept her distance and looked down at him. Sitting on his pallet placed him at a disadvantage. She looked him in the eyes, not once lifting her gaze. It would have been a sign of fear or of weakness to do so. She watched him intently, praying silently, 'Lord, give wisdom, give strength.' The time seemed like an eternity. So intense was Jo's concentration, she was unaware of people standing motionless behind her. She had no sense of time and wondered how long this would last. He was waiting for her to weaken, to break down. 'Lord, don't let me do that; I know you are here.'

And then a sudden, ear-piercing siren broke the silence and the spell. Voices and movement behind her made Jo turn around, the door opened and people pushed their way out. Jo saw her moment for escape—wasting no time she followed the crowd out to freedom. Marie was still there. Jo grabbed her arm, 'Quick, run, before they shut the door on us. I'll talk later.' They ran out of the building, found their bicycles and sped home as fast as the wheels would turn. Was ever a siren more welcome? 'Thank you, Lord!'

A concerned Lieut. Johanna Nelwan and Min were anxiously waiting for them. Marie's first words made them laugh, 'O, Min, we need a strong *koppie tubruk*...all of us, including you!' The cup of coffee helped everyone to 'unwind' from the tensions of fear and uncertainty. Jo knew they were curious as to what really happened in the commander's office. Even Marie did not know all that took place. Jo referred to their joint ministry; each with a different task, but united in a soul-saving, caring ministry. She recalled how early that morning the three of them had shared in prayer asking for the Lord's protection over her when visiting the Japanese commander and how that carried her through the day. She mentioned how she knew God's presence with her. He kept her calm and gave her a clear mind. God answered their prayers in an amazing way. 'This is a story just for the three of us, not to be shared with anyone in the home. Let me tell you what happened…'

Later, Jo expressed the thought that the men standing behind her were there to force her to comply with the commandant's demands when he gave the signal. But it never came to that. Her main concern was for the young military wives who would be terrified if they heard this story. 'If you are asked where we were this morning the best answer is: the commandant was seeing many people this morning. However, I don't believe we have seen the last of him. I was so grateful to see Major Marie still sitting there waiting for me. It was such a relief to see you, Marie. Thank you for being there! And Lieutenant, thank you so much for taking charge here today. I know Min would have looked after you. But now we all need a good rest; it's time for bed.'

Jo, however, did not sleep. Following the events of that day she knew their days at the Open Door were now limited. Staff needed to be prepared for a departure day. This included everyone. Tomorrow could have its challenges. I have no doubt that she prayed for wisdom that evening.

Preparing the staff for closure

A couple of days later Jo had a serious conversation with Min regarding the closure of The Open Door in the near future. She explained they would probably receive a date when the building had to be vacated. All the Europeans would be put in camps, including the women and children who were resident at The Open Door. Min and the other employees would need to return to their home villages or kampongs; it would be too dangerous for them to remain in Malang. Jo asked if Min understood what she was saying. Did he have any questions? His face was strained. He was afraid. Not all the workers came from the same village. Some had family. Jo suggested that Min bring all the workers together and talk to them about it, emphasising the message: 'Do not remain in Malang!'

For some time, Jo too had been preparing for the day of their departure. She was a meticulous seamstress. I cannot remember her being without a sewing machine. She made all our clothing and often embroidered with small floral designs. She completed a backpack for Joan and was pleased with the result of the design. Already Jo had made a large one for herself. Having done so, the thought suddenly occurred to her what she would do with the sewing machine when they had to leave. They were only allowed to take what they could carry. What a waste to leave it here. Who would benefit from it? In the meantime, she worked on a small backpack for me. I had celebrated my third birthday the previous month.

While tidying her room and putting away her sewing equipment, her mind was busy with the events of the last few days. She recalled the time of prayer when Marie and Johanna had asked God to protect her when she had been summoned by the Japanese commander. It was a very special moment and the Lord had answered their prayer. Here were three women, each from different backgrounds, yet serving the same Lord together through the Spirit. 'We need to set aside a time each week to pray and read the Bible together; it will draw us closer together and to the Lord.' As she was closing the sewing machine she realised that the most logical person to give her precious treadle machine was Johanna Nelwan! Jo could not imagine life without it and felt close to tears at the thought of parting with it, but reality took over. Think what an asset it will be in a village situation, she told herself.

The first priority was to discuss Johanna's departure. Her officer-parents were not in Java at that time, but her relatives in Central Java would take her in. These relatives could not be contacted, but she knew where they lived. Jo explained that Johanna's departure was a case of urgency: all Europeans would soon be in camps and The Open Door would be closed.

Jo then mentioned the sewing machine. 'Oh!' Johanna put her hand to her mouth in surprise, 'You are giving me your sewing machine?' Her excitement knew no bounds! Jo suggested they spend a couple of days together for Johanna to learn how to use and care for the machine. It would then be packed in a special box. The big challenge was how to travel with it.

As usual, Marie managed to get a good train seat for Johanna with space for the sewing machine box. There were tears and hugs and a farewell prayer from Jo for a safe journey and arrival for Johanna. 'God be with you till we meet again.'

An angry commandant

The day they feared eventually came. The Commandant in his formal outfit including his sword made his entrance with his entourage. This time there were no smiles, just the demeanour of an angry man. Jo stood her ground silently. She looked at him and listened to the angry tirade of the military chief: 'Finish Salvation Army, no more uniform!' He ripped the S's off her collar and ground them under his boots. She watched them leave the building...her heart thumping, full of fear. It was then at that very moment she was overwhelmed by a great sense of the Presence of God, and a peace never experienced before came over her. Fear was gone and the realisation came that all the externals were unimportant except for the knowledge of the Lord's Presence. The Salvation Army had not disappeared because she could no longer wear her uniform. God had not changed! He was still in control and he would continue to go before. 'Thank you, Lord!'

Within moments of the commandant's departure Marie was at her side. 'Min told me "Mr Nips" turned up again with his minors.[d] But what did he do to your trimmings?'

'He came to tell me that there was no more Salvation Army, and no more uniform and he then proceeded to pull off my S's and ground them under his boot. He was not a very happy man. But the Lord was with me. We need not fear. He is in control. However, I believe the day for our departure could be any day now. We will be interned and need to know what we can and what we need to take with us. I will need to speak with the other women to do the same thing. This may be a suitable time to distribute some of the spare linen including the towels. We need to face reality.'[e]

In East Java, the internment of Dutch women and children generally occurred almost a year later then in West Java. We lived

---

[d] 'Nip/s' and 'Mr Nip/s' were nicknames for members of the Japanese military derived from Nippon or Japan.

[e] The Japanese did allow clergy to wear small crosses on their collars.

at The Open Door with the 12 families until March 1943. Jo had the arduous task of having to inform our faithful staff and boarders that The Open Door would be closed during the second week in March. For our domestic staff this meant leaving the security of The Open Door where some had lived and worked for many years. She called Min to the sitting room. He knew she was going to say something serious. Jo explained that all the *Totoks* or Europeans would be transferred to De Wijk. It would not be safe for him or the other staff to remain in Malang any longer. Most employees had been away from their home villages for many years and they feared rejection from family if they returned without substantial wealth. Jo promised they would be given some travel money and advised them to go as soon as possible and not to remain in Malang.

De Wijk

De Wijk, or The District, was our first internment camp. This was the hillside suburb of Malang. From 1942 to 1944 the suburb served as a large civilian camp mainly for women and children. It commenced during November–December 1942 as a 'protected neighbourhood' surrounded by barbed wire. The number of internees was ultimately 7,000 women and children.[32] Jo recounted:

> Early in 1943 European women and children in Malang were instructed to transfer to De Wijk. Marie and I received notification of the house number and the date we were expected there. It was the European district and every house would accommodate four or five families. It was the first stage of a POW camp. The difference was that we were free to move around The District and buy our food supplies but were not permitted to communicate with anyone on the other side of the barbed wire fence surrounding the district. European men were transferred to the Marine Camp in Malang.[33]

Jo's reaction to the move to De Wijk indicates the financial strain both she and Marie had been under with the additional 12 families who demanded full board and lodging:

> For 18 months, we survived on a tight budget and meticulous accounts kept by Marie [in the last 12 months]. When she took over the responsibilities of The Open Door accounts we continued to draw our own salaries. What a blessing this proved to be. The twelve women with their children were transferred to another women's camp. I thanked God that the end of that nightmare was over. Not one of these women ever contributed a penny; yes, they had three meals a day including their morning and their afternoon refreshments. When the home was eventually closed, we had five guilders left in the account. God was faithful. He provided.[34]

My mother, Joan and I, together with Marie and Jantje, arrived at De Wijk on 16 March 1943. We received one large room for the five of us. The camp was surrounded by barbed wire and bamboo supports. De Wijk camp consisted of many houses, the owners of which had already been transferred to other areas. There were some sentry boxes at the gates with Japanese or Indonesian soldiers here and there, to ensure that we did not try to escape! Camp residents were given oil and rice. Water was scarce. There was a small hospital. Because the camp also functioned as a transit camp for evacuee transport, the number of people in the camp changed continually. Five doctors and many nurses were among the internees.[35]

The Japanese called the camp a 'protection camp' against the local people who saw the Dutch as their enemy. They organised enforced parades including youths and local workers who were not permitted to wave to people on the other side of the fence. Min was in one parade close to the fence and gave a small smile in our direction.

Because the camp was completely enclosed, it was safe for Joan and Jantje to play games at the nearby green gardens. The house was full of adults and the two children had fun exploring the area. On one occasion, they saw Min on the other side of the barbed wire fence; he beckoned them to come over. They were so glad to see him and ran over to where he was standing. He asked for the 'Mrs Nonya', so they ran home to find Jo, who hoped there was no-one in the sentry boxes.

'Nonya, I will come and work for you,' was his plea.

'Oh, Min, we cannot get out and you are not allowed in the camp. I cannot help you and I am very sad,' Jo replied with her hand on her heart. She was close to tears.

He placed his hands together as if in prayer and said: *'Selamat tinggal'* – Goodbye.

Jo repeated the farewell, *'Selamat tinggal*, Min.' They waved him goodbye.

The event left Jo very teary. To change the sad moment to positive action she said: 'Quick, who can get to the steps first?' And off went the two champions. 'That deserves a biscuit when we get home.'

On the rare occasions Joan and I have time together in our retirement, we invariably reminisce about our childhood. Joan, in particular, has memories of those last days we were in Malang.

> Mum and Dad never talked about what would happen with the servants; they were all good people. Well, Mum's heart bled for Min the senior houseboy. When the *'orang blanda'*—the 'white people'—left, both he and his fellow workers would have been in dire straits; without work and thrown back on their own devices without an income. I am surprised at the lack of memories I have of Indonesia. As a child, I was happy. The servants adored us and the days followed each other in the long string of happy times,' said Joan.

I realised that my own memories of those days did not go back as far as Joan's and I asked her, 'Didn't you have any fears?'

'No,' was her answer.

This surprised me. 'How different your pre-war childhood days were to mine and this includes my post-war experiences as well. I recall tensions and fear from the time I was very young—the fear of uncertainty; flashbacks of camp incidents or hearing a Japanese voice... I've had many through the years, memories associated with fear; many of the post-war experiences were like that for me as well.'

Joan listened quietly and nodded. 'Yes, yes I know,' she said.[36]

On one occasion, Jantje and Joan were sitting on the front doorstep of the house where we were living in De Wijk, taking in their new surroundings and the large beautiful houses on the wide Idjen Boulevard on the other side of the barbed wire fence. Unbeknown to the two youngsters, they were looking at what used to be the houses of the 'white business elite' who lived in luxury and possessed cars. These homes were now empty, the owners interned or imprisoned. Japanese generals were now living in the empty houses. There was very little traffic on the road. Oh, there was a car! It slowed down and stopped at one of the beautiful homes. A Japanese soldier got out and walked up the steep steps. The two little children looked with great interest at the distant scene. The door opened before he reached the top step. He must have been expected. An important-looking Japanese soldier came out of the house and began to beat and kick the visitor until he fell to the ground. When he tried to get up the big soldier continued to kick the man. After a while the big soldier went inside and shut the door loudly. The visitor got up very slowly. He was wiping his face. Was he was crying or bleeding? Slowly he walked down the steps, got into the car, shut the door and the car drove away. Joan and Jantje looked at each other. 'Oh, that was bad,' said Joan. 'I must go inside and tell Mummy about that.' This incident left a negative impression of the Japanese on Joan's mind as a child.

The journey...to Solo

On 30 November 1943, the barbed wire fence and the gates of De Wijk Camp were unlocked and opened. Bringing with them what they could carry, 450 women and children were counted and had their identity cards checked in an orderly manner. Mattresses, mosquito nets, pillows, linen and other special things were tightly rolled, wrapped and labelled. These would be transported separately and returned to their owners on arrival in Solo, Central Java.

We were transported in motor trucks from De Wijk to the Malang station. Marie and Jantje, together with Mum, Joan and I, stayed close together as we climbed into the truck which took us to the railway station. Fortunately, both Joan and I have only vague memories of this journey. At the station, we were pushed into long train compartments. The shade slats on the windows were nailed, shutting out much fresh air and any possibility of seeing the names of stations. Any attempt to force the windows open was met with an angry, *'Tutup'*, meaning 'Close!' or 'Shut!' The point of a bayonet held by an invisible person at the window reinforced the command. We had to sit on dirty floors, and there was no toilet. Mum had taken a toilet-potty with her for me and other the small children. Little children started crying, especially when the train stood still, sometimes for several hours, while the sun was shining on the roof. It was unbearable. We didn't know where we were being taken; we could hardly see anything at all. This horrible journey took more than 24 hours. There was no water to drink in the train. With her usual great foresight, however, Mum had brought both water and food.

CHAPTER 6

Solo and Banyu Biru

Solo (Surakarta)

Jo was familiar with the city of Solo. In May 1935 Ryer and Jo had their first appointment in the Netherlands East Indies there: nine months full of new experiences and surprises. Solo was also their first experience managing both a Military Clubhouse and adjacent Salvation Army corps.

The city of Solo did not initially play a significant part in regard to the internment of prisoners of war. Eventually, however, both Ziekenzorg—literally translated 'sick-care'—and Boemikamp hospitals in that city became gathering places for European men, women and children awaiting transfer to an assigned prisoner of war (POW) camp. Under Japanese control both hospitals were cleared and the patients transferred to the Missionary Hospital in a neighbouring town. These two empty hospitals provided the Japanese authorities with the large rooms needed to accommodate hundreds of prisoners of war. The connection between the two centres was a narrow lane with a Japanese surveillance post at each end. During the final stages of the war from November 1944 until the evacuation of POWs at the end of May 1945 to camps in Central Java and Semarang, both Ziekenzorg and Boemikamp increasingly lacked space and were ultimately amalgamated.

As the war progressed, POWs were constantly being rotated from one camp to another. During 1943 many internees such as ourselves were moved from East Java to Solo, Central Java, to Boemikamp. Among them was another Salvation Army officer named Major Geziena Smid, known as Sister Smid. She was a strong leader. Writing about Major Smid, Melattie Brouwer said she was made head of the camp with 5,000 women in an old hospital precinct.

> It was here, too, in Solo that the Major risked her life when she refused the Japanese to procure young women for entertainment in brothels. 'God gave us strength and grace,' she wrote.[37]

Give us this day our soya beans

As food was a growing preoccupation and concern across our time in internment, a brief digression is in order, to provide the background for the stories that follow.

During the early days of our internment in De Wijk (1943), the Japanese informed us that we were placed in camps to protect us from the local people who regarded the Dutch as the enemy. At that time, there was freedom to move within the enclosed area and buy our own food. Gradually, this freedom diminished. During the early months in POW camps, soup contained some meat, and the serves of rice were reasonable. As time went by, however, food rations were gradually reduced. From the end of 1943 onward the main meal was usually a bowl of starch-like soup, some slivers of meat and perhaps some bone-broth with a few green leaves and a cup of cooked rice. However, the daily rations continued to drop in quality and quantity.

Joan remembered that in Solo we were given cooked maize initially. But Major Smid was able to get soya beans. Knowing the nutritional value of soya beans, she really pressured the Japanese for this change. Although initially there was little support from some of the POWs because of the unpleasant taste of the unprocessed beans, the Major said to the women: 'Eat it! Maize has very little food value but soya beans are rich in multiple vitamins. Make your children eat it. Put some sugar in it!' Jo too, went around and spoke with the mothers: 'Set the example to your children, even if you don't like the taste. Eat it! It could be that you get through this war if you eat what you are given.'

POW camps are equalisers of society. Rich and poor rub shoulders and there are no favourites in the food queue. Initially some adults refused their soya bean breakfast, but soon realised that drinking extra water did not cure their hunger. Reminiscing about the now distant past, Joan commented, 'So the second half of our stay in Solo was a healthier breakfast than the earlier part. Well, I do not really remember a "starchy" breakfast while we were in Solo...it was grains from the start.' Whether of maize grain or soya beans, breakfast at Solo was of far higher nutritional quality than breakfasts at later camps.

Boemikamp

Joan recalled a related incident after we were transferred to Boemikamp. An attractive young mother with two little children refused to give her children food they did not like. She also failed to look after herself and the children followed her example. Jo remonstrated with her and again took time to explain the nutritional value of the food. The woman's husband was a doctor and all she would say to Jo was, 'Yes, but they need vitamins and my husband has given me these.' We do not know what happened to this family and many others with the same attitude.

In the early days of the camp families were given rations of brown sugar. People went wild when it arrived and many devoured it all in one day. Others sold their children's portion in exchange for cigarettes. Our mother was different! She carefully measured each quantity with a spoon from one bag into another and dated the filled bag. She then worked out how many spoons were required for a month if we each had one level teaspoon a day. Then, when a new supply came, and if there was anything left, we could have a double quantity and slowly lick the sugar. Mmm …what a feast!

Joan recalls the following:

> We were in a small room in Boemikamp where Mum,
> to her great surprise, meets a woman who had been one
> of her teachers at a girls' domestic school...with her
> grown-up daughters...and would you believe it...in the
> same room! We were all on trestles, and had our own
> kapok mattresses.[38]

Prior to her departure from Solo, Major Smid looked for reliable leaders and asked Jo to take charge of one of the 15 long barracks of Boemikamp which were surrounded by a *gedek* or bamboo and barbed wire wall. Each barrack accommodated about 100 women and their children.

Writing about Major Smid's ministry, Melattie Brouwer gives us an understanding of the situation and conditions Jo inherited. During her less then 18 months in Solo Major Smid conducted 106 funerals.[39]

Jo was kept very busy. Women from all walks of life suddenly found themselves surrounded by strangers. Privacy was gone. Space was limited. Courtesy and patience were essential qualities when communicating with unknown neighbours. Food was a constant concern, with the quality and quantity continuing to decline. Soup was watered down. Rice was reduced. There was no fruit. Milk was no longer available for the very young. Jo and the other women were aware of increasing physical exhaustion. The children lost weight.

Family time

Camp life was a constant reverberation of women's and children's voices echoing through the endless corridors of Boemikamp. Despite her oversight of camp responsibilities for 100 women and children, Jo made time for her two very precious girls; we too required her time. Ever practical in her planning, she had packed some simple education books, writing paper and reading material for Joan. Although I have no memory of this, my mother would have had something to keep me busy. She had included a supply of embroidery thread and some of my old, well washed and worn tropical napkins. The material of these was ideal for cross stitching. Joan learned to do beautiful designs from patterns our mother had brought with her. Grace was said before meals, even for soupy-starch made from cornflour! There was always a Bible story before bedtime, with hug and kiss before a 'tuck in' of the mosquito net. Joan recalls an amusing incident not long after the family arrived at Boemikamp.

> From the room allotted to us in the camp, looking at the fence outside, there was a white painted, brick wall. We couldn't look over it but there was one thing that stood out which told us it was an Islamic burial ground: it was a thin stick above the wall with a half crescent moon on it. Then one night we had an unbelievable tropical storm, there was an unholy 'crack', the lightning struck and the moon was blown off. The next day only the tip of the stick was visible. If we stood on the steps leading into our room, we could just peer over the wall to see a few gravestones but that was the only thing clearly visible.

I was only four years of age at the time, but recall that in Boemikamp we played on our bed; it was our 'home'. Sometimes we had pillow fights. On one occasion, the pillow knocked out one of my front teeth; it was a big event in my life! Then one day the seam of the pillow came unstuck and clouds of kapok fluff wafted through the air. Kapok is the Malay word for a silky fibre made from the fruit of the silk-cotton tree, used for insulating and padding. Our mother gave us the next game: find the fluff! It took us hours!

God became real

The following is a family-related story of another sort, told by Joan about an incident that took place in Solo's women's POW camp, possibly sometime during 1944.

It was about that time I believe and I could not have been more than nine—I turned 10 in Solo—when something had obviously gone wrong with the war and the Japs would take it out on us. And using a mild example, if we had grown anything such vegetables or tomatoes, we would have had to destroy it. But this time all the leaders of the barracks were to front up at the office. Everybody knew when they were called for no particular reason, something must have gone wrong and we had better be prepared! And the women were terrified. Mum told us that on such occasions, 'When we got there I would take my glasses off and put them in my pocket because the Nips would go "bang, bang" in your face' (indicating slapping).

All the leaders stood there in a long row, and they were all interviewed; they were all scared to death, shaking in their boots. But Mum decided that she was going to be defiant, to keep quiet. She gave all the answers, but she never stopped looking him [the interrogator] straight in the eye. But the big concern for me was you: this big burden. 'What am I going to do with my little sister?' I didn't know what to do with you... I was only nine and you were four...

Anyway, I began to pray: *'Dear Lord, don't let them beat her!'* And that in my child's mind was the worst thing that could happen...the human emotion...that thing could happen, that slap, slap, slap. My worst fear that she would be beaten and I prayed, *'Don't let her be beaten, don't let her be beaten'*. So, you can imagine, she comes back and I said, 'Oh, how did you go, how did you go?' And I only had one question, 'Were you beaten?' and she said: 'No, and I was the only one' [on that occasion].

That was the first time that God became real to me as a young child, because he had listened![40]

The journey continues…to Ambarawa

In late May 1944, both Ziekenzorg and Boemikamp Hospitals were evacuated as the numbers of POWs became too many to accommodate in the two facilities. The internees were dispersed to different camps including Muntilan, Ambarawa, Banyu Biru—sometimes written Banju Biru [and often referred to in documents by its former name of Banjoebiroe]—and Semarang.

At very short notice the group of 450 women and children, including Marie and Jan Luitjes, Jo, Joan and I, were transferred on 30–31 May 1944 to Banyu Biru 10 (BB10), via Ambarawa.[41] This town is situated in Central Java and was the rail-hub for train connections to Semarang on the north coast, Magelang, Yogyakarta (Yokya) to the south and also to Surakarta (Solo).

Annual monsoon rains provided an abundant water runoff from mountain rivulets into Lake Banyu Biru, which in turn fed the swamp and the surrounding agricultural landscape with its rice fields and vegetable gardens. With the exception of a few scattered villages, most local farmers had probably lived there for generations; nothing had changed much over time. The locals knew the dangers of the swamp—they knew the stories of lives lost. At one time, there was a rumour that the Japanese considered forcing the POWs from Banyu Biru into the swamp. Fortunately, it did not come to that.

At that time, modernity did not appear to have encroached on this beautiful, but isolated, agricultural backwater. On the southern-western horizon, Gunung Boetak (Mount Baldhead, probably because of its lack of vegetation), a part of the foothills of Mount Telomoyo, dominated the view. The downwards slope of the mountain was covered by a moving tapestry of lush green forest which gradually levelled out towards the rice terraces. In the camp, we could see the tops of tall palm trees over the wall.

The *Geïllustreerde Atlas Van De Japanse Kampen In Nederland-Indië* says of the camps in this area:

Both Ambarawa and Banyu Biru camps were situated in the lowlands surrounding Lake Banyu Biru, and the swamp, Rawa Pening, c. 45km south of Semarang. During December 1942 large numbers of European women and children from Central and West Java were interned here... not only women and children...but from September 1944 increasing numbers of boys aged ten, or even younger, were taken from their mothers and placed in camps with sick and old men... During the final months of the war the Ambarawa and Banyu Biru camps jointly, accommodated 15,800 internees.[42]

Sadly, because of this history, Banyu Biru is not primarily known for the lake's enchanting name, meaning 'Blue Water' or its beautiful countryside with its peaceful surroundings, but for the horrors of war and the deaths of many innocent people.

Banyu Biru 10

Banyu Biru (BB) Camps 8 to 12 were all situated in the Banyu Biru district, with Camps 10, 11 and 12 being the predominant BB camps. Facing south, away from the lake and across the dirt road, was an old prison known as the 'Boei', about 5 km south of Ambarawa. A map showing the plan of the prison dating back to the days of the 'Cavaliers', the Dutch cavalry regiment based there during the Java War of 1825–30s, includes large horse stables within the camp, facing a gate in the west wall, which opens directly on to the grassland behind the camp. The prison was built to accommodate a maximum of 1,000 prisoners. The NEI Government decommissioned the prison and closed it many years prior to WWII; however, the Japanese re-commissioned the prison as BB10.

From August 1943 to February 1944 what became BB10 was used as a transit camp for men who had previously been employed as agricultural farmers in Kesilir, East Java. Considering the number of years the prison and its multiple barracks had been exposed to the elements, one wonders if these farmers were brought in to clean and repair the camp. I do have a hazy memory of a vegetable garden in Banyu Biru. Could this have been a legacy left by the Kesilir farmers?

From March 1944 the prison, with its outbuildings and agricultural land, was officially designated as Camp 10.[43] From February 1944 until the end of December 1945, Banyu Biru 10 became a gathering place for women and children from all over Java.[44]

The main road takes a right-hand turn at Camp 10, with BB Camp 11 less than 500 m further down the dirt road. During early internment days, the women in Camp 11 were free to walk outside and visit each other for a limited time each day. Although, this 'freedom' was of short duration, it temporarily diminished the sense of 'prison' for these internees.

Internees of BB10 had none of the above-mentioned freedoms. Was it because of the invincible walls and the high gate with its lock, or was it the definitive statement on the gate, 'Roemah Penjara', meaning 'prison', that discouraged the Japanese from opening the gate for even a few hours a day to allow the internees of BB10 a measure of freedom during the early days of internment[f]? What we only appreciated later was that, unlike the stone walls of BB10, the external walls of camps BB11 and BB12 were not sturdy and were often in a state of disrepair. Most of their walls were a combination of split bamboo and wood with barbed wire fencing, none of which were bulletproof. There was the danger the walls would fail to provide adequate shelter against external militant hostilities, a situation that made internees extremely vulnerable, particularly towards the conclusion of the war.

Thus far I have yet to find one good word about the facilities and conditions at BB10; it was known as one of the worst camps in Central Java. It was dirty, unhygienic, short of water and electricity, and alive with bedbugs. It is described in Shirley Fenton Huie's, *The Forgotten Ones* as:

---

[f] Former POWs at BB10 have visited the area post-war and found the camp still there, with the gate locked. On request, however, the resident guard will open the gates for visitors.

> A terrible place full of rats and cockroaches with only
> hard planks to sleep on, with a 40–45 cm bed space for
> each person...there was only one area where women
> could wash—a big open tank. The Japanese guards
> stood watching the women at their ablutions.[45]

An antiquated sewage system required daily clearing; the faecal waste was initially carried to a latrine pit outside the camp first by young boys but eventually this task was taken over by the young women when the boys left.

Proximity to the large, stillwater lake meant that clouds of malaria-bearing mosquitoes invaded the camp each evening. As would be expected, this caused a high rate of malaria in the camp. As Elizabeth van Kampen tells it, the irony was that when the war was over and the supply store was cleaned out, 'many boxes were found of anti-malaria tablets, quinine, and several other medicines that could have saved lives of the many who died in prison'.[46]

Every evening Jo would tuck the mosquito net under our thin mattresses. She also kept a close check on the net, and tiny holes were carefully stitched. Our little family was blessed not to have caught malaria during our time in Banyu Biru despite large numbers of mosquitoes from the lake.

Banyu Biru—the journey to the end of the dirt road

In notes about the end of the war, Jo wrote:

> Final episode, starvation.
> May 30–31, 1944 saw us transferred to our last camp,
> Banyu Biru 10.

Our little family found itself on the next stage of the journey with Marie and Jantje and hundreds of other women and children from Solo. The women went through the wrapping, packing and labelling of their diminishing goods. It was reassuring that these would be taken to the camp for them; however, no-one had any food for this journey, only water. Truck upon truck seemed to arrive from nowhere to transport the luggage of these hundreds of women and children to Solo Station. There was the usual shouting from the Japanese military as they pushed and shoved women and children into the filthy railway cabins. Again, we found ourselves in 4th class shuttered cabins in total darkness, this time for 22 hours from Solo to Ambarawa. As well as the noise of the train, we could hear the crying of sick children; some had whooping cough and others dysentery. The stench of faecal material and urine all over the floor pervaded everything. The *Tutup*—'Shut!' or 'Close!'—command was shouted continually as it was on the journey to Solo. For most of the journey Marie was a silent traveller. Jo was also physically exhausted. Drained of energy she wondered, 'Will this be the end of the road for us?'

Arriving at Ambarawa Station the following day, exhausted, weak, hungry and thirsty, the women expected to be taken to the camp by trucks. However, this was not to be. Instead, the exhausted travellers were informed they had to walk the 5 km road to Banyu Biru. There was running water to fill their bottles for the journey. Prior to their departure, however, the women were provided with food wrapped in banana leaves. I have no real memory of what happened that day. I can only imagine women and children looking for shade; perhaps a cool wall to lean against while they savoured their food.

Many elderly women feared they would not be able to complete the long walk in the heat of the day. Some removed their shoes and consequently burned their feet on the hot asphalt. As the group set out, tired mothers strapped their little ones on their backs, allowing them to use their hands to carry the bags. We were pushed on by soldiers armed with bayonets. Few words were spoken on the long walk; each carried her own burden. Even at times like this, though, one exhausted woman would relieve another woman's load by offering to carry one of the two children she was carrying. Others would give strength by walking arm in arm with an elderly person. Some would sing Dutch national songs. Few would have noted the beautiful, green, agricultural countryside. For most, each step just brought them closer to the end of the journey.

The scene changed. The exhausted stragglers could see the end of the journey was in sight. There was evidence people lived in the area, with native villages on their right and large paddy fields and a lake on the other side of the road. A distant, high, whitewashed wall confirmed they had arrived at Banyu Biru Camp 10. As the women looked at the gate a wail of horror was heard when they read the notice on the gate:

ROEMAH PENJARA (Prison)

At the sound of hundreds of women's and children's voices, the gatekeeper opened the large gate and we began to enter our new accommodation. I have no memory of either the long walk or our arrival at the camp gate. Jo recalled that most of the women were just relieved to arrive at their destination. They were too exhausted to think about tomorrow.

More than 2,000 women and children were already resident in the camp prior to our arrival. Some had been there since early February 1944.[47] We were assigned to Block III, ward 18. Block III had a very long and wide verandah typical of a colonial building in a tropical country. Our block was divided into 10 sections called 'wards', numbered 14 to 23, each measuring approximately eight metres by five metres. Perhaps these were former communal cells for accommodating multiple low-risk prisoners. Each ward had provision for sleeping accommodation on slat-based bunks on either side of a narrow walking space and was provided with two small steps across a gutter onto the compound's circuit road. I have no knowledge of the number of women and children accommodated in a block; however, increasing numbers of POWs were transferred to BB10 from nearby camps because of the security afforded by its high and secure walls.

Despite the large group of women and children requiring bed-space and baggage storage, the allocations appeared well organised; our allotted 45 cm mattress-spaces had been carefully marked out on wooden slats. This would be our home. The women were exhausted and wondered what would happen next. When our luggage came, our mother unrolled the now dusty mattresses and found some sheets. By the time she attached the mosquito net, it almost felt like 'home' again. Marie and Jantje were accommodated in a ward further down in the same block.

While I have no clear memory of what followed immediately, I like to think that after a night's rest, Jo took our little family for a walk to explore our new surroundings. We would have met so many women and children. We would have walked around the compound and seen several barracks like our block. There was a big well where the women did their washing. We passed the kitchen and looked at the big mountain from the front of the camp and then were glad to get 'home' to our bed-space. What I do know is that our mother's former teacher from Vlaardingen, and her two daughters, had also been transferred from Ziekenzorg to Block III.

A block 'Leader' was responsible for the neatness, cleanliness and good behaviour of the internees in the block. She was also required to provide the daily statistics for the morning and evening roll calls of the sick and hospitalised and those who had died. 'Helpers' were assigned to each ward and were to support the Leader, who they met with twice a day. In the case of a deceased person the Helper of that ward was required to inform the Leader, who arranged for the removal of the body. Block Leaders were also responsible to organise teams for gardening, cleaning toilets, cooking and general cleaning. The elderly, those over 60 years, were not given labour tasks or night duties. Jo was a Helper for Ward 18 for some time, but eventually her health declined to the point where she could not continue in this role.

Childhood memories

At the age of five years I remember standing with my back close to the front of the camp wall. From that distance, I could see the tops of palm trees and the long green leaves of banana trees directly behind the back wall of the camp. In the distance, higher up, was the mountain surrounded by green forests. The memory of this scene has remained with me throughout my life. I can clearly remember sitting on the top step of Ward 18 surveying my surroundings. Across the path, I could see trees in a grassed area with a well in the centre. I knew about trees, and grass, and wells—they were familiar things and made me feel safe and secure.

We discovered that the daily menu in BB10 was similar to that in Boemikamp. I was most amused to discover that Elizabeth van Kampen reported the familiar daily camp menu in her book:

> Tea early in the morning before roll call
> Breakfast: a bowl of starch (cornflower)
> Lunch: a cup of boiled rice, a heaped tablespoon of boiled green cabbage
> and a heaped teaspoon of sambal, a sort of Spanish pepper
> Tea: in the afternoon
> Dinner: starch soup with leaves of cabbage. One could count the small pieces.[48]

Most POW camps had a similar menu. It rarely varied. It was a 'slow death' menu. Sadly, the food in BB diminished in quantity and quality over time. Even slivers of meat disappeared. I remember receiving my bowl of starchy soup one day and noting what appeared to be a bright green piece of cabbage. On closer examination, it turned out to be a well-cooked green worm! Small as I was, I can still 'see' it floating in the bowl. Finding floaters in our camp soup was not unusual. Internees tried to supplement the diet with snails, frogs, rats and cats, when they could catch them. There was always the danger of being caught by the Japanese guards, but it was worth the risk to make a snail broth in a small saucepan on a stick and grass fire. Some women had small saucepans—just the right size for a snail broth!

While having our rice meal one afternoon I saw a little plant which had pushed its way through a crack in the concrete of the gutter below the steps on which I was sitting. I could not see any soil. It just came out through the crack. I asked Mum for some water so I could run it into the crack. Mum was interested and came with the water bottle. She gave it a good look and said: 'It looks like the leaf of a tomato plant. How exciting is that?' What was a tomato? I had never seen or tasted one. I watered it every day. Time went by and it developed little flowers. Eventually the plant developed a good size green tomato. We waited for the sun to ripen it. Then one day 'Mr Nip' passed by our steps and caught sight of the tomato plant. Oh dear, here was trouble! Gesticulating with his hands, he garbled angry words we did not understand. Then, in one enraged sweep of his hand, he pulled the plant out of the crack and squashed the beautiful tomato under his boot. He then walked away, pleased at having done a good day's work! My grief knew no bounds, but I was too small to verbalise it. My tears said it all. I have no recollection of what my mother said in reply to my teary question: 'Why did he do that?' I suspect my wise mother would have replied something like this: 'I really don't believe he is a very happy man.' I remember though that she did say, 'But you know what? One day you will grow your own tomatoes, and you already know how to do it.' Neither of us knew that was a prophetic statement at the time—my husband and I grow tomatoes every year.

A number of internees in Block III had been in BB10 for some time before we arrived. Most of these women appeared in a poor physical condition. A white rice-only diet ultimately resulted in severe beriberi, the consequences of a consistent lack of vitamin B. Evidence of this was seen in women and children with extended abdomens. Others suffered from painful red legs; some had festering wounds which failed to heal. Some women had cut strips off their sheets to cover their legs. Resident doctors in the camp had neither drugs nor other tablets to relieve headaches. Bandages were in short supply. The hospital section of the Banyu Biru prison had some internee nurses who cared for the extremely ill. Most women refused a transfer to the hospital section, fearing they would never return to their ward.

About this time, Jo became concerned about Marie, who remained in bed, covered by a sheet. Jantje looked lost and wandered listlessly around the camp. Jo mused in silence when she saw the body wrapped in a sheet. She took a risk and with a clear voice close to Marie's ear said, 'Marie Luitjes, what are you doing in bed?' The shocked response was instant. Off came the sheet, and a surprised and ruffled-looking Marie sat up. 'I am tired and sick and just want to die!' I believe Jo took a firm tone with Marie, reminding her of Jantje. Jo was adamant he needed his mother's love and attention. He was a little boy who needed his mother and Marie needed him! Jo was a very determined person! She would not allow Marie the 'pleasure' of sympathy by giving up without a fight. So, Jo began to spoon-feed Marie for every meal, with the help of Joan and Jantje, who was about nine, two years younger than Joan. Having chattering children present made it difficult for Marie to resist. This added responsibility required Jo to be active and on her feet. Who knows whether keeping an eye on Marie was an unwanted gift from the Lord? Jo's weak legs, depression and exhaustion had to be put aside to look after a fellow comrade worse off than herself! Looking back, I believe if it had not been for Joan and me, our mother may well have gone the same way as Marie. We kept her on the move doing things like reading a story, teaching Joan to embroider and teaching me the alphabet.

Revised regulations

Jo would have heard from internees who had been in the camp during the earlier part of 1944 that the behaviour of the Japanese towards the women had changed. They were more aggressive; slapping and kicking incidents occurred more frequently. The rumour spread: 'They know they are losing the war!' Camps were notorious for rumours, but any glimmer of hope was welcome.

As of April 1944, internees such as us were officially given the 'status' of prisoner of war, including POW numbers. For the civilian internees, the transition to a military administration meant a more uniform and a stricter regime. The attitude of the Japanese rapidly changed as a result. Former 'internees' became POWs and were treated as such—including their children.[49] When the military administration took control of the camps, the internees lost both their freedom of movement and speech. One of the first rules set in motion by the Japanese in July 1944 was the separation of boys aged 10 and older from the women's camps in Java.[50]

On the occasions when all ambulant women were called to the roll call, everyone feared the worst! Someone may have been seen behind the prison block doing a black-market deal under the camp wall, perhaps to buy some cigarettes or selling clothing to secure more money. If some irregularity came to the ears of the Japanese Commander via an informant or sympathiser, the guilty person had to confess. If no-one came forward everyone was punished. Sometimes women were forced to stand for hours in the blazing heat or a tropical downpour. If a woman fainted due to exhaustion no-one was allowed to help her up.

A compulsory two-hour night guard duty was introduced between 2am and 4am. Nights were often cold in the mountain district and no-one had warm clothing.[51] The women considered this a 'fatigue' exercise—another way to limit the women's rest periods. Guard duty did not exist prior to the rulings of April 1944. From whom did we need to be protected in a high-walled POW camp?

The person or persons on duty were required to walk around the barrack building. If a Japanese soldier showed up, those on duty had to recite, in Japanese, the number of the ward and the number of the occupants. The women were terrified and Joan recalls that Mum would often walk with them as she was unable to sleep and would recite the report for them. 'A good memory for me was that Mum used to make a flask of coffee for those occasions and she would hand me a cup through the little window near our bed, to help with the hunger pangs.'

Fixed times were set for going to bed and getting up in the morning. Internees were to rise at 5.30am and go to bed at 8.30pm. We later heard similar regulations were imposed on internees in other camps. With the transition to a military administration, Japanese leadership appeared determined to put the women to work and physically exhaust them. These rules were indiscriminate, particularly for mothers with young children.

A different group of women was on a cleaning roster each week. Jo found her name on a cleaning roster for toilets and bathrooms. This was not a task for the faint-hearted! The camp had many problems. The toilet sewers drained into open buckets. With the great increase of POW women, the buckets had to be removed every day, taken outside the camp and emptied into a type of latrine pit. Goodness only knows where the contents were deposited! I recall Mum talking about this in a humorous way years later: 'We were given ammonia to clean the toilets and wondered if the Japs were afraid of cross-infection. Best of all, however, when the job was done we, the cleaning ladies, were the first to have the opportunity to use a clean loo!' The so-called 'loos' were deep holes in the ground covered by two planks with a space between them and the bucket underneath. It was not a comfortable arrangement; in fact, it was particularly dangerous for the young and elderly.

Some women worked in a vegetable garden and cutting grass, of which there was very little in the camp; this was regarded another 'fatigue' exercise, usually allocated to younger women. The rules were strict! 'No talk, no laughing, just work!' Kneeling was not permitted. The women had to squat on their haunches—making it a painful activity. It usually required an hour. Disobedience could mean an extra hour. The workers were supervised by 'Mr Nip' who carried a whip. Rule-breakers felt the painful whip of 'Mr Nip'!

I was deeply moved to read one woman's voiced frustration:

> ...so in the morning I spend an hour scrubbing toilets, in the afternoon an hour cutting grass, and at night an hour on guard duty. What time is there for children...for mending and the washing? These are fatigue duties, a means of wearing us out. There are so many sick children and elderly in our block...that is why we 'strong' women must do two or three nights a week on night watch.[52]

A caring ministry

There were 2,000 women and children at BB10 at that time. Towards the end, 10 to 12 people a day were being buried. Despite all that was going on there was a great ministry undertaken, although strength was almost gone for most.

Jo came to know some of the women and discovered a prayer and bedside Bible reading ministry, particularly for those women who were close to needing a transfer to the hospital section. Many internees who had been in the camp since early 1944 were low in physical strength; hope for some was almost gone. But prayer and the Word of God lifted their spirits. Women discovered the power of singing, particularly hymns and carols, and also some national songs. Much was made of Easter and Christmas celebrations, and secret Bible studies were held.

Sunday worship and singing were permitted in the camp. Jo was delighted about this as the two previous camps, Ziekenzorg and Boemikamp in Solo, did not allow Sunday services or any expression of Christian worship. Jo knew the value of singing, particularly for the sick and the depressed; it was something she did as a young Salvationist in her home corps. She was asked to be on the list as a speaker for Sunday services. The women were also allowed to celebrate birthdays. Some made small hankies with floral designs using coloured threads from a towel.

When my parents entered The Salvation Army Training College, Ryer in 1929 and Johanna in 1930, every cadet had the same Dutch edition of the Bible, printed by the London Bible Society in 1926. The size of these Bibles was 9 cm x 13.5 cm. I still have my mother's Bible with the red Japanese stamp on the inside cover page. The Japanese needed to give approval for the possession of any book—especially a religious one. In this Bible I found two small pieces of paper, a scarce commodity in a POW camp (see page 113). The first one was 7 x 7 cm, and on it was written the dates and Bible references for two weeks, including the number of a church hymn for each day. It was written in neat, miniscule print and dated, '16–30

September', probably 1944. The second piece of paper of 5 x 7.2 cm suggests Bible readings for 'Advent 1–15 Dec 1944'. With some coloured pencils, a woman's artistic hand had drawn a tiny red candle with an equally tiny yellow flame, some green holly leaves and red berries, reminding its recipients that Christmas was close. Here was an expression of faith, undeterred by gloom and doom. The Light of the World, the Prince of Peace came to bring hope and peace to a sick and cruel world.

One wonders how many of these Bible reading snippets went out each fortnight. Jo obviously treasured them. It must have been an enormous encouragement for her to meet these Christian women in Block III. Despite frailty and suffering, their faith and hope in a loving and merciful God did not waver. Seventy-one years later, I found these reminders of God's grace in this small Bible my mother had with her throughout the war. Again, I am deeply moved by the faithfulness of our Great God. As I am writing this, a well-known Christian chorus comes to mind:

> How great is our God, sing with me,
> ... How great, how great is our God...
> ...My heart will sing: how great is our God.[53]

The last days of the war

Eventually Banyu Biru camps 10, 11 and 12 respectively had 5,300, 2,400 and 1,100 women and children. You will recall that one of the first rules applied once the status of internees changed to that of POWs was the removal of boys 10 years and older.

> By August 1945 a total of approximately 3,600 boys of the youngest age category, sometimes younger than 10 years, ended up either in camps for men or special camps for boys scattered in a number of provincial cities in Java.[54]

Reading the above paragraph brings tears to my eyes. Some of these lads had already seen their father taken away by the Japanese.

Then, at the age of 10, sometimes younger, they were torn away from their mother. I heard of women who went through this ordeal of seeing their frightened little boys taken away and the cries of grief as a truck took them to an unknown destination. It also happened in Banyu Biru. I am so grateful I knew nothing about these brutalities of war. Fortunately, Jantje was too young to be taken in this way.

Then something very exciting happened. Even Jo came out to see it. Sometime during August or September 1945, a small, single-engine reconnaissance plane, with the English red, white and blue insignia on its wings, circled over the camp. The plane flew low enough for us to see the pilot wave his hand. Women and children cheered as they watched the small plane circle around the camp. All eyes watched as it moved away towards the lake. The pilot appeared to do a final farewell circle, but went too low. He was unable to lift the plane and it nose-dived into the swamp. The high camp wall prevented the women seeing the accident. Gradually the plane sank into the murky waters of the swamp. Hope and excitement changed to cries of grief when the women realised what had happened. From the camp gates, the wrecked plane was visible with its tail up in the air. No attempts were made to rescue the pilot at that time. It was probably too dangerous because of the quicksand in the bog.

Jo's health declined noticeably. By now every internee, old and young alike, was affected by beriberi. Painful limbs zapped the body's energy and slowed activity. Some were worse off than others. It was the insidious 'norm' of a consistent starvation diet; we were now receiving 90 grams of rice per day. The young did not comprehend this, but for mothers with small children this was a nightmare. Many children died.

Hunger often leads people to smoking. A couple of desperate women were smoking their last cigarette near the trees away from the wards. The inhaled smoke briefly dampened their hunger. A whiff of smoke drifted from beyond the trees to where Jo and many others were resting. The fragrance of the smoking tobacco surprised Jo who suddenly yearned for a cigarette. It made her sit up, realising the futility of such actions. Yet at the same time she was concerned for these two women who had probably bartered some clothing under the camp wall for the cigarettes. They smoked to stop their hunger and in so doing had become addicts.

Signs of change

Things began to change in the camp. Initially it was difficult to pinpoint a specific motive. The Japanese were visible, but no longer 'walked' the camp with bayonets. The soldiers mostly remained in their quarters. Fatigue work ceased, yet no verbal announcements were made. Daily food rations improved in quantity and quality and compulsory work outside the camp ceased. Work rosters ceased until the women's camp committee took control. New rosters were made for the cleaning of toilets and maintenance of camp cleanliness. But the gate remained closed!

One of the things that kept Jo going was feeding Marie her soup three times a day. Jantje made sure she had her cups of tea and water during the day. But eventually Jo consulted the hospital section staff. The day for Marie's transfer to the hospital was set for Friday morning, 24 August 1945.

(Top left) Arie van Kralingen
(Ryer's father).

(Top right) Hermanus and Petronella
van Kapel (Johanna's parents),
with their eldest child, Jan.

(Left) Grandmother Johanna Klos
and Grandfather Gerard Klos at
their 50th wedding anniversary.

Ryer (extreme left) and Johanna (extreme right) with other young adults of Vlaardingen Corps, (from left) Gerrie van Rij, Geer van Kapel, Maja van Rij [who eventually married Geer] and Jo van der Lugt.

Bandmaster Geer van Kapel, Jo van der Lugt and Ryer van Kralingen of Vlaardingen Corps.

Johanna van Kapel

Ryer van Kralingen

Wedding photo of Ryer and Johanna van Kralingen, 1933.

Map of Java showing the most significant places in this story.

Map of Java showing the most significant places in this story

Joan and Sonja with their mother
and pet dogs at Malang Open Door
before Ryer left for Tarakan.

Joan (left) and Sonja outside
the Open Door military
rest house at Malang before
Ryer left for Tarakan.

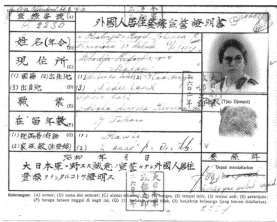

Official photograph of
Mrs Adjutant Johanna
van Kralingen c. 1942.

Johanna's identification card as a
Japanese prisoner of war using the same
official photograph. In the original,
the stamps were in red ink.

(Top) An aerial view of Banyu Biru 10 POW Camp in 1945.

(Centre) The view of Mt Baldhead (a foothill of the
Telomoyo Range) from Banyu Biru 10 POW Camp which
the author remembers. (Joost van Bodegom, 1986)

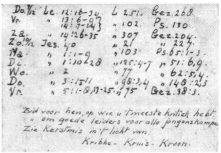

(Top row) Scans of the front and back of small 7.2 cm x 5.0 cm cards that the Christian women in the Jo's section of Banyu Biru 10 made using pencil and crayon. They outline Bible readings and hymns for the Advent season in 1944. The original coloured version show green holly leaves, red berries, red candle and a yellow flame.

The final lines on the back of the card translate as: 'Celebrate this Christmas in the light of the Crib – Cross – Crown.'

(Left) This similar homemade card, 7 cm x 7 cm lists reminders of daily Bible readings from 1 Corinthians and Psalms for 16–20 September 1944 for the Christian women in Banyu Biru 10.

(Above) The threatening, yet ultimately protective, walls of Banyu Biru 10 as at 1986, with Mount Baldhead in the background. (Joost van Bodegom, 1986)

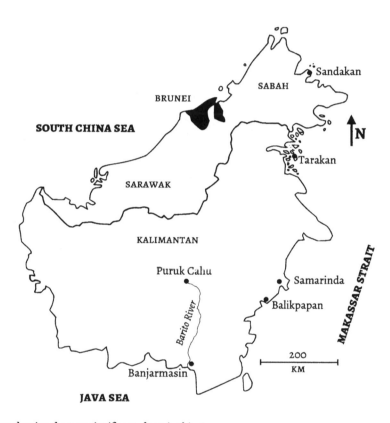

Map of Borneo showing the most significant places in this story.

Official photograph of the opening of The Salvation Army Open Door Military Clubhouse in Tarakan in 12 November 1941. The Roman numerals indicate: I, Dr A. Colijn, BPM Administrator (front row extreme right); II Lieut-Colonel Simon de Waal, Military Commander (fourth from the left, front row); and III Adjutant Ryer van Kralingen, Manager and civilian chaplain (extreme left, second row).

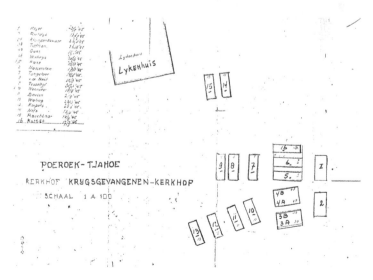

Ryer van Kralingen's sketch of where in the graveyard he buried those Dutch troops who died in Puruk Cahu before the War concluded.

Place.	Date.	Hour.	Summary of Events and Information.	Remarks and references to Appendices, Diaries, &c.
BANDJERMASIN	21	0930	1 Pl 2/1 Wk Bn to relieve HQ Coy d posts at radio stn.	
		1345	Municipal bldgs incl Java Bank, coal and oil dumps and power house under amt Pd.	
		1100	200 Dutch PWs and Internees arrived from POEROEK TJAHOE with 17 Jap gds with their arms.	
	22	0900	CO and party visited released PWs in our own and NICA hospitals	Appx B.
			The Dutch soldiers were suffering from malnutrition and malaria and some had bad skin diseases.	
		1000	CO and party to Jap HQ where he publicly denounced HONO and staff. He told Japs they would be held responsible for the condition of released PWs and proper action would be taken to deal with the perpetrators of the atrocities. He then ordered that the Japs remaining in BANDJERMASIN would march to MANTAPOERA the following morning.	

AUSTRALIAN WAR MEMORIAL

RCDIG1027403

Page from War Diary and 2/31st Battalion AIF, Banjarmasin, September 1945 recording release of the group of Dutch prisoners of which Adjutant Ryer van Kralingen was a member.

116

Adjutant Ryer van Kralingen in
a borrowed Australian uniform
and wearing the metal insignia
that the Japanese Commandant
of the POW camp in Balikpapan
ordered to be made for him.

Joan (centre back) and Sonja
(extreme right) with the cousins
(from left) Ben and Eddie
van Kapel in the Netherlands
after the War in 1946.

The front of The Salvation Army Military Clubhouse 'The Open Door'
at 55 Jalan Kramat Raya, Batavia (later re-named Jakarta) which Ryer
had managed to secure for Salvation Army purposes in 1947.

(Above left) Sonja with a pet goat at Jakarta (c.1948).

(Above right) Sonja with her precious pet dog, Siep, at Jakarta (c. 1952).

(Right) Jo, Joan and Ryer with the motorcycle Ryer used for his public relations and fundraising work for the Army in Jakarta c. 1953.

Jo (extreme left) and Ryer (extreme right in adult group) with Dutch immigrants to Australia who participated in a Salvation Army Congress meeting in the Melbourne Exhibition Building in 1954.

Sonja in her first Australian Salvation Army uniform at Port Melbourne 1956.

Senior-Majors Ryer and Johanna van Kralingen with Sonja and Joan at Clayton 1957.

Jo and Ryer's precious retirement home at Elmore Avenue, Croydon, Victoria, in 1960's.

(Above) Johanna [left front] and her war-time colleague and companion, Mrs Brigadier Marie Luitjes [right front], at a 1969 reunion of those who trained as Salvation Army officers together in Holland in 1930. Between them is Commissioner Arend Beekhuis who had been their Training Principal, and later their Territorial Commander in the Netherlands East Indies.

(Right) Ryer and Johanna's immediate family in January 1970 just prior to Sonja, Ian and their baby Sharon [left] leaving for Zambia, Africa, on missionary service with The Salvation Army. On the right of the picture are Joan [seated] and George Stolk with their three children, Ingrid, William (Bill) and baby Patricia.

120

CHAPTER 7

Freedom gained, lost, regained

Freedom gained

News in the camps came by telephone to the Japanese quarters and was only passed on to internees if it was deemed relevant. By 15 August the military at BB10 knew that the Empire of Japan had surrendered unconditionally but this was not immediately announced. We knew that changes were afoot, however, as several days before the announcement the food situation improved dramatically. This would surely indicate that the quality and quantity of the rations could have been much better than those we received.[55]

On 17 August, although we did not know it, Sukarno announced himself as President of Indonesia. It was not until Friday 24 August that we were told an important announcement was going to be made. By that time, however, there was little interest in hearing 'good news' from the Japanese. Joan reminded Jo of the announcement, but she no longer had the energy to walk the distance and suggested that Joan could go and find out what it was all about. Perhaps other parents made the same suggestion. A few moments later, the children ran back to their blocks, shouting 'The war is over, the war is over!' Joan arrived back very excited: 'We all sang "Het Wilhelmus!" [the Dutch national anthem]. The gate is open we are allowed to go outside.' The women looked at the excited children. Their response was silence! No-one believed it! No-one moved. They just sat!

'Mum, the gate is open! There are many people outside selling food and other things. Can I go outside, please, Mum? See if I can change the potty for something else; and can I take your green bag to put things in?' Jo could not remember seeing her 11-year-old daughter so excited. As if in a dream, she gave Joan her old green-lined, drawstring bag. And off she went! Joan knew how to barter and there were many other people doing the same thing. This was real fun!

Sometime later an excited Joan returned with five large duck eggs and two mangoes! When did we last have such luxuries? The five eggs included one each for Jantje and Marie. Before long, women were coming from all over the camp. Forgotten for a moment were their aches and pains. There was a new hope and laughter as they walked to the gate. Gradually, Jo and other 'disbelievers' stepped outside their wards, their smiles becoming tears and laughter all at the same time.

Jo walked to Marie's ward, also in Block III. This was the very day Marie was to be transferred to the hospital. But it never happened. Much to Jo's surprise Marie was sitting on her mattress and greeted Jo with, 'The war is over and I'm not going to the hospital!' Jo laughed, relieved to hear the determination in the voice of Marie. Her voice briefly reminded Jo of Marie in Malang—an energetic, on-the-go businesswoman. It was a momentary light relief for Jo who found herself unprepared for the sight of Marie's almost skeletal appearance. She saw a skin-and-bone person at death's door with unwashed, uncombed black hair, looking at her through sunken eyes. Jo wanted to cry, but restrained herself. She knew Marie was not a sentimental or emotional person and a prayer would have been water off a duck's back that moment.

Suddenly, Jo did the unexpected. 'Marie, the war is over, we are free! From here on things are going to change!' And before Marie could protest, Jo bent over, giving Marie a sudden underarm body lift while telling her, 'Stand up and feel the floor with your feet while I lift you!' Marie had no option but to do as she was told while Jo kept her standing on the floor. In retrospect, Jo wondered how she managed this, knowing how feeble her own legs were. Admittedly, Marie was no weight at all! But it was a triumph for Marie. She had not stood on her feet for some time; although shaky, she had made the effort and found the ground beneath her feet while Jo held her.

Within days of the gates opening, people were out on the road and fresh food was streaming into the camp. Most of the internees expected that there would be a swift political transfer to the Americans and British. However, during this time, leaflets were dropped on the camp with the message to internees to remain in the camps; it was not safe to travel. Despite this warning, hundreds of internees left the Banyu Biru and Ambarawa camps to commence the journey to their loved ones and return home.

Freedom lost

Sukarno's declaration of independence on 17 August 1945 came as a complete surprise to the internees. How the world had changed for them during those three or four years locked away from loved ones and society. The call for independence, naturally, generated great excitement among the Indonesian people. The news rapidly filtered through to the surrounding villages. Gradually the friendly atmosphere in the market changed. Indonesians did not want to return to the Dutch colonial government. They would now be in charge! This was the time for *Bersiap!*—a national revolution. In Bahasa, *bersiap* means 'be ready' or 'be prepared'. The call to a war of independence trickled through even to the quiet and once peaceful surroundings of Banyu Biru.

The supposed 'liberation' and happy anticipation of freedom changed. We were told to return to the camp—the gates were closed for our security. The message was that the *Pemuda,* young untrained nationalists who supported Sukarno, had taken up arms against the Dutch and Indo-Europeans. Their plan was to target POW camps and the Japanese who soon became our protectors! This was not how Sukarno had envisaged becoming the President of Indonesia.

It was washing day back at our camp. A number of women were at the central well of the camp when shots were fired from a tree behind the back wall of the camp. There were screams and panic. A bullet narrowly missed one of the women. The civil war had come to Banyu Biru.

From this point onwards, I can only give brief memories of our 'liberation'. Many of them are associated with deeply embedded 'fear scars' best understood by kindred spirits who have been through similar childhood war experiences. In my case, as a six-year-old, the fear came from uncertainty: the gates were opened and they were shut again; the war is over and there is more shooting! Added to that—my mother was not well.

The BB camps 10 and 11 were situated in a most isolated and vulnerable area, 5 km south of Ambarawa which itself was a further 40 km south of Semarang, bereft of news and transport. There was so much fear and uncertainty in the camp. Why was the camp gate closed again? Why were we now protected by Japanese without weapons? No-one believed the war was over. If the war was over, why were we internees kept behind the gate? Why was no-one celebrating? Was 'freedom' a Japanese stunt? What really happened to bring about this sudden change?

In August 1945, due to both our isolation as POWs and the fast pace of events at an international level, there were many facts we didn't know that are now common knowledge.

- The terms of the unexpected Japanese surrender on 15 August.

The Americans dropped two atomic bombs, the first on 6 August on the city of Hiroshima, and the second on 9 August on the city of Nagasaki. The dual shock of these events forced Emperor Hirohito to accept the terms the Allies had agreed to during the Potsdam Conference held in July 1945: The Declaration demanding an immediate capitulation by Japan *with all Japanese soldiers required to hand in their weapons immediately.*

- The Netherlands East Indies transferred to British military oversight.

In a 2014 article, 'A Common Approach? The British and Dutch in the Netherlands East Indies, 1945–1946', Maikel Vrenken writes,

> There was the sudden boundary change between the American South West Pacific Area (SWPA) and the British South-East Asia Command (SEAC) which transferred the Netherlands East Indies (NEI) to the British sector, a change that the Dutch government had not been consulted about at the time.[56]

American forces withdrew from the Western Pacific to concentrate on moving through to the Philippines to occupy Japan. The matter had been discussed by the British early in 1944, but it is not clear at what level of government this had happened.

- Britain was now responsible for reoccupying the NEI until the Dutch Government was ready to take over.

Large numbers of Dutch troops in NEI had been POWs. When liberated many of these men were sick and were quickly transferred to Holland. Any reinforcement troops had to wait in Asian countries such as Burma, Thailand, Singapore and Australia before they could land in Java in 1946. The Netherlands had already commenced reconstituting its own armed forces. Holland was one of the last Western European countries liberated. It had hardly any troops in the Netherlands and for this reason it had even fewer in the SEAC area. Neither Britain nor the Netherlands had the required numbers of military personnel to support their objectives. Both the Netherlands and Britain were waiting for supplementary support, the British initially from the Nepalese Gurkhas. The first regiment, the Gurkha Rifles of 800 men, would not arrive in Java until 19 October 1945, and the British Indians (Sikhs) arrived even later. The Netherlands had to gather its troops from the homeland or those who had been scattered to the islands when NEI had been invaded. As all transport to and from Europe was by ship, this took time!

As the Dutch Government had neither been consulted on the

matter nor invited to the Potsdam Conference, these decisions were severely criticised by its parliamentary enquiry commissioned after the war.

- The declaration of independence by Sukarno on 17 August 1945.

Understandably, the NEI experienced a political vacuum. There was no leader to govern and no military to protect the country when Japan suddenly capitulated on 15 August 1945. Without an established government, what was to be done with perhaps thousands of Japanese soldiers without weapons?

> Almost immediately after the Japanese surrendered, on August 17 1945, Sukarno and Mohammed Hatta declared Indonesia's independence from Sukarno's home in Jakarta. They had effectively been forced to make the declaration after being kidnapped by military youth groups. A new constitution was made the same year. The move was made with the tacit approval of the Japanese— who remained in Indonesia until a formal surrender to the British—before the Dutch had returned. It would be another four years, marked by sporadic fighting, before that declaration was realized.[57]

When Sukarno declared himself the first President of Indonesia, the pro-independent youth movement, known now as *Pemuda* took advantage of the situation. Within a short period of time hundreds of these young untrained youths exerted their authority and confiscated hundreds of weapons from the Japanese. Most of these youths had never used weapons of war. A weapon meant power! Their numbers grew into thousands as they went on a rampage against Europeans and Indo-Europeans, Chinese and other island groups, and killed hundreds of Japanese. Commencing from central Java, they moved to the western provincial cities of Bandung to Batavia and the coastal cities. They took the law into their own hands as the Indonesian National Revolution spread. Apparently Sukarno also told the Allies that if any troops from the Netherlands were allowed to land on Java at that time he would permit the slaughter of POWs still in Central Java. This may also help to explain the six-month delay in their arrival until February 1946.

Without this information, the continuing presence of Japanese soldiers in the camp was a source of puzzlement and anxiety. Of course, not all Japanese soldiers were unkind during our internment. In Banyu Biru 10 one Japanese soldier refused to participate in any disciplinary treatment of the POWs. He was often kicked by his fellow soldiers as a punishment. And what about the soldier in another women's camp, a friendly man with a smiling face! He loved the children who sat on his knees and played games with him. He was eventually removed, and a 'tyrant' took his place. These were exceptions though.

What we couldn't know then was that the position of the Japanese in Indonesia had changed dramatically. During WWII, the colonial powers in East Asia were regarded by the Japanese as the 'enemy'. Japan wanted to extend its territory and for many years systematically infiltrated the islands of the NEI archipelago. They presented themselves as the benign, friendly and industrious people they appeared to be when not engaged in brutal war. Most Japanese men would regularly return to Japan, supposedly to visit family and friends. The real reason for these short visits was for continued military training. Japan's sudden capitulation left thousands of Japanese soldiers outside of Japan vulnerable to attack from other nations. On Java, Japanese soldiers were brought back into military service to support the British and Dutch military against the fury of the civil war. The Japanese soldiers were remarkable in their support, and they saved many lives. During the revolutionary attack on Surabaya, a number of evacuees were protected by the Japanese soldiers and brought to safety and were full of praise for the way the Japanese soldiers protected their camp.

One cannot say life was dull during and directly after those fearful and uncertain days of a continued war. 'Things' happened almost every day. An occasional plane circled over the camp and dropped large quantities of tinned food by parachute. The food was carefully distributed.

On 28 October, Nepalese Gurkhas came into the camp.[58] There were less than 10 and a young British captain was in charge of them. They set up six mortar guns, virtually outside our quarters and we could see them from our block. They were polite, friendly and helpful to the women. They were on duty both day and night and became part of our daily camp life. Their presence was appreciated and showed we had not been forgotten by the world outside. The Gurkhas were also a great novelty for the children!

Some Gurkhas were placed at guard posts on the camp wall during the day. Others remained with the machine guns and were in contact with soldiers on the wall to check on movement behind the wall. Machine guns were placed in the front of the camp facing the mountain and the forest directly behind the back wall. The Gurkhas were usually active during the night because, while the extremists could not be seen, their shooting was heard at night. For many weeks after the gates were closed, we were attacked from the trees behind the camp where men or boys of the Bersiap revolution roped themselves onto tree trunks or branches so they could aim their shots at any movement in the camp. Some internees were hit, fortunately none severely. Unknown to the internees at the time, a small group of Gurkhas went on a reconnaissance check behind the wall and discovered a number of dead bodies hanging in the trees. The intermittent gunfire night and day was exhausting and terrifying. Yet, strangely, although it disturbed the lives of every internee, it brought the realisation that this was happening to clear the roads for our protection. But how long would it go on? Freedom when? How safe would we be in freedom?

The battle for Ambarawa

Aside from seeing occasional planes overhead, we really had no idea what was taking place five kilometres away in the Ambarawa camps and townships. The details that follow are the briefest summary of what I have gleaned since.

Heavily armed Pemudas invaded the area of Ambarawa and blocked roads in an attempt to prevent military trucks from rescuing and transporting POWs to freedom. During 27 November to 1 December, a major battle took place around Ambarawa and Banyu Biru camps 7, 11, and 12. Pemudas used their weapons to target internees in at least two camps; eight lives were lost. The war in and around Ambarawa was intense. Pemudas blocked sections of the road from Ambarawa to the coastal city of Semarang with two-wheeled bullock carts called *grobaks* wedged into each other on specific sections of the road. These literally blocked off food supplies to Ambarawa and the surrounding population including ourselves. As a result, from 20 November food supplies for Ambarawa and Banyu Biru 10 came by packages dropped by parachute. Many of these youths infiltrated the local villages along the road. They targeted POW rescue transport going to Semarang.

Under the protection of large military trucks, sick internees from camps BB10, 11 and 12 were transferred to a hospital. Most of the camps mentioned above, with the exception of BB10, did not have high stone walls. More able-bodied internees from camps BB11, 12 and Ambarawa camp 9 were transferred to BB10 for better protection behind its stone walls. The new arrivals in our camp told us of fierce battles in and around Ambarawa where Pemuda extremists went from house to house and dragged people out of their homes, then shot them. Eventually, British artillery and Thunderbolt planes went into action and stopped the carnage by the extremists on 1 December.[59] Many lives were lost.

Without the victory of Ambarawa by the British and Gurkhas troops, and the clearing of road obstructions to Semarang, we would have had to remain behind the wall and gate indefinitely. When we were next on the list for evacuation past Ambarawa to Semarang and to freedom, there was no time to be wasted. It was 'all hands on deck'.

Freedom regained—evacuation from Banyu Biru

Early in December 1945, the evacuation of 1,500 internees from Banyu Biru to Semarang took place.[60] On the day previous to our departure, the Japanese soldiers in the camp announced that military trucks would come the following day to take us to the evacuee centre in Semarang (45 km journey). We were to take bottles of water and the minimum luggage. British soldiers would be there to help us into the trucks which would come into the camp. We were given less than an hour to exit the camp. It was a very exciting day. For some it was almost too much to deal with—so much excitement. Jo had her concerns about Marie who would be in the same truck with us. Many of the sick had already been transferred to hospitals elsewhere.

Everyone had to be ready inside their ward and wait until the soldiers opened the back of the truck. 'Go to the truck nearest to you!' was the order. Finally, what seemed an endless convoy of huge troop transport vehicles slowly wound its way around the circular road in the camp. Many were already covered with mattresses as a protection against bullets. Spare mattresses could go on the metal floor of the trucks and on the roof, to shield us from the sun and more stray bullets on the journey.

Each vehicle had two soldiers in the front-cabin. They were amazing in their care for the frail elderly who were lifted up and gently placed in the truck. Everyone had to sit on the floor. As ward leader, Jo was inside to assist with the seating; it would be a tight fit! The children were excited! Marie and Jantje travelled with us. Half an hour was set for getting the right number of people in each vehicle. In the rush and excitement of it all, I lost my mother; I could not see her face anywhere. I was afraid and began to cry, 'I want my mummy!' The big strong hands of the soldier picked up skinny little me and said, 'Here is your mummy', handing me over to Mum, who gave me a hug. She had been there all the time and knew exactly where I was, but she had her back to me while making sure all the people on her list were present.

At a given time the trucks began to move towards the gate. However, the Gurkhas with their special armed vehicles and loaded machine guns came out first and placed themselves in a position where they checked every truck coming through the gate, initially remaining at the back of the convoy. They then moved at great speed from behind the last truck to the front of the convoy and waited until all the trucks had passed. They did this at regular intervals. When we passed villages, they would remain in one position near the village until the convoy had passed, in case of hidden and armed Pemudas.

None of us had any knowledge of the battles that had taken place to clear the roads for our rescue journey to Semarang and freedom. Early in our journey we passed through Ambarawa. Damaged buildings and homes, cut electricity lines and partial blockades of streets were evidence of recent heavy fighting. From there we continued directly north to Semarang. Several times we passed through still smouldering villages where extremists had only recently sheltered. The fires were part of clearing the road to give our convoy a safe journey to freedom. I will never forget the smell of burning flesh as we passed these roadside villages. They had probably been cleared that very morning. Once upon a time these were safe places where kindly people lived. The internal war brought hate and destruction, even here. Yet, somehow, we felt secure within the mattress-covered metal truck.

After all the excitement of the day, some of the children and adults closed their eyes for their afternoon nap. Forty-five kilometres from Ambarawa was a long journey. But we had thankful hearts for peace and hope for a better tomorrow.

Semarang

Semarang was the 'gathering place' for the post-war refugee camps for POWs from East and Central Java. It was in operation from November–December 1945. POWs awaited evacuation in Semarang from NEI to their countries of origin. Writing about this period, H.Th. Bussemaker notes:

During 2–13 December 1945 another 7,700 people were brought to the safety of Semarang. Among them were 1,100 Indo-Europeans and people from Ambon, and 1,095 Chinese from Ambarawa. From 23 November to January 1946, 27,500 people were evacuated by ship or plane, to Batavia, Singapore, Ceylon, and Australia.[61]

Late in the afternoon the day we left Banyu Biru we entered the city of Semarang. We were much surprised by the very visible presence of armoured Japanese guards, protecting the evacuation centre and its surrounding streets. We still had to discover the Japanese were now our friends who would protect us against nationalistic militants.

It had taken the British just over two months after the Japanese surrender before the first contingent of 800 Nepalese Gurkhas landed in Semarang on 19 October 1945. The third battalion, 10th Regiment Gurkhas Rifles, were under leadership of Lieut-Colonel H.G. Edwards. By 20 October a platoon of 40 Gurkhas was stationed at Magelang.[62] Due to the limited numbers of British soldiers, Lieut-Colonel Edwards deemed it necessary to keep the Japanese Commandant Kido in Semarang to maintain order and peace. They gave outstanding service and eventually the Kido-battalion became part of the British military set-up in Semarang. The first Dutch military contingent of 3,000 men took until April 1946 to arrive in Semarang from the Netherlands. This journey would have taken at least six to eight weeks by ship. Other groups followed later.[63]

This provincial capital of Central Java was well placed to be an evacuation centre. It has an ideal harbour that could berth several large passenger ships at one time. Evacuees from camps in Central and Eastern Java arrived in military trucks on an almost daily basis. Hundreds of family tents were set up in numbered rows and looked like a tent city in a super-size sports field. Our names and nationality were registered. Evacuees were placed in nationalities close to their national flag or emblem of their country. Embassies dealt with their own nationals or at least had qualified persons to assist their refugees. This was required for legal matters, especially for issuing passports and visas.

To our surprise, Major Smid was in the Semarang holding camp when we arrived from Banyu Biru to welcome the recued ones! What an amazing woman!

Vouchers for clothing, footwear and other personal requirements were provided free onsite. I know we had a tent, but have no actual memory of what it was like. There was even a dining tent for food! What a wonderful distraction for a tired and hungry six-year-old. Everything was for free—even the good food!

Health checks were required and arranged for all adults and children prior to their departure to their home countries. In addition, all the children were required to see a dentist; this was an amazing provision for them. I do recall being in a large room on board a ship with many dentist chairs in a row. Mothers were there with their children and each child had their teeth checked. It was the first time I went to a dentist.

My memories of the evacuation processes in Semarang are vague. But I felt free and secure. There was space to run and lots of food. For a six-year-old who had associated 'safe' with the boundaries of Banyu Biru's high stone prison walls, Semarang was like a green field full of daisies, with a kite high in the sky tugging the string to fly higher. It was a *safe place*. Continuing from her story about the occasion when God became real to her through answered prayer in the Banyu Biru, Joan remembered related impressions from Semarang:

> Later in Semarang when we had been rescued... Now, our home was a holding place for people. The very first night, I was just about to lie down on a mattress on the floor of the tent and there was distant shooting and I sat up instantly, listening. And a Voice said, *'Go to sleep, it won't come here!'* And I went to sleep. These are things you remember now—then it fades again. But God had laid a foundation. I don't think I ever, from that moment on, stopped trusting God...as God. Whatever else happened while I was growing up, post-war and during the independence revolution, in Indonesia...I knew...God was to be trusted.'[64]

The war had separated families and the first question was usually, 'Where can I find information about my husband/wife and family?' Jo would have asked that question! For some it was a long, anxious and sometimes painful process of waiting for information. For Jo, however, waiting in the Semarang Red Cross mailbag was a letter from Ryer written after he arrived in Brisbane and dated 23 October 1945. When Ryer wrote his letter to Jo he did not know that Marie and Jo were together during the war. I believe Ryer mentioned in his letter that Adjutant Tjeerd Luitjes, Marie's husband, was one of the Dutch officers who escaped the war and lived in Brisbane. The timing of this letter was significant for both women; they knew their husbands were in Australia and both Jo and Marie with the children could travel together. How wonderfully God provided for both these women and their families! Jo was excited to learn Ryer was in Australia and going to Melbourne. This gave Jo and Marie the direction for the next step of their journey—not to the Netherlands, but to Australia! Both Jo and Marie and the children required Dutch passports, and visas from the Australian consulate. All these things required time and patience—hundreds of people were doing the same thing, but the staff at the refugee camp were friendly, patient and organised. We were in a *safe place*—there was much for which to thank God!

To Batavia (Jakarta)

On 13 December, Jo and Marie and we children departed from Semarang on an American troop ship bound for Batavia once our nationalities, health and destinations had been cleared and confirmed. Jo's comment about the ship was, 'Terrible!'

Having arrived in Batavia three days later, we were taken to a holding camp. The management there would provide us with bookings for a plane journey to Singapore. Hearing where they were staying in the city, Marie suddenly sat up, her eyes were bright: 'I know all those places, even where to do the bookings for the plane.' Joan was delighted! At last, a positive response! She asked Marie in which district of Batavia she had lived before coming to Malang. It was just a question to get Marie talking again. The moment passed, though, and Marie became quiet again. That was so unlike her. Her eyes had lost their sparkle; she was not well and her usual vibrancy was gone.

A few days after our arrival in the capital, Joan was not well and it was soon obvious she had the nasty and highly infectious measles. Within a matter of a few days the news had spread through the camp like wildfire. During a measles epidemic on a passenger ship en route to Europe recently, a large number of children caught the disease and died—and had to be buried at sea. So, a ruling was made that all evacuated children were required to have had measles before travelling overseas. This had to be confirmed with a signed doctor's certificate. As a result, mothers brought their children to Jo and asked if they could sit close to Joan. Each day the room was filled with children who wanted her to 'breathe' over them. Alas, Joan was too sick to talk, let alone breathe over a dozen kids. Fortunately, Joan improved and there was time for her to recover her strength before the next leg of our journey. Jo was thankful for a caring local doctor and that Joan had the measles in Batavia, before leaving for Singapore. I cannot recall having the measles myself at that time. Perhaps I had it in the camp earlier and was so allowed to travel.

Singapore

Travelling to Singapore by plane was an exciting new experience for us all. A staff member from the Singapore Evacuation Centre was there to greet us. We were allocated a room where there were mattresses on the floor.

During the following days, Jo met some resident English Salvation Army officers who had been POWs in Singapore. She was also surprised to find an elderly Norwegian officer, Brigadier Hiorth, who had served many years in the NEI. He survived the war as a POW in Java. He was now waiting for a ship to take him to Norway. He was a sad old man. His gentle little wife, Anna Kristine, died on 3 July 1945 in camp Banyu Biru 11 and was buried in Semarang.

His beautiful teenage daughter, Ella, had survived the POW camp where her mother had died. Ella was supposed to return to Norway with her father when she became sick with meningitis in Singapore and died a few days later, about a week before Jo and Marie arrived. What tragedies! The Brigadier had an officer-daughter in Norway, named Ingrid. Years later Ingrid helped me with my first corps cadet lessons when we lived in Jakarta.

Joan's 12th birthday on 16 February provided a more cheerful note to the visit. Who would have thought she would celebrate on a lovely Singapore beach? This was probably the first time we children had seen such wide open spaces and in the far distance that place where sky and sea seem to meet each other. What a wonderful experience to paddle in the sea and build sandcastles!

Singapore received large quantities of tinned food from the Americas. This included family-sized, oval-shaped tins filled with sardines in tomato sauce. I remember Joan sitting with a large tin from which Mum had taken the lid. It smelled wonderful! Joan ate the fish with her bare hands until they were gone and slurped up the leftover tomato sauce before licking out the tin. Her nose, cheeks, hands and face were covered with tomato sauce. After her enthusiastic example, I was not far behind her. It was the most scrumptious, delectable and delicious food I had ever tasted. In POW camps we never had protein-rich food and our bodies craved it. Our tomato-covered faces were a testament. I also learned something about tomatoes that had been allowed to grow. Yummy! It was great to see Mum laugh. Joan and I decided that after we eventually lived in a proper house again—I am not sure if we really understood what a 'proper house' was—we would have sardines in tomato sauce every day!

We enjoyed six weeks of holiday in Singapore waiting for the next boat to Australia. We loved to play on the beach and swim in the water. What a good thing we did not immediately go to Australia. For Jo and Marie this was a wonderful opportunity to unwind from all they left behind in Indonesia, to rest without fear or tension, to have unharassed opportunities to share in worship and sing familiar hymns with other believers.

The Singapore evacuation centre arranged bookings for the two families on another cargo ship bound for Brisbane. The ship's captain warned Jo that the boat was loaded with ammunition returning to Australia. 'Well, I've been living with ammunition for years, and survived, so I'm not worried about your cargo,' was Jo's untroubled reply.

Sometime late in February 1946 our little family comprising Jo, Joan and me, and Marie with Jantje, commenced our journey to Australia to meet our dad, who Mum called Ryer. I wondered what he looked like. I really wanted to meet him.

CHAPTER 8

Ryer in Tarakan

The island of Tarakan

Tarakan is situated four kilometres off the east coast of Borneo, a triangular-shaped island, roughly 24 kilometres long and 18 kilometres wide (see map of Borneo page 114). In the 1940s much of the coastline was swampy mangroves surrounding the island, stretching up to one and a half to two kilometres inland. Most of the island consisted of steep, densely forested hills, just over 30 metres high. Situated just three degrees north of the equator, it has a regular temperature of 32°C with a relative humidity of 90 percent.[65] This makes the climate permanently hot and damp. The rainy season is from October to March and the driest season is from July to September; however, frequent heavy downpours are not unusual at any time.

Prior to WWII, Tarakan was part of the NEI and an extremely important oil production centre. There were 700 oil wells on and around the island including a refinery and an airfield. The two oilfields produced 80,000 barrels of oil per month in 1941.[66] These rich oil resources on the island were a likely target for attack by Japan. A garrison of about 1,300 men from the KNIL was stationed in Tarakan in mid-1941.[67] So were numbers of BPM resident staff, with their wives, employees and medical personnel. A number of women, nurses and wives of men from the oil company remained to care for the men and any casualties in case of war. Apart from the few employees of the oil company and some indigenous people from Tarakan Township, the soldiers were alone.

Arrival

Adjutant Ryer van Kralingen with his assistant, Lieutenant Estefanus Simatupan, and Major Ramaker, arrived in Tarakan on Saturday 21 September 1941. On the following day the chapel was officially reopened as a corps.[68] Up to that time there had only been a military home with an adjacent chapel for the KNIL. Major Ramaker returned to Java on Monday taking with him the Dutch officers, Captain and Mrs Sterk, who had been stationed on the island up to that time.

A warm welcome awaited Ryer from the military; the administration appeared pleased to accept a 'civilian' chaplain. This designation indicated that he was not appointed by the military, but by the government. An orientation tour was arranged and he was provided with a map of the island showing relevant landmarks, military installations, the airport and separate hospitals for military and BPM staff.

From the day he arrived in Tarakan, and throughout the duration of WWII, Ryer carried his small 9 x 14 cm Bible in the pocket of his trousers. After his early morning devotions until his return to quarters in the evening he would keep it there for those who needed comfort and reassurance—and there were many!

A state of siege had already been declared prior to Ryer's arrival. He was informed that families of military personnel had been sent home to Java due to the dangerous situation. The morale was low among soldiers due to the absence of their families and the threat of an invasion.[69] It was among these soldiers that Lieut. Estafanus Simatupang, a gracious and caring person, found an open door for ministry. He too left loved ones by coming to Tarakan and could relate with their grief, as could Ryer.

Recreation was limited to the local bar and the indigenous village. The situation had become grim and intolerable. Soldiers were more often drunk than sober and sometimes incapable of doing their duties. Ryer could now better understand the tense situation and the 'urgent' request to The Salvation Army Headquarters in Bandung, 'for a person experienced in work with military personnel'. Checking through the existing facilities, he found the situation worse than anticipated. The recreation centres looked tired and neglected. A thorough clean-up and repair of equipment was needed. Ryer had been given free rein by the authorities to clean and upgrade the facilities. It still proved quite a task, but he was given support when he asked for it.[70]

A chapel and a friendship

BPM staff provided considerable support in Ryer's clean-up. Mr Gerrit van Geffen was the public relations person for the BPM in Tarakan and continued in this position post-war in Batavia where he met up with Ryer in 1947. The two men became good friends almost from the day they met each other in Tarakan. Both men and their wives migrated to Australia and sometime during the late sixties they met each other in Croydon, a suburb of Melbourne.

Many years later, in a moving tribute at Ryer's funeral in 1971, Mr Van Geffen spoke of his friendship with Ryer during these years. The tribute covered Ryer's life and activities during those four months prior to the Japanese invasion of Tarakan in January 1942, and in the years immediately after the war when they met again in Jakarta (1947–1953). It was Van Geffen who confirmed that when Ryer arrived in Tarakan, he served as welfare officer with the Dutch 7th Battalion Infantry and Artillery which was stationed on the island. Van Geffen remembered Ryer as a quiet, peaceful man, deeply committed to the service of God and the care of his men or, his 'boys', as he was known to call them. His influence for good on hundreds of servicemen during the WWII was not forgotten, as became evident years afterward. Following the funeral service, Van Geffen gave his notes to my mother, which she treasured greatly.

We know from Van Geffen's tribute that The Salvation Army had a small citadel (chapel) on Tarakan.

There had always been some sort of cooperation between Van Kralingen's predecessors and my wife. Apart from the work among the indigenous civilian population, there was their work among the Dutch troops stationed there... Mrs Van Geffen had a class for young indigenous girls at the chapel and taught fancywork.[71]

A surprising find and a visitor

Even the mundane routine of clearing cupboards can have an unexpected touch of the sublime. Hidden under a stack of papers and broken equipment, Ryer was surprised to find a cloth bag. Both the colour and texture of the cloth reminded him of the long, brown robes worn by the Franciscan fathers in the heat of the tropics. Unwinding the cord, he opened the bag and found a communion chalice with some small bowls. For some moments Ryer held the chalice in his hands. He sensed the sacred—a holy moment in the midst of tension. Once upon a time this had been given to a young man at his ordination as a priest—a lifetime commitment. Had there been a priest here at some time? Where was he now? Surely, no priest would leave his chalice behind! What happened to him? Ryer was intrigued. Here was an untold story. Carefully, he returned everything into the bag. That evening, he washed the bag and its contents and returned it to the same cupboard the following day. Someone would know, he thought.

The following morning, Ryer visited the sergeant (NCO) on duty and asked him about the 'treasure' in the cupboard. On the basis of what my father told me and my memories of his style of speaking, I imagine the conversation may have gone like this:

'Tell me, is there a priest on the island?' Ryer's question was unexpected.

'Yes, there is...was,' came the hesitant reply. 'He was a loner... some difficulties living on a military base; it all became too much for him. He got lost in the bar, befriended the locals and followed them home to the village and remained there.' The NCO's cautious reply alerted Ryer that there was much more to this story.

'Where can I find him?' Ryer asked.

'Well, most days you'll find him in the bar. Just recently he opened a brothel as well and is using some of the bar facilities for his business.'

The sergeant's words confirmed for Ryer the urgent need for wholesome recreation activities for the men. Most of them were grieving for their wives and families in Java. He shared their grief; he too felt the pain of separation from Jo, Joan and Sonja every day. The men had been let down by their spiritual mentor, one who was supposed to pastor them. How sad; how very sad!

'On a lighter note,' continued the sergeant, 'your presence may induce him to reclaim his bag! He's a tall man; you can't miss him, but,' with a sterner voice, 'should he desire to resume his previous position, tell him, on behalf of the camp leadership, that his services are no longer required!'

Ryer pondered if this was another reason for the 'urgent' request to headquarters in Bandung, 'for a person experienced in work with military personnel'.

Sometime following that discussion, a tall man matching the senior sergeant's description came to see Ryer at the clubhouse, accompanied by a couple of village women. One look at the pale-faced visitor confirmed for Ryer that he was looking at the erstwhile priest. However, the shabbiness of the visitor's appearance surprised him. Ryer introduced himself as the chaplain and welfare officer for the troops. Years of wearing the long brown habit had protected the visitor's body from the sun. But the habit had been exchanged for an old shirt and ill-fitting just-below-the-knee trousers, exposing his white legs and sandalled feet. His unkempt hair added to the sad picture of poverty and neglect—a man who had lost his way. Ryer's heart went out to the man.

'Would I be correct in assuming that you have come to collect the bag with the communion chalice?'

An almost aggressive 'Yes' confirmed this to be so.

Intuitively Ryer sensed that behind the 'Yes', was an angry man. Facing him was a priest without his habit, dressed as a pauper, with uncombed hair and looking for his communion chalice! What was the real story?

Ryer took him to the small room and offered the visitor a comfortable chair.

'Not long after my arrival in the camp I began a clean-up of the clubhouse and commenced with this room. Imagine my surprise when I found this bag. I took it home and washed the bag and its contents; it had obviously not been used for some time,' commented Ryer, and placed the bag on the table.

'I am most concerned about your current situation,' said Ryer. 'What caused you to leave your appointment?'

The question disturbed the visitor. Within moments there was an outburst of long bottled-up anger. Heated emotions connected to the past broke through in short, angry outbursts. His voice reverberated in the confined space of the small room.

'I was happy with my previous work. I did not want to be here! No-one listened; they were all too busy. When I arrived here there was nothing to do. I don't relate to this work!'

In the silence that followed, Ryer looked at the angry man opposite him who refused to look at him. The man changed his position; he was uncomfortable. Was he embarrassed? Ryer's quiet pastoral response was to the point.

'Having expressed your anger, I suggest you put it behind you. Commit yourself to God and make a new start. Is this not what the communion chalice is all about? Christ gave his all. Can we do less? As members of the clergy, we are required to go where we are sent. We are in a war situation! There is no time to squabble! You mentioned earlier that there "was nothing to do". Many of the soldiers are depressed and grieving for their families...living under constant tension of a military invasion. There is fear; there is anger... they need a listening ear and friendship. But, above all, they need to hear about a loving, caring God who understands their pain and fear. Is that not the basic message of the communion chalice—a loving God who gave himself for the sin of the world?' A long silence followed.

Ryer changed his approach.

'But, tell me, what alternative attractions on this island enticed you to desert your post?'

It took some time for the priest to respond, but when he did it was on the defensive.

'The village people were friendly. They cared about me. They offered food and lodging'

'And, you accepted their hospitality and just disrobed, forgot your chalice, walked out and shut the door on your holy calling? Was it really as simple as that?' Ryer's voice was very quiet. 'Or was it because indefinite hospitality and lodging requires a reimbursement of some kind, preferably money? That is the custom. And so to retain hospitality you set up a bar and opened a brothel to cover the costs for board and lodging. Would I be correct in that assumption?' A long silence confirmed this to be case. The indifference in the man's face saddened Ryer as he spoke with him.

'Your current lifestyle is sufficient reason for you to withdraw from conducting communion services for the troops. I have been instructed to inform you that your service is no longer required in the camp. Before the end of this week both the bar and brothel will be closed for good. I suggest you take the next ferry to Java; it may be the last one. If you need financial support for the journey, please let me know. I understand the communion chalice has great significance for you. May it remain a constant reminder for you of the love of God and the blood of Jesus shed on the cross that we might be forgiven with the assurance that one day, we will see him face to face.'

Ryer handed the bag to the priest who took it and left, taking his two companions who had waited for him outside. Ryer never saw him again.

That same week the bar was closed, the brothel cleaned up and the workers sent home. With generous support from the oil company, Ryer was able to open two recreation centres in a relatively short time.

A celebration for a home away from home

On 12 November 1941 the Christian Military Home for the KNIL, Tarakan, was officially opened. There was quite a celebration! The Ambonese Military Flute Club played for the occasion. Present were Lieut-Colonel Simon de Waal, Military Commander, Tarakan, KNIL members, and Dr A. Colijn, the BPM Administrator, with staff from the oil company. Years later Van Geffen recalled the above event as if it was yesterday. Those who attended the opening were amazed how Ryer had transformed The Salvation Army's ramshackle clubhouse. For obvious reasons it could not be much of a house...

> ...but those who went there, and there were many, knew they could find there convivial surroundings, understanding of their problems, and counsel, a place where they could lose their feelings of loneliness and boredom and...frustrations.
>
> It was to a great part, thanks to his efforts, that The Salvation Army acquired a larger accommodation in the Shell Company's residential area... After extensive restoration and alteration, which were planned by Van Kralingen, it was not only a clubhouse but also a hostel, where a man who had been on duty for some time on the coastal batteries and in the bush, could recuperate if he wanted. It was a nice place to stay...and it was good playing billiards and other games...being a mate to his 'boys' as he called them. To many of the men, it was...a home away from home. It was in this work among the soldiers that Van Kralingen seemed to be at his very best.[72]

It was during this time that the men began to call Ryer 'Stip'. His Salvation Army rank was 'Adjutant,' and the insignia for this rank was a * (star) and an S, that is '*S'. 'Stip' is the Dutch word for 'spot' or 'dot' or, in this instance, 'star'. The name 'Stip' remained through the war and beyond as a term of endearment and respect.

God be with you

With the dark clouds of war building at an alarming pace across the NEI archipelago, The Salvation Army leadership in Bandung, Java, encouraged national officers to return to their home towns and villages. The organisation would eventually be banned by the Japanese military command on 6 May 1942 and the wearing of uniform forbidden. In anticipation of this likelihood, The Salvation Army advised officers that those who wished to remain in their appointments were permitted to do so, but assured those who returned home that they would be reaccepted when the war was over.

Under the leadership of Lieut. Simatupan, the newly reopened Tarakan Corps had made a good start with a Bible study group and a Sunday fellowship. The Military Flute Club used the hall for an occasional practice. The lieutenant was well received by members of the KNIL; however, with the increasing political uncertainties in Tarakan, Ryer was concerned for the young man's safety if he remained on the island.[73] He decided to discuss the matter with the lieutenant, who came from a tribe on the east coast of Borneo, in Kalimantan. Ryer encouraged the young officer to return home as soon as possible while there were still boats available to take him across to the east coast. The lieutenant was most grateful for Ryer's caring concern. Prior to his departure, Ryer took time to pray with the young officer, encouraging him to remain faithful to God and his officer covenant. Although saddened to see him go, Ryer knew he had made the right decision. As he waved him off he called out: 'God be with you till we meet again!'

Most European women and children had been evacuated to Java in May 1941 due to the uncertain situation in Tarakan. Approximately 20 women without children remained behind, including the wife of the Administrator of the BPM complex, Dr A.H. Colijn. She was in charge of the BPM Hospital. In December 1941, it was decided to set up an 'emergency' hospital between the military and BPM hospitals. Casualties were expected in Tarakan.[74]

No turning back

On 7 December 1941, the Japanese attacked the US Naval Base at Pearl Harbor, Hawaii Territory. The following day, the Netherlands declared war on Japan, meaning that their colony, the NEI, was also at war. By mid-December 1941, and following the attack on Pearl Harbor, tensions were high throughout the Pacific region. Expectations of an imminent attack, the limitations of entertainment, particularly on a small island like Tarakan, and concern for family back home, were part of a soldier's life. Ryer and Jo kept in contact through a weekly letter exchange.

A week prior to Christmas, Ryer received a request from Commander De Waal to see him. The commander was a busy man with enormous responsibilities. Ryer sensed the reason for this interview and knew what his answer would be. The commander addressed Ryer as 'Adjutant Van Kralingen' and commended him for what he achieved in a relatively short time in regard to repairs to both the recreation centre and the 'clubhouse', as the soldiers called it.

'You have completed the task for which you came and we are grateful.' The Commander's face was serious. 'An attack on Tarakan is expected, not in weeks, but within days. The last boat to Java leaves this weekend and for the sake of your safety we suggest you take this opportunity to return home to your wife and family.'

Ryer was quiet for a few moments and, looking at the man on the other side of the desk, he said: 'Commander, your offer is most gracious and I appreciate your kindness, but my place is here with the men. The recreation centre is a temporary thing; it won't last. I believe I am here because of what is yet to be. I also believe that I am in God's hands—this is where he wants me to be. I am staying!'

The commander pushed back his chair and stood up.

'Very well, Adjutant, you are a good man, welcome!' And with that they shook hands. That ended the interview.

A few days later the last ferry departed for Java. It was torpedoed by the Japanese. There were no survivors.

The Australian edition of The Salvation Army's publication, *The War Cry*, dated 4 April 1942, provides an interesting footnote to Ryer's interview with Commander S. de Waal. Charles Palstra, a son of Dutch Salvation Army officers, and resident in Australia, visited The Salvation Army Headquarters in Bandung, Java, early in 1942. Prior to leaving on the last plane out of Bandung to Australia, Mr Palstra had a brief interview with Commissioner Arend Beekhuis, leader of The Salvation Army in the Netherlands East Indies.

> Some splendid instances of self-sacrifice were mentioned. The Officer-in-charge of The Army's Military Home at Tarakan, in the oilfields, is a married man, but as no women were allowed on the island, he had, on taking this appointment, to leave his wife and family on the mainland. When there was still time to get away from Tarakan, this Officer was included in the list of those who were to be evacuated. Notwithstanding his love for his wife and children, he said: 'My soldiers are here, and I will stay!' This act of sacrifice made a great impression, and was referred to in the local press as a very noble action.[75]

Ryer never knew this article appeared in the Australian edition of *The War Cry*. Nor would Ryer have forwarded a report of this interview with Commander De Waal to The Salvation Army Headquarters in Bandung, other than indicating to his leaders that he was remaining in Tarakan. I believe this was sent by Commander De Waal to the government, who in turn notified headquarters in Bandung, to explain the reason a civilian chaplain had remained in Tarakan instead of returning home to Java with other civilians.

A few days prior to Christmas 1941, Commander De Waal asked Ryer to prepare some 1,500 small Christmas parcels for the troops. One of the ladies from Tarakan would assist him in getting this done. Using a mobile canteen, by Christmas Eve Ryer managed to reach even soldiers stationed in isolated coastal areas with a small gift to remind them that they were remembered. As Mr Van Geffen recalled: 'It must have cost him days and nights to distribute the parcels in time to the men who at that moment were already scattered all over the island.' Working at this pace, though, time passed quickly.

Some 22 years later, in 1964, a discussion arose at my place of work about the significance of the invasion of Tarakan. As a result, I wrote to my father asking a series of questions about this event. His reply dated 20 May 1964 provides us with brief glimpses of events in Tarakan prior to and following 10–12 January 1942. Also in his post-war report to the Dutch military on his WWII experiences, Ryer wrote of himself as follows: 'I was a manager of two military homes in Tarakan and had a mobile canteen when the island was bombed by the Japs on 10 January 1942.'[76] In his letter to me, Ryer mentions that mobile canteen again, recalling that an American reporter had written of his work and included a photograph of him with his motorised canteen in one or more articles. Ryer recalled the reporter, and was also told about the articles by Dutch Salvation Army officers who had worked in the Netherlands West Indies (Suriname). These papers were also sold in the Netherlands. His friends informed him about the photos on his return to Holland in 1946–47.[77] At the time of writing this history, I remain unable to locate these articles.

Ryer writes how little prepared England, the USA and Australia were for war, either in their homelands or colonies. By comparison, he writes, Indonesia was well prepared, although the small number of troops was nowhere near enough to protect the over 900 permanently inhabited islands, large and small. In this context, he continues, 'Tarakan was very well defended, with 1,550 men plus a minesweeper, the *Prins van Oranje* and a small warship'.[78]

Japanese invasion, 10 January 1942

On 10 January 1942, reconnaissance information from a flying boat and an old patrol boat alerted Commander De Waal of the approach of 16 Japanese transport ships escorted by a marine squadron which, aside from several patrol ships, included 14 fighter planes and six minesweepers. Without further delay Commander De Waal with his 1,550 fighting men and limited equipment, deployed a well-trained demolition unit to destroy all the oilfield installations. According to Dutch historian, Dr L. de Jong, everything moved according to plan and by the end of the day all the oil wells were destroyed and the tanks of oil ablaze.[79] Ryer's 1964 letter provides his memories of these events:

> ... the approach of a marine fleet on Saturday afternoon 10 January 1942, attacked from the sea and the Japanese attempted to make a landing...that same afternoon the soldiers immediately began to destroy everything making it level with the ground including oil wells which we blew up... Our men were involved in heavy fighting for almost two and a half days. During the battle we lost about 60 men... The Japanese did not find a litre of oil—everything was destroyed (the estimated value was 160,000,000 pound sterling). Our military coast batteries also managed to destroy a heavy cruiser, two light cruisers and a destroyer...[80]

I recall my father describing how the noise of battle was lost in the thunder of exploding oil installations; some of these carried as much as 100,000 tons of petroleum. The heat of the fire was intense and fearful to observe and thick black smoke obliterated the sunlight for days. Burning oil began to flow toward the coast following the trenches where the men were stationed, and on into the sea. Everything in its way was destroyed: buildings, roads and the tarmac of the airfield. It requires some imagination now to appreciate the circumstances. Many people on the island would have been affected by the darkness, the heat and the fumes of burning oil.

Not so the Japanese Sakagoetsji brigade. They succeeded in landing about 6,000 fighting men on three separate points on Tarakan's isolated south coast on the night of 10 January. The Japanese captured 30 soldiers, threatening them with death if they failed to give information on a shortcut to Tarakan Town and the oil rigs. They refused to comply with the demand. On 12 January, all but one of 30 were stabbed to death with bayonets.[81]

Ryer supported the soldiers during the battle as best he could. His mobile canteen was filled with food and drinks. He placed himself where he could be seen. As the battle intensified, he assisted the medical staff moving the wounded from the firing line.

Ryer recalled that on the morning of Monday 12 January, Commander De Waal was left with 'less than one company in reserve'—insufficient soldiers to resist in the longer term—and believed it unwise to continue the battle. Rather than sacrifice more lives, the commander decided to surrender with all his troops on 12 January. The battle lasted just 24 hours.[82]

The commander's immediate concern was then for the 215 KNIL soldiers at the most distant, southern coastal batteries. They were unaware of the surrender. The Japanese military commander appeared sympathetic and advised the Japanese marine commander to hold back from giving his minesweepers instruction to sweep the mines laid in the river passage by the Dutch *Prince of Oranje*. The marine commander refused to accept this suggestion. As a result, two of his six minesweepers were destroyed and Japanese sailors in the water were fired on. However, the Japanese military commander assured Commander De Waal that the soldiers of the coastal batteries would not be punished, and with that promise Commander De Waal reluctantly moved to personally encourage the soldiers to surrender to the Japanese.

That same day the BPM plane left for Java with the remaining company staff. Ryer was offered a *third* opportunity to return to Java to join his family. He again declined the offer with the firm conviction that he was to stay with his 'boys'.

Lest we forget

On 17 January 1942, the Japanese marine commander took over the control from the military commander. The next day, the 215 prisoners of war on the southern coastal battery were taken to sea, their hands and feet were bound and their bodies thrown overboard at the very place where they sank two Japanese minesweepers.[83] During his years of internment, both in Tarakan and in Borneo, Ryer somehow managed to keep a record of dates and names of the people he buried. At the end of the last list of names, he wrote the following 'obituary' in Dutch, translated: 'Monday 19 January 1942—215 men from the 7th Battalion and Artillery "Tarakan" were beheaded by the Japanese. The names of these people are not included in these lists.'[84] It would appear from the wording of the 'obituary' that Ryer never found out how these men died. Most of the 215 men were members of the KNIL. Many came from the islands of Ambon, Celebes or Java. Ryer knew these soldiers. He had played board games with them and listened to their stories, prayed with them and shared in their mutual grief of separation from loved ones. They were amongst those who called him 'Stip'. Many of these men were Christians and were pleased to share fellowship with him.

Amongst my father's personal papers were several copies of the above obituary, each on a separate page, not together but among other war documents. It is only now, many years later—as I journey with him with pen and paper—that I catch a glimpse of what he was trying to convey. He still grieved over their loss. I believe it was significant that he included this obituary on the final list of names with the last person he buried in September 1945. 'The sea is their grave, but let us remember their names. Lest we forget!'

I have often thought about the impact of all this on my father. He was such a quiet and peaceful man, without military training or any experience with firearms. A friend and fellow prisoner with Ryer later mentioned to my mother and Joan, that Ryer never carried weapons during the war. The welfare of the soldiers was his first concern. He never spoke about the war except when asked about a specific matter. Undoubtedly, my letter stirred many memories for my father. I believe that, as he wrote his reply, he relived the roar of fires from burning oil tanks, the annihilation of infrastructure and the ruthless destruction of human life by the Japanese in less than three days. His memories of names, dates and events were sharp. However, I think it is also significant that he wrote this letter in the month following

Anzac Day—the anniversary of the landing at Gallipoli, Turkey, by the troops of the Australia and New Zealand Army Corps (ANZAC) on 25 April 1915. Anzac Day has subsequently been used to recognise and remember the sacrifices of Australian service personnel in all wars. This was always a very emotional day for him. I recall seeing him weep on Anzac days. Both mentally and emotionally, he was geared up days before, with the anticipation of the annual Anzac Day march down St Kilda Road in Melbourne as he joined with fellow Salvation Army Red Shield service personnel behind The Salvation Army Melbourne Staff Band. He could visualise the forecourt to the Shrine of Remembrance and hundreds of other military services personnel marching with their regimental flags and emblems. Anzac Day, a day to celebrate peace, freedom and friendship, was also a time for some to grieve—hence the tears.

Facing the firing squad

One thing was obvious: the Japanese military commander was furious because of the utter destruction of the oil installations. There was also the 'loss of face'—the failure to save the precious oil for the Japanese war effort now so evident everywhere. Oil seeped into the ground and ditches; even the sand on the beach was tainted by it. Well over 2,000 of his fighting men were lost during the two-day battle. He must have wondered if there was anything else worth saving on this little island of Tarakan aside from oil.

By midday on the day of surrender the men were ordered to stand in lines for execution. Ryer was lined up with the second group. Unobtrusively, he leaned against the wall to rest his back and closed his eyes. Was it a moment in the presence of the Almighty, a prayer for his men or Jo and the children? All morning the men stood in the blazing heat. On three separate occasions the firing squad had lined up and three times they were called away at the last moment. Then word came that the men were not to be harmed because they were carrying out orders of their superiors. Ryer's faith was tested and he found God to be faithful! Ryer witnessed executions on other occasions, however.

POW camp Tarakan

I believe it is fitting to include part of Ryer's report on the situation in Tarakan after the surrender on 12 January 1942, recorded on 23 November 1945.[85] Part of the report held in the War Archives follows below:

> On the 13 January 1942, I was interned at Tarakan till the 3 July, 1942 in the POW camp. This camp was exceedingly bad, little food, very bad sanitary conditions, in consequence of which dysentery and beriberi broke out... Beating was frequently done... [86]

Needless to say, there was no opportunity for the men to return to barracks to collect any personal items. Although Ryer was within a short walk of his accommodation, he never returned there. Suddenly he became aware that his most precious possession—his Bible—was in his deep, right hand trouser pocket.

Following the military surrender to the Japanese, the local people, including the Chinese, began to ravage the houses of Europeans. They demanded rings, watches and jewellery from both citizens and soldiers; even senior Japanese officers participated in the rampage.

Approximately 1,250 men were incarcerated in five long, narrow passageways; each one was 25 metres long and four metres wide. They were without any sanitation facilities, food, water or a mat to soften the stone floor they had to sleep on. Officers were placed with groups of six to nine men in small rooms not big enough for all of them to sit or stretch out to sleep. Windows were shut and nailed down preventing ventilation or light penetrating. Many of the men had been beaten and kicked, and the humiliation of defeat and imprisonment sank in. The stench of human waste pervaded both atmosphere and clothing. Heat and lack of air caused some to faint as did hunger and lack of water. Men collapsed with exhaustion. Strength was gone. The Japanese military commander knew how to disengage an adversary swiftly.[87] Wounded soldiers were removed from the military hospital and nurses were locked in at the hospital to care for the Japanese wounded only, under humiliating conditions. Reports would suggest dreadful things happened to these women.[88] Later that day, as light began to fade, voices quietened and countless exhausted men tried to find the most comfortable position to sleep. Most would have found a clean spot or wall to lean against. Lack of light and ventilation brought an early night, with added exhaustion due to a lack of clean air.

I believe Ryer too would have found a place to sit and lean against the wall. Whatever went through his mind that evening, of one thing I am certain: he entered the presence of the One who never sleeps and who hears our prayers. It may well have been that he said, 'O God, where do I go from here? I've not walked this road before.' I believe God was with him and enabled Ryer to sleep despite the horrors of the past few days.

The voices of hundreds of other men waking up and the overwhelming stench of human excrement woke him the next morning. It was difficult to find a clean place to stand; men were weak and dehydrated. Some could only sit. Ryer wondered what the day would bring. He slipped his hand into his right pocket for his Bible and turned to Psalm 73. The early part speaks of the rich, the wealthy, and those who ignore God. But this time Ryer's attention was drawn to the latter part of the psalm where God, the All Sufficient One, draws him into his presence. In this heavily pencil-marked Psalm 73, verse 17 became significant for Ryer on the morning of 13 January 1942, and that morning or later, he noted the date in the margin.

> All day long I have been plagued; have been punished every morning. If I had said, 'I will speak thus,' I would have betrayed your children. When I tried to understand all this, it was oppressive to me—till I entered the sanctuary of God, then I understood their final destiny.[89]

For some brief moments, I believe Ryer would have closed his eyes, shutting out all distractions as he sought the presence of the One who was on this journey with him. As he entered into the presence of God, his peace was restored and his trust confirmed. He knew God was in control. The Lord promised his presence, and Ryer was to trust him. The book of Psalms in Ryer's Bible is full of markings in different colours; he obviously ran out of pencils and used what was available. Many years later Ryer spoke of this moment in his still-broken English to cadets on a Spiritual Day at the Officer Training College in Melbourne in 1967, quoting verse 17: 'till I entered the sanctuary of God, then I understood their final destiny'. I was one of those cadets, yet at that time I failed to comprehend the full significance of his experience. The Psalmist concludes on a positive note:

> Yet I am always with you; you hold me with your right hand. You guide me with your counsel, and afterwards you will take me into glory... I have made the Sovereign Lord my refuge; I will tell of all your deeds.[90]

Missing people—Tarakan 1942 and 1944–1945

In his personal report, Ryer mentions the names of 11 persons who went missing in Tarakan during the battle from 10–12 January 1942. There were also four prisoners of war, including a woman (a wife of a soldier), who Ryer buried at the cemetery of the Dutch Royal Merchant Navy (KPM). These four names are recorded on Ryer's lists of deceased military personnel. Initially he placed their names on the back pages of his Bible. The names of the 11 soldiers are also recorded, but as *missing,* because he was not familiar with the names of these 11 men, nor did he bury any of them.

The disappearance of a second group of 11 people known to Ryer, in April 1945, was another unsolved 'mystery' for him. I suspect he assumed the worst—correctly! *Geïllustreerde Atlas van de Japanse Kampen in Nederlands-Indië 1942–1945* gives the following information which may provide the answer. Allow me to share what I discovered in the small print of this amazing 'War' Atlas.

> 16.12.1944: The last 85 European POW men transferred to Balikpapan.
> Only 15 European POWs remained in Tarakan, three officers and 12 sick people.
> 17.02.1945: One European patient died.
> 13.04.1945: At 20.00 hours, 11 sick patients are transported and disappeared.[91]

Towards the end of the war when the Japanese knew they had lost the battle it was not unusual for people to 'disappear'. It was a quick way to clear the POW camps and hospital beds.

I do not recall my father ever speaking publicly about atrocities carried out by the Japanese. He did not deny these things occurred. But when asked about specific incidents he would nod his head, answer with quiet restraint and carefully redirect the conversation to a humorous incident he recalled of camp life. Ryer had a dry sense of Dutch humour and knew how to tell a good story. Though the memory of war and the pain of friends lost was ever there, I believe he chose to put the war and hatred behind him and forgive. Only then could peace become a reality for him.

Oil at Balikpapan

The destruction of the oil installations in Tarakan was a huge setback for the Japanese. The military commander of the Sakagoetsji brigade considered how to prevent a similar disaster in Balikpapan. He chose Captain A. Colijn and Commander De Waal's adjutant, Captain G.L. Reinderhoff, to convey his instructions to the KNIL commandant of the 6th Battalion Infantry stationed in Balikpapan. The two men commenced their 600-mile journey from Tarakan to Balikpapan on 16 January on the large motorboat of the BPM.[92] Arriving early on the morning of 20 January, they knew time was crucial. The two senior military leaders stationed in Balikpapan expected the two men. They were quickly informed of the threats made by the Japanese military leader—any destruction of the oil installations in Balikpapan would mean the death of all military personnel who had participated in the destruction process, including countless Dutch citizens. Despite this ominous threat, the KNIL commandant was prepared and ready to commence an immediate destruction program of all oil installations. All flying boats were to return to Surabaya; these provided an escape to Java not only for Captains Colijn and Reinderhoff, but also for some who had been on the demolition team of the oil installations.

When the Sakagoetsji brigade departed from Tarakan on 21 January to capture Balikpapan, the oil installations were burning! Three days later, on 24 January, when the Japanese Sakagoetsji fleet arrived in Balikpapan all oil installations were destroyed. Dr L. De Jong describes the horrific death of 78 innocent people which followed.

> On 24 February, a month after the capture of Balikpapan, the Japanese military leader put into action the threat he had made to Colijn and Reinderhoff which they delivered to the KNIL Commander, Lieut-Colonel C. van den Hoogenband. A wide representation of Balikpapan European residents from all walks of life who observed the destruction of the oil installations, civil servants, lawyers, engineers, patients from their hospital beds and many more, including three priests and a minister of a church—78 people in total—were brought to the beach. A large group of Indo-Europeans and other citizens had been gathered to witness what took place. Two men were beheaded. The other 76 were told to walk into the water up to their chest where they were shot one after the other. It was said that the eldest priest tried to mediate with the Japanese and comfort his friends until he too was shot. These people were never buried; their bodies were left to drift with the rising and falling tide.[93]

CHAPTER 9

Ryer in Borneo

Balikpapan, 5 June 1942 to 19 February 1945

Balikpapan means 'upside down ship'—an excellent description of the local topography. The town is situated on the south-east coast of Borneo and built on a plateau that resembles a flat hull, with sides coming down to the plain.

Ryer's 1964 letter records: '2 June 1942, transferred from Tarakan to Balikpapan, arrived on 5 June.' This transfer was the first and involved 450 military prisoners of war. 'The crossing was well organised by the Japanese...'[94] This date was confirmed in red on the blank pages at the back of his Bible.[95] On their arrival in Balikpapan, military prisoners were placed in a concentration camp. Smaller groups from Tarakan followed later until the last active Europeans had been removed from the island.[96] Ryer's official war report mentions military officers who were transferred from Tarakan to Balikpapan in the same group as Ryer.

> From 3rd July (1942) till the 19th February, 1945, we were
> interned at Balikpapan. Our Camp Commandant was 1st
> Lt. Lamers. Early in 1943 a small group of officers had a
> discourse about what to do if an allied invasion occurred.
> This conversation was reported in one way or other, and
> was considered by the Japanese as a plot. The first four
> on the list were transported from Balikpapan to Tarakan

on the 23 February, 1943, to the Kampei, interrogated there and severely tortured. After 1½ years they were returned to the camp but later on they were transferred to the prison at Bandjermasin [*sic*]. Lt. Lamers died however, in consequence of torture and dysentery as early as May 1943. The other three persons were condemned to 10 years imprisonment by Japanese court-martial, but were murdered a short time before the capitulation. The then Commanding Officer, Capt. Brouwer wrote a report on it and handed this to the Australians who arrested the Japanese who were responsible for these murders...[97]

The above report suggests that the Japanese military command chose Balikpapan as the mustering place for all military prisoners from the Borneo zone. Eventually, the various brigades of POWs from North and East Borneo, Samarinda 1 and 2, Tjolok Bajur, Banjarmasin and Tarakan were all transferred to Balikpapan and put behind a barbed wire fence.[98]

Insignia story

By 24 April 1942 wearing The Salvation Army uniform became prohibited throughout the Asia Pacific region. The Japanese considered the organisation an ally of Britain, therefore anti-Nippon and dangerous. This information was quickly dispersed on the island of Java; however, it failed to reach Japanese commanders on distant islands such as Tarakan, Borneo or Celebes (Sulawesi). Being unaware of these restrictions, Ryer continued to wear his Salvation Army uniform.

All European military prisoners of war from Tarakan and Borneo were transferred to the Balikpapan POW Camp. Not long afterwards the prisoners were informed that the chief Japanese military commander for the region would visit the camp for an inspection. On a given day prisoners were instructed to assemble in their brigades. Ryer stood with the 7th Brigade Infantry. A platform had been set up to allow the visiting commander to view the prisoners. A hushed silence came over the soldiers as all eyes focused on the man who stepped onto the platform. The chief military commander had the stature and bearing of a leader—a quality instantly recognised by the prisoners of war. Not a man to be ignored! He was a head taller than his compatriots who faded into the background behind him. He was observant and took time to view the long lines of prisoners.

Ryer, standing near the front of his brigade, was aware that the commander's eyes moved in his direction several times, and knew his insignia had been noted. His heart began to beat faster. What next? Again, the commander focused his attention in Ryer's direction—and he consulted with the camp commander who was then instructed to bring Ryer to the platform. Ryer knew it was his uniform that had attracted attention and wondered what would happen. The visiting commander smiled as he looked at Ryer and, with the aid of an interpreter, he said: 'I am familiar with your uniform. My best friend is the leader of The Salvation Army in Japan; his name is Commissioner Gunpei Yamamuro. He is a good man!' Ryer knew the name and smiled, nodding his head. 'Yes!' The chief commander continued: 'Because I know the true mission of The Salvation Army, you will also be a good man. You are to wear that uniform all the time and be free to do your work here in this camp. I will write a letter to you that you are to wear this uniform all the time. If anyone stops you, show the letter to them and keep it with you at all times.' True to the chief commander's words, the letter was waiting for Ryer in the office of the camp commander that same day. However, the commander retained the letter in his office.

That evening as quietness settled over the barracks, Ryer followed his usual evening routine and, kneeling beside his bunk, entered into the presence of Almighty God. He poured out his heart in gratitude to God for his protecting mercies and his perfect timing of the events that day. Ryer's prayer was, 'O God, give me the strength to fulfil this task.' In the darkness of the night, God's promise to Joshua echoed in his mind, 'Do not be terrified; do not be discouraged—I will be with you!'[99]

Both by his words and letter, Ryer's position as chaplain for all military personnel in the camp was confirmed by the visiting Japanese military commander in the presence of the Japanese camp commander, his staff and all POWs. Not once was his position as chaplain, spiritual leader or preacher questioned throughout his imprisonment. After some time, however, the washable S's on his collar became threadbare and wore out and Ryer found himself summoned to the office of the Japanese camp commander. He was questioned as to the reason why he was not wearing his insignia. Ryer showed him his shirt and the commander understood his situation. He forthwith instructed the camp metal worker to make two exact copies in aluminium of the Adjutant's rank collar badges, including the red colour behind the *S. These are now part of our family heritage.

God's hand at work—'I will stay'

Several instances demonstrate for me the hand of God in Ryer's life at that time. One was his conviction that God wanted him to remain with the troops in Tarakan. During their interview Commandant De Waal had warned Ryer that war was imminent and graciously suggested that Ryer take the last ferry to Java, but Ryer said: 'I will stay'. Then, there was the tragedy of the last ferry from Tarakan, which was torpedoed by the Japanese with the loss of all on board. This news must have been a great confirmation of Divine guidance for Ryer. Then, following the surrender of the military to the Japanese, the administrator of the oil company offered Ryer a seat on the company plane returning to Java with staff. Again, Ryer said: 'Thanks, but I will stay with these men.' Next was the incident of the firing squad in Tarakan—Ryer near the front line—with the execution being called off and many lives spared. Ryer exhibited a quiet determination to remain faithful to his holy calling as a Salvation Army officer as well as the appointment given to him. His cloth insignia may have become frayed and worn but he refused to abdicate his calling—he knew the One who goes before. On his arrival in Balikpapan he would have heard the story of the massacre of the 78 people including four members of the clergy. He would have grieved over this loss. As other brigades swelled the number of prisoners of war in Balikpapan, no other clergy/chaplain came with them and he would have realised the almost impossible task ahead of him as the only chaplain for hundreds of men. But how amazing is God's provision! Who would have expected that a senior Japanese military commander would provide Ryer with a personally signed letter allowing him complete freedom to fulfil his position as chaplain to the military and his calling as a Salvation Army officer? With hindsight, was this another reason for the 'urgent request' to The Salvation Army Headquarters in Bandung, from the NEI government, 'for a person experienced in work with military personnel'? Only God knows!

Food, starvation and unexpected blessing

Food was in short supply for almost the entire duration of their imprisonment. Ryer reported: 'The camp in Balikpapan (1942–43) was worse than that at Tarakan. The rations were 400 grams of rice per day. Treatment was bad, sanitary conditions awful and in consequence of this many persons died...'[100]

Ryer and other prisoner representatives did all they could to obtain more food, but before long many men became ill with the early stages of beriberi due to a daily diet of white polished rice and a consequent deficiency of thiamine (vitamin B_1). Unless treated, the deficiency can have a terminal effect on many systems of the body, including nerves, muscles, heart and the digestive system. The camp had a makeshift hospital with some qualified doctors among the prisoners, but medical supplies were limited. It was in this context that Ryer made an unexpected discovery. Bill Stolk, a nephew of the writer, records the incident as told to him by Jo:

> On one occasion, Ryer was taken from the camp with a working party to a place near the camp's storage sheds. He slipped away from the party, and took a look around the

> sheds. In one he found a crate containing bottles of pure Vitamin B—the very thing needed to combat beriberi... Being fairly simple folk, the soldiers had never smelt pure Vitamin B before, and so Ryer had little trouble convincing them that it was food that had gone off. He was subsequently put in charge of disposing it! As soon as he could, he delivered the crate to the camp doctors in their makeshift hospital, who were naturally overjoyed with the discovery.[101]

This was one of several instances where the limited education of many Japanese soldiers was evident to prisoners. It was noted, for example, that many of the Japanese soldiers were not familiar with modern equipment such as telephones and electricity. Most of them did not know how to use a telephone and were hesitant to touch one. Some thought the voice at the other end of the phone was a spirit-voice delivering the message. Electricity was still a novelty to most of the Japanese soldiers who watched with awe when military technicians repaired electrical cables with bare hands without receiving a shock. It did not occur to them that rubber-soled shoes protected the men— and no-one enlightened them. The electricians were happy to leave them in the dark about these mysteries.

Slower paced pastoral ministry

Living with death changes people's perspective on life. The men avoided going to the hospital knowing it was usually the last journey for those who went there. Ryer made daily visits to the terminally ill in the hospital and in the barracks. He would sit with ailing soldiers and prepare them for their final journey. It was not unusual to have men admitted with wounds from beatings and other maltreatment by the Japanese. Most soldiers had a church background. Some requested communion before they died; others asked for a prayer of forgiveness or a favourite Bible story.

Ryer had a good sense of humour. During his early-day experiences in the fishing trade, the boats he worked on moved up and down the coasts of Holland and Belgium, and the east coast of England. During those years he picked up provincial witticisms and humour from the men who pulled in the nets with him, and from people he met in small seaside villages. He understood the gist of these sayings and sometimes used them in word play, much to the amusement of his audience. A POW camp is a great leveller of society. It amused Ryer how some well-qualified professional soldiers would join in on a discussion about 'customs and "sayings" spoken in my home province' in Holland. It was simple entertainment and usually brought back memories of youth and laughter.

As the war progressed, however, the number of debilitated men increased, as did the number of funerals. The insidious presence of beriberi affected everyone. It was not uncommon to see men in the early stages of beriberi massaging calf and arm muscles or squeezing elbow or knee joints. Later beriberi was seen by the careful way men placed their feet when walking; foot movements became limited to small steps to avoid the pain of bending the foot when stepping. Towards the end of the war many walked on bare feet; their shoes had worn out or it was too painful to wear them.

Ryer too became aware of aches and pains in body and limbs when he moved; however, he preferred to keep active. His daily round to his sick and dying comrades was slowing down, but a slower pace was preferred to staying in bed and Ryer maintained a daily routine. God's command, 'Be strong and courageous...' still applied to him.[102] The fact that he was permitted to continue his work as chaplain meant he was available to provide encouragement and pastoral care to men in extremis. He also officiated at all funerals.

In his personal report to the military, Ryer mentions, 'All the military personnel who died in Balikpapan [while I was there] were laid to rest by me.' This included transferees to Balikpapan from both Tarakan and other areas in Borneo.

> When I had to conduct a funeral, and sometimes there were
> several on one day, the Japanese would come and check
> that I had my 'buku', the Bible. I carried this in my pocket

every day; it was my only and most precious possession. I gave each person a Christian funeral regardless of their denominational affiliation. The Bible was read by the open grave and a relevant message was given, followed by a prayer. The Japanese never stopped me from reading the Bible or saying a prayer. Japanese officers and their minors, who regularly attended, would listen respectfully, with heads uncovered until the service was concluded.[103]

There was a degree of respect shown for this process of burial by the Japanese. They called him a 'Hadji'; in so doing they recognised him as a religious leader. In his funeral tribute, Van Geffen reflected on Ryer's contribution during this period and the immediate post WWII years in Indonesia.

What stands out for me is that everyone who is alive today and who lived with the Brigadier [Ryer's post-war rank] during these years will not forget his never-faltering faith, his urge to help and comfort. I can still picture him as I have often seen him, after work, in his cubicle, either surrounded by eager listeners or more often in serious conversation with somebody who was in danger of succumbing to his own sorrow. I can still see him... when he escorted somebody to his last resting place and gave him as decent a burial as was permitted under the circumstances.

Early signs of hope—clouds across the 'Rising Sun'

D-Day, 6 June 1944, was the day of the Normandy landings when the Western Allies joined their efforts to liberate mainland Europe. As they moved further east into central Europe, countries from the west to the east were progressively liberated from the Nazi invasion, culminating in VE Day, 8 May 1945, which marked the Allied acceptance of Nazi Germany's unconditional surrender, ending

WWII in Europe. In the East, the war had a different shape and dragged on into 1945.

In a series of dates in various reports and in the back of his Bible, Ryer gives glimpses into the slow progress toward freedom in his part of the world.

> On 13 August 1943, a heavy air attack by 30 American Flying Fortresses caused huge damage. The Japanese were furious and took out their frustration and anger by merciless treatment of the prisoners for a number of days. But for the troops it was a great morale booster.[104]

On another date, 16 December 1943, Ryer grieved over the unexpected news of the death of military Captain Van Walsum, whom he knew: a teacher of French at the local high school of Banjarmasin. For unknown reasons, the Japanese took him outside the camp and killed him.[105]

Another pencilled date and comment at the back of Ryer's Bible, 'April 21–23, 1944' records the tragic circumstances: 'Deceased flyers, buried at Balikpapan'.[106] Apparently, this incident took place on a full-moon night a few days earlier, well outside the camp perimeter; the crash was heard and seen from a distance. He later included the following in his report:

> Four men in an Australian flying boat were attempting to lay mines in the Bay of Balikpapan at night. There was a full moon but the boat crashed and sank. On 21 and 23 April, I buried four (4) members of the crew at the BPM cemetery.[107]

By December 1944, Ryer and his fellow prisoners were living in extreme and threatening circumstances. They were devoid of any world news beyond the two-metre-high, barbed wire perimeter fence.[108] By the latter part of the war, Australian and American troops were preparing for a final assault on Tarakan. Writing about that assault, Ryer commented to me:

When the Japanese entered Tarakan in 1942 it was in a mess because the NEI Oil Company had burned the oil refinery and its surroundings. The Japanese rebuilt only the refinery to keep the oil flowing for their fleet of 12 ships, but they left the rest of Tarakan in chaos! When the Americans and Australians came to reclaim Tarakan in 1945 they attacked from the sky and from the sea for at least one week. This was the second time Tarakan, an island of 24 km long, was destroyed.[109]

In preparation for the attack on Borneo, Allied planes dropped pamphlets over Balikpapan (and probably elsewhere) stating that all remaining prisoners of war in Tarakan were to be transferred to 'a safe place'.[110] The pamphlets were seen by POWs who realised the Allies were gaining the upper hand. The entrance of the Americans on to the war scene was a warning to the Japanese of more to come.

Next to another date, 16 December 1944, Ryer wrote: 'A further 85 European POW transferred from Tarakan to Balikpapan'.[111] Although Tarakan was a long way from Balikpapan, it is likely that the Japanese there understood that they too would eventually come under attack. 'The Japanese commander knew the war was a lost battle and there were strategic reasons for preserving prisoners of war.'[112] The presence of prisoners may have been seen as a deterrent to Allied fire; and their deaths, if killed accidentally by Allied fire, as a final form of retribution.

In response to the pamphlets dropped by Allied planes, the Japanese began to transfer the first contingent of about 382 prisoners of war from Balikpapan to Banjarmasin; the exact number of men transferred is uncertain. Many of these men were originally based in Banjarmasin, Samarinda 1 and 2, and Tarakan. The journey by long, slow boats was arduous, taking several days/weeks. Most of the men had been prisoners of war for more than three years. They were severely malnourished; most were not able to stand for long periods; several had malaria. In his official war report in 1945, Ryer records the following:

On 19 February 1945, we went (from Balikpapan) to Banjarmasin where we stayed till 29 June, 1945. Here the rations were 165 grams rice per day, which, owing to Captain Brouwer, was increased later on to 200 grams. Many died of hunger, oedema and dysentery.[113]

From Banjarmasin to Puruk Cahu 1945

In his letter to me in 1964, using his memory rather than a copy of his earlier report, Ryer noted the next stage of his journey:

About the middle of January 1945 we were transferred from Balikpapan to Banjarmasin where the prisons were filled to capacity. On 29 June 1945 we were evacuated from Banjarmasin to Puruk Cahu 600 km up the Barito River in the heart of Borneo on a slow boat.[114]

As the boat moved into open waters to commence the 600 km journey up the Barito River to Puruk Cahu (often referred to in documents by its former name of Poeroek Tjahoe), a heavy air attack by the Americans—one of a series between 30 June and 7 July— caught everyone by surprise. The attack was brutal. Ten soldiers died by the end of July due to severe injuries following the air raid and lack of medical supplies. Another two men succumbed by 8 August 1945, bringing the total to 12 deceased.[115] Only eight were mentioned in his personal report and I assume that these were the only names Ryer remembered during the post-war interview. However, 12 names are mentioned in a list found among Ryer's possessions after his death under the heading 'Deceased POWs in Borneo'.[116] During the journey, the Japanese 'captain' would anchor the boat at a suitable place to dig the graves for the deceased in the dense forests on the way to Puruk Cahu. The boat carried several shovels and spades. Weak as they were, a group of POWs including Ryer would assist with the digging. A list of the names of the deceased was prepared, and Ryer would conduct the funerals. In less than three months he conducted 30 funerals for men whose life journeys had come to a painful end—all weakened by extreme starvation and beriberi.

> We arrived in Puruk Cahu six weeks later in mid-August, under horrible circumstances. The conditions were so extreme that between 14 August and 17 September, 30 soldiers died due to starvation. Rations of rice per day were 200 grams. On 27 August 1945, we received the news that the war was over.[117]

The last funeral he conducted in Puruk Cahu was on 17 September 1945.[118] On his return to Jakarta in 1947, with the above tragedy still clear in his memory, Ryer recorded a brief report for the military. He made a detailed map of the mortuary and grave sites of the 18 soldiers he buried at the Puruk Cahu Cemetery for prisoners of war. (See page 115)[119] After the war, their remains were exhumed and transferred to the Military Cemetery in Batavia.

Ryer must have been reading from the prophet Isaiah for his daily devotions during August and September 1945. There are several markings and dates next to passages where the prophet speaks about freedom, hope, the need for repentance and thanksgiving (chapters 60–66). In Ryer's neat and precise handwriting, I found the following at the end of Isaiah 63, in pencil: '8/9 '45 Puruk Cahu 1.30pm. The first Australian plane with food and *obat*.[g] Hallelujah!'[120]

End of WWII on 15 August 1945

On 6 August 1945, the Americans dropped the first atomic bomb on Hiroshima. A second atomic bomb was dropped three days later on the city of Nagasaki. On 14 August 1945 Japan signed 'The Instrument of Unconditional Surrender'. The following day, through a pre-recorded radio broadcast, Emperor Hirohito addressed the subjects of his empire, announcing that:

---

[g] 'Obat' is a Bahasa word for medicines.

> To strive for the common prosperity and happiness of all nations, as well as the security and wellbeing of our subjects, is the solemn obligation which has been handed down by our imperial ancestors and which lies close to our heart... The enemy has begun to employ a new and most cruel bomb, the power of which to do damage is, indeed, incalculable, taking the toll of many innocent lives. Should we continue to fight, not only would it result in an ultimate collapse and obliteration of the Japanese nation, but also it would lead to the total extinction of human civilization.[121]

The formal Japanese surrender took place on 15 August. Despite the great news that Japan had surrendered and people were free, there was a power vacuum. People were happy to be free, but were bewildered—who will rule our country? Who will protect us against crime? People began to feel insecure. 'Who do we/I trust?' Suddenly there was no political power to 'rule' or to control crime due to the sudden surrender of Japan. It took several weeks for the Allied forces to provide a secure takeover. It would take some time before the POWs would know what had turned the tide from war to peace and freedom. It was nonetheless a time to rejoice.

In the narrow space between the pages of his Bible, next to Psalm 71:8, Ryer wrote in pencil: '27/8/'45 Declaration of peace with Japan, Puruk Cahu, Borneo'. The verse reads: 'My mouth is filled with your praise, declaring your splendour all day long.'

The return to Banjarmasin

In a brief line, Ryer recorded for me the final stage of his journey:

> On 27 September, we returned to Banjarmasin and were liberated![122]

Ryer had concerns for some of the men and wondered if they would survive the down-river return journey to Banjarmasin. When every man was accounted for, the boat moved into the open waters of the mighty Barito River for the return journey. Ryer noted an unusual buzz of conversation—even laughter, not heard for some time. The 'P' word—PEACE—was quietly lifting the air of despondency. Even the very sick could smile. There was a new hope of freedom, food, and family life. Some had tears, as did Ryer. For a fleeting moment, he saw in his mind three people at the gate in Malang, as they waved him off to Tarakan. 'O, God keep them safe,' he prayed.

> On 29 September, we were back in Banjarmasin by 8.00 in the evening and were warmly welcomed by the Aussies.[123]

The Australian Military War Diary for the 2/31st Infantry Battalion confirms the arrival of POWs from Puruk Cahu (see page 116):

> 21 September,
>
> 14.00 hrs 200 Dutch POWs and internees arrived from Poeroek Tjahoe with 17 Jap grds with their arms [sic].
>
> 22 September
>
> 9.0 hrs Commanding Officer (CO) and Party visited the released PWs in our own and NICA[h] Hospital. The Dutch soldiers were suffering from malnutrition and malaria and some had bad skin diseases.
>
> 10.00 hrs CO and party to Jap HQ where he publicly denounced GOTO and staff. He told Japs they would be held responsible for the condition of released PW's and proper action would be taken to deal with the perpetrators of these atrocities...' [sic]
>
> Commanding Officer, Colin Campbell Dunbar[124]

The Battalion Diary gives the arrival date of the (first) group of POWs from Puruk Cahu as 14.00 hrs, 21 September 1945 rather than

---

[h] NICA: Netherlands Indies Civil Administration

the 29th, a discrepancy which probably reflects the fact that Ryer and the other POWs and their guards had been without watches and calendars for some time.

Ryer remained in Banjarmasin with the troops. Supplies were brought in by plane and boats. Like most of the Dutch POWs, he was in need of medical care and nourishing food. It was amazing how quickly freedom, good food and medical care began the physical healing process.

I recall Ryer mentioned lectures given to the soldiers by visiting medical personnel and psychologists, prior to their discharge from military service. They emphasised the importance of allowing time for physical and psychological recovery; and to be patient with themselves. Other topics included family life and employment outside the military.

An international search

At this point of Ryer's story, let us turn our attention briefly from Banjarmasin to the International Headquarters (IHQ) of The Salvation Army in London. As an international movement, The Salvation Army was much affected by WWII. In 1973, General Erik Wickberg of The Salvation Army wrote in his preface to General Frederick Coutts's *The History of The Salvation Army Volume Six,* that the volume deals with

> ... the Second World War, when at one time a very large part of the Army was separated from its central leadership. That its unity of spirit and its strong international idealism should have survived all nationalistic upheavals and pressures is something of a miracle...[125]

As Allied forces began the process of liberating Europe, and then with the coming of VE Day on 8 May 1945, IHQ was anxious about its losses, especially among the officers—their ordained personnel— and set in motion an enquiry to all relevant territories. In the East, this was much more difficult to do so because the war dragged on until the relatively sudden surrender of Japan in August 1945.

In response to the inquiry from IHQ, The Salvation Army THQ in Bandung, Java, reported 28 officers had been 'promoted to Glory' during the war. The overseas officers who died represented several European countries and most of the 16 expatriate officers who died were interned in concentration camps on the island of Java.[126] Some of these missionaries had lived and worked in the NEI for 30 to 40 years. Two European male officers were taken by the Japanese to work on the Thai-Burma Railway. Both died within two months of each other in 1943. THQ in Bandung expressed concern about the whereabouts of Adjutant Ryer van Kralingen who was appointed in September 1941 as Welfare Officer and Chaplain to the NEI 7th Battalion Infantry and Engineers. His last contact with THQ was from Tarakan, December1941, to inform the Territorial Commander that he was not returning to Java, but would remain with the troops. The Japanese invaded Tarakan on 10 January 1942.

This concern about Ryer activated the unique international network of The Salvation Army. Sometime during August 1945 an 'urgent' telegram from IHQ, London arrived on the desk of Major Arch McInnes, Chief Commissioner of the Red Shield Defence Services at The Salvation Army Australia Southern Headquarters, 69 Bourke Street, Melbourne. It simply read: 'Request urgent search be made for Adjutant Ryer van Kralingen in Borneo.' The chances of Ryer being alive, let alone meeting up with a Salvation Army representative, seemed remote. As the Chief Commissioner of the Red Shield Defence Services, Arch McInnes sent the following telegram to all Australian military commanders and Red Shield Service representatives assigned to both the RAAF and Australian Imperial Forces (AIF) in South Eastern Borneo: 'Find Adjutant Ryer van Kralingen in Borneo', signed, 'Chief Commissioner', without further reference to The Salvation Army.

Major William (Bill) Parkinson was an experienced Red Shield Service representative. He was appointed to the RAAF in November 1942. In 1944, he was attached to the No. 2 Bomber Squadron at

Hughes Field, Darwin, awaiting an assignment to Balikpapan sometime during August to September 1945. I believe the telegram signed 'Chief Commissioner' prompted a flurry of action and that William Parkinson was confident that with a committed team it was possible to find Adjutant Van Kralingen. It was in these circumstances that William Parkinson found himself serving as a Red Shield officer with the Australian troops in Borneo. Many years after my father's promotion to Glory, I received an undated, typed letter from retired Lieut-Colonel William Parkinson, in which he wrote:

> It was during the last month of the 2nd World War that I met Adjutant Van Kralingen in Balikpapan, and bid him goodbye as he boarded a plane for Australia.[127]

I can only imagine Ryer's great joy when he recognised The Salvation Army insignia on Major Parkinson's Red Shield uniform at the now RAAF-occupied airfield in Borneo. Neither could understand the other's language, but the Major would have had Ryer's name with him and this would have confirmed for Ryer that The Salvation Army was taking care of the situation. The Lord had answered his prayer and he was in safe hands.

Ryer's sudden departure from Banjarmasin leaves some questions unanswered, however.

Ryer did not leave any information for his family about his 'sudden' departure from Banjarmasin to Australia; nor did he mention his first contact with Major William Parkinson at the Balikpapan airfield. If this was the first and only time the two men met each other in Borneo, how did William Parkinson know the day Ryer would be in Balikpapan and the day of his departure to Australia? In the absence of further information, I am inclined to believe that William Parkinson had been notified that the 'lost' Adjutant Van Kralingen had been found, and that he was there at the airport to reassure Ryer that The Salvation Army was looking after him.

Let us return to that telegram from the 'Chief Commissioner'. The telegram was addressed to commanders of both the RAAF squadrons and AIF brigades. When Ryer returned to Banjarmasin from Puruk Cahu with more than 200 POWs, men from the 2/31st Australian Infantry Battalion were there to greet them. There did not appear to be a representative from the Red Shield services with this brigade. The telegram from the 'Chief Commissioner' would have been received by the military commander, however, and it is likely that he would have enquired if there was someone called 'Ryer van Kralingen'. I assume that when the 'slow boat' arrived Ryer was told that he was wanted by The Salvation Army. His health required attention, as it did for many others. A military doctor would have advised he remain there until fit to travel to Australia. In this context, it is important to note that Ryer was well enough to conduct a thanksgiving service for his men on 29 September with the 2/31st Australian Infantry Battalion. It was the first service he was allowed to conduct since January 1942. This significant event is recorded in Van Geffen's tribute to Ryer at his funeral. As soon as he was considered fit, the military would have attended to the travel arrangements for his departure to Australia and notified the Red Shield services of Ryer's departure via Balikpapan. Bill Stolk gives us some additional detail from Jo:

> When he was eventually found, weak and emaciated, he was told that he would be flown to Australia with other refugees. He protested at this, preferring to find his family first, but was assured that they would follow him to Australia with the other women and children. Upon arrival in Australia, Ryer immediately wrote to Johanna through the Red Cross. Seven months [actually seven weeks] later the letter finally got through to Johanna and his two daughters, who were overjoyed to find that he was still alive. It was their first contact with him in five years.[128]

No doubt, Ryer would have been overwhelmed with gratitude to God. He had been located through The Salvation Army Red Shield network and with the assistance of the Australian defence forces. He was safe; he could relax. God was faithful and he was in control. This was the end of the war for Ryer.

CHAPTER 10

After Liberation:
In Australia and Holland

A safe arrival

Stepping on to the plane in Borneo, Ryer was heading to an unknown country, people and language. His strongest memory of the journey was the intense coldness in the plane. Most passengers were POWs with limited clothing; there were no blankets so everyone huddled as close together as possible. Ryer's only possessions were the clothes he was wearing—and his Bible.

Ryer arrived in Australia in October 1945. The plane landed in Brisbane where the Dutch government had its 'embassy in exile' for the Netherlands East Indies (NEI).[129] Ryer wondered who would be there to meet him, but he need not have worried. In cooperation with the military, The Salvation Army Red Shield services had followed him all the way to Brisbane and a surprise welcome awaited him. Aside from a local Australian Salvation Army officer, two Dutch officers from NEI, Adjutant Tjeerd Luitjes and Major Geus, were present to welcome him at the airport. These Salvation Army officers were in Ambon when the Japanese invaded the island. They managed to find a motor boat and, with some other refugees, set sail towards Australia without maps to guide them; they eventually landed in Queensland and remained in Australia throughout the war. These two friends acted as Ryer's interpreters for the duration of his stay in Brisbane. They helped to arrange appointments for him with the Dutch Embassy for legal matters and a passport, and with the Red Cross for medical checks. At one of these checks, Ryer was questioned about his military uniform. This opened the door for him to request an interview and formal discharge from the military. This matter was noted and would be followed up.

On 23 November 1945, Ryer appeared before a Dutch Military Ensign, Th. Ens. R. Meindersma. This officer was in charge of the investigation concerning war criminals and collaborators in the NEI at Tarakan-Balikpapan-Banjarmasin-Puruk Cahu, and Barito River.[130] The content of the inquiry or interrogation, which was in Dutch, was limited to a closely typed, one-page report including an index page. The copy Ryer received of the report was in English, which would have been difficult for him to read in 1945. I assume the interview took place at the Dutch Embassy in Brisbane before Ryer departed to Melbourne. As well as the details Ryer provided in that official report, he made his own more detailed report for the Dutch military authorities on burial sites in Balikpapan, Banjarmasin and sites along the Barito River. This was recorded in the second file forwarded to the Netherlands Institute of War Documentation. When my husband Ian and I visited this Institute in Amsterdam in 2004–05 and enquired if there was a war record of my father, the staff presented us with a copy of his report and a copy of the interrogation by Ensign R. Meindersma.[131]

The Red Cross advised Ryer to write a letter to Jo while he was in Brisbane and to forward his new address in Melbourne to her. That letter was no doubt transmitted by the Red Cross mailbag and directed to Semarang where POWs from camps in central and eastern Java were being registered by nationality for evacuation to their homeland countries. When his own process of identification and the health checks were completed Ryer was ready for the next leg of the journey. According to my mother's notebook: '26 Oct '45 [*sic*] Information from Ryer'.[132] This must have been the date Ryer wrote the letter—well before Jo, Joan and I arrived in Semarang.

I do not have an exact date of Ryer's arrival in Melbourne, but his last appointment in Brisbane appears to have been on 23 November 1945. On his arrival at Essendon Airport in Melbourne, Ryer was greeted warmly by an Australian Salvation Army officer and to his great surprise and joy he also saw the smiling face of a British Salvation Army officer, Brigadier Leonard Woodward, noticeable by his grey hair and beard. Leonard too was in Melbourne with his wife, Maggie, to recuperate from their war experiences in Celebes.[133] The brigadier spoke perfect Dutch and accompanied the Australian officer as his interpreter. Despite the language barrier the warm welcome made Ryer feel instantly at home. He knew he was among friends and momentarily felt a huge load lifted from his shoulders. He had reached his destination. But his mind was in a spin. Unspoken concerns carried deep in his heart overwhelmed him. The cumulative strain of caring for sick and dying men of war, the hasty departure from his POW comrades in Banjarmasin, and the whirlwind plane journey followed by formal processes in a strange land and language, suddenly took their toll. He was exhausted; drained of energy. In addition, while physically he was in Melbourne, another part of him was preoccupied with Jo and the children, and living in the grief of their absence.

The two officers who had come to collect Ryer were kind but concerned as they looked at the thin and harrowed-looking man. Leonard understood and he said to the Australian officer, 'He's been through a big change. He's concerned about his family. He needs rest and food and a quiet place. I'll take him home with me.' 'Home' was a temporary arrangement for Ryer; the Woodwards were accommodated at The Salvation Army Training College, 68 Victoria Parade, Melbourne, and Ryer would remain at the college until almost the time Jo and the children arrived.

Leonard and his wife, Maggie, had been prisoners of war in South Celebes (Sulawesi) and interned in separate camps from 1942 until the end of the war. They too were released in a relatively weak condition.[134] The Woodwards came to Indonesia in 1916, halfway through WWI; they had no children. The two men held each other in high regard and had been friends for a number of years despite their age difference. Although each encountered different deprivations during the war, they both experienced separation from their spouses as well as internment.

Ryer and the Woodwards had their meals with the College training staff. Although Ryer enjoyed the meals he found it difficult to eat all that was on his plate and wondered why. The Woodwards went through a similar experience. He needed to put on some weight yet his body slowed him down. A memory niggled him for some days when suddenly he remembered: 'Don't force yourself to eat everything on your plate, as Mother used to tell you! Remember, your stomach has shrunk during your incarceration! Allow your body time to get back to normality, slowly.' Ryer recalled the laughter from the soldiers when the medical practitioner spoke about being 'patient with your body's recovery'.

The Training College timetable was nearing the end of the academic year, with the commissioning—now referred to as ordination and commissioning—in January. Seeing cadets was a real delight for Ryer. He thoroughly enjoyed his own year at the Training College in Holland. He was asked to speak to the cadets about some of his war experiences. Ryer drew on Leonard's support for this discussion. He was amazed to learn the cadets had never met a person who did not speak English. Some listened with open-mouthed astonishment. Many were also surprised by Leonard's language skills: 'How could an English tongue speak another language?' Perhaps the events of Pentecost and Jesus' Great Commission to his disciples took on a new meaning for them that day.[135] It certainly brought home to Ryer the isolation of Australia and its people from the rest of the world.

Leonard loved reading and when he wasn't walking he could be found in the College library. He was good company for Ryer, who felt isolated by the language barrier. Leonard suggested they explore the city of Melbourne. 'It'll be good for both of us,' he said. He invited Ryer for a 15-minute walk to The Salvation Army THQ in Bourke Street. Ryer was delighted to discover the close proximity between THQ and the College.

Leonard was the proverbial Scot: he turned every penny over

twice in his pocket— even for a tram ride. Rather than paying the required fee of tuppence for a return tram ride around the city of Melbourne, he preferred to walk the distance. There were, however, times when he forgot to turn the penny over. For instance, it was during the last month of spring in the southern hemisphere and the mercury was rising daily. What better day to introduce Ryer to Peters Ice Cream as they walked the streets in Melbourne. Between licks of ice cream, Ryer saw an opportunity to raise the delicate matter of Leonard's footwear. He had noted that the soles of Leonard's shoes were full of holes and held together by some brown sticky paper and a piece of string. Feeling somewhat out of place wearing his own new shoes, Ryer queried Leonard: 'I notice the shoes you are wearing are well worn. Weren't you provided with new shoes when you arrived?' A rather indignant Leonard looked at him, 'Why wear new shoes when the old ones will get me there?' was the brusque reply. 'You're not in the backblocks of Sulawesi, nor climbing mountains or riding horses to get to your appointments. If you wear your new shoes now they'll just be right when you get back home,' Ryer replied. No further mention was made on the subject, but Ryer was pleased to note a very smart pair of shoes on the feet of the person sitting next to him during the morning service the following Sunday.

Bringing closure

One of the first things Ryer arranged on his arrival in Melbourne in late 1945 was an appointment with the RAAF Headquarters in Melbourne.[136] He asked Leonard to accompany him. He wanted to bring closure to matters related to the war. The incident in which an Australian flying boat crashed in the Bay of Balikpapan on the moonlit night of 19–20 April 1944 was a subject close to Ryer's heart. The officers who interviewed Ryer were extremely grateful for his report, including a detailed description of the burial sites. These matters were considered of utmost importance. Up to that time the four men were still listed as 'missing'. He was assured that an attempt to return the remains of these men to Australia would be put into action that very day! Ryer mentioned that each soldier was given a Christian funeral and expressed his desire to personally visit the parents of these soldiers; he believed this would bring a 'closure' for the parents and for himself. This was accepted with the suggestion that he delay the visits until there was a confirmation that the remains of the soldiers had been successfully returned to Australia. After an exchange of contact addresses the interview was closed. Only a few weeks later a phone call from the RAAF informed Ryer that the remains of the soldiers had been found and returned to Australia; relatives had been notified. In his personal war correspondence, Ryer wrote:

> Several family members of the deceased, including the father of the pilot, visited me personally in Melbourne and thanked me for the Christian funeral.[137]

Another visit on Ryer's agenda was an appointment with Major Arch McInnes, Chief Commissioner of the Red Shield Defence Services. Ryer thanked the Major for his urgent telegram that led to him being found in Banjarmasin, and for the tremendous cooperation between the Red Shield Defence Service and the Australian military.

Ryer was a man of faith; he thanked God every day for his love and faithfulness. He believed in saying thank you. During the limited time Ryer had been in Melbourne he had been deeply moved by the many Salvationists who told him that they prayed for the safe arrival of 'your wife, your children'. He heard these words frequently and sometimes felt that his 'thank you' was inadequate for such expressions of love. They often brought tears to his eyes.

Settling and preparing

It was during those first weeks in Melbourne that Ryer was reunited with Major William Parkinson, the Red Shield Welfare Officer who was at the Balikpapan airport to wave him off to Australia. After the war, Red Shield welfare officers returned to their regular appointments. Major William Parkinson and his wife were the corps officers of the Canterbury Corps, a suburb of Melbourne. In an undated letter to me, the then Lieut-Colonel Parkinson mentioned how he involved Leonard and Ryer in some activities associated with the Canterbury Corps:

> We spent many happy days together...conducting women's gatherings and occasionally doing religious instruction in schools...the Woodwards and Ryer were engaged in speaking tours around Melbourne. The last occasion we were...at the Mangarra Girls High School, Canterbury, when Brigadier Woodward and Adjutant Van Kralingen were invited to conduct a thanksgiving service in the Assembly Hall for the whole school, for God's wonderful preservation of the two missionaries.[138]

The presence of the Woodwards provided Ryer with an open door to speak of the faithfulness of God. He was thankful to God for allowing him this period of some normality despite his inability to speak the language. Following the experience of the previous five years, freedom had turned his world upside down. While physically well and experiencing something like normality, he struggled mentally. Memories were vivid and his mind was often elsewhere. Some people who remembered him from this time spoke of Ryer as 'the man who wept at the sight of young mothers pushing their babies in prams and walkers'. No doubt it was the memory of his own children who he had not seen for so long. Would they recognise him, he may have wondered.

What is joy? Joy is receiving a letter from the beloved—to know that Jo, Joan and Sonja were well and in a safe place. It took six weeks before Ryer received Jo's reply letter through the Red Cross: 'We received your letter...we are safe and in Semarang.' It was the first letter from her after five years.

It was several months later, sometime during March 1946, when Ryer was notified that Jo and the children were on their way to Australia by boat from Singapore. During his own arrival in

Australia, and again during the arrival process of his family, Ryer experienced one of the wonderful things about the internationalism and networking of The Salvation Army—the close contact between territories and IHQ, and the care of the organisation for its people.

The Salvation Army had an old but comfortable rest home in Healesville, about an hour and a half from Melbourne by car or by train. Both Jo's letter and the great news of the family's imminent arrival prompted Ryer to move to the rest home in Healesville. He wanted to familiarise himself with his new accommodation and the surroundings of the little township.

In the late 1940s, Healesville was a quiet backwater. The local population knew about the war but few, if any, had been personally involved. The 'refugees' at the rest home were probably a novelty to some of their neighbours. The home itself was situated on a hillside overlooking the main street of the township below. To this day the town is surrounded by forests of tall eucalyptus trees with well-marked walking paths and slow, meandering streams fed by small waterfalls from the surrounding hills. For refugees who had experienced the horrors of war and the noise of battle, Healesville was a haven of peace and rest. It was an ideal place for a family to recuperate and to begin the process of reconnecting after years of separation.

Ryer also wanted to link up with the young officer couple, Adjutants Henry and Willie Hotvedt, who were living on the first floor with their toddler, Conrad. Henry was an officer from Canada. Willie was born in Indonesia to Dutch Salvation Army officer parents, both of whom had died in POW camps during the war.[139] Henry and Willie themselves had been interned in separate camps, and they too were in Healesville to rest and recover after the war.

A family reunited

On 4 April 1946, Jo's ship arrived and docked at Brisbane where a number of people disembarked, including Mrs Adjutant Marie Luitjes with her son Jan. Her husband Tjeerd was waiting for them at the wharf. Jo, Joan and I continued our journey along the east coast of Australia, to Sydney. Jo wondered who would be at the wharf to meet them, but she quickly recognised The Salvation Army navy uniform. It was a most reassuring sign for her—they were expected! She waved her hand in recognition and knew, regardless of language, that they were amongst friends. We were welcomed, cared for, and then seen to the next part of our journey on the night train to Melbourne, *The Spirit of Progress*. Each day of liberation was a new experience. We were taking this long and exciting journey to meet Dad. Dad! Who was this man? I was only 22 months old when he left us and I wondered what he looked like.

What excitement the train journey was for Joan and me, whose home for three and a half years had been a makeshift family bunkbed, less than half a metre apart from the next bed in a long, doorless barracks. I was six years old and knew nothing better than a bunkbed shared with Joan and my mother. It had been home, school and where most of the family's day activities took place in a POW camp. In comparison, I recall the excitement of being on this train where you could pull out the seats to become beds, and the beds were beautifully made and straightened by someone who came to the cabin for that purpose. As if this wasn't enough, the cabin had a toilet and its own hand basin so we could wash our faces and get ready in the morning. And then there were the train windows and so many things happening outside as we passed. There were animals in the fields which I had never seen. 'Yes, that's a cow,' the conversation went or, 'No, that's a sheep.'

Eventually, on 7 April 1946, we arrived at what I remember was a very big station with many trains. It was Spencer Street (now Southern Cross) station. There were people everywhere. Mum had said that things would be different with Dad. The important thing was that we would be together as a family again; together, no longer separated. By this time Ryer had already been in Melbourne for four months. He looked well and had gained weight. He wore his new Salvation Army uniform and he was not the 'thin and harrowed man' who arrived in Melbourne just a few months earlier. Dad recognised Mum and Joan, and I was the 'little one'. He began to run towards Mum, the woman with the two girls, one already in her early teens. I remember Mum being bear-hugged by this strange man. Then he hugged Joan and me, and he had tears, but he laughed and was happy too!

Lieut-Colonel William Parkinson recalled the moment in his own inimitable way, almost 50 years later:

> We were on our way to Melbourne...to witness a wonderful sight, the uniting of the family which had been separated during the years of the 2nd World War, being interned by the Japanese. One can never forget such a unique occasion, and give thanks to Almighty God for his wonderful providences during those years of separation & severe testing...[140]

We journeyed together to Healesville, which for us was this beautiful, quiet place. What a blessing it was for our family to have a place to call our own in that rest home!

Life was full of adjustments, good and challenging. I can remember some of the toys that I was given, including a ball. How exciting it was to play with a ball on the road at the front of the house! Clothing and customs were so different to those in the Netherlands East Indies.

I remember Dad giving me an apple. An apple! What was an apple? I was told it was sweet and good to eat, so I bit into it. I didn't really like it. It was hard. So, when no one was looking, I thought, 'I'll put it in the bin.' My father, who was not used to young children, was appalled! He said, 'Don't do that! That's good food. It's beautiful fruit to eat. You don't throw it away!' And I was frightened of this man who was my father. So, I went to Mum and said, 'That man over there,' pointing my finger at *that man*, 'growled at me.' He wasn't my father yet; he was 'that man'.

Healesville was a great place for such adjustments; there were things that we could do together as a family. We saw some unusual animals in the nearby forest and beautiful birds and the kookaburra, a bird that laughs! We went for long walks, and Dad introduced us to the lovely Peters ice cream that he had enjoyed while he was out with Brigadier Woodward. These things brought our family together in very simple ways. We prayed together, we read the Word of God together, and gently began to create a new normality together.

The Australian Salvation Army comrades were generous to our family. Women from the home league, Salvation Army women's fellowships, knitted beautiful jumpers for Joan and me. We learned to eat meat pies with tomato sauce and how not to get it all over your face. Then there was fruit cake. Yum! And could we ever forget double-layer sponge cakes covered with thick cream. Never had we tasted such delicious food. In Healesville young boys came to the door to sell skinned rabbits for sixpence. Many people refused to eat them, but to us they were delicious; Mum knew how to cook them. For us, Australia was the land of 'milk and honey'!

Returning to Holland

After three months of rest and recuperation in Healesville—for Ryer, this had been longer—my parents were ready to commence their 'homeland' furlough in Holland. When, after medical checks, we were deemed healthy and well enough, it was time for us to take the journey to Holland. On 21 June 1946 we departed from Melbourne for Holland on the ship *Bloemfontein*. Most of the passengers were troops returning to Holland. There were also a number of Dutch evacuees on board who escaped from NEI during the early stages of the war and were given shelter in Australia.

In the late 1940s a sea journey from Australia to Holland took six to eight weeks. For Ryer the journey could not have been better—it was perfect; he loved the sea. Having worked on fishing boats for eight years he felt totally at home on a ship. This return journey to Holland to meet his family was an unexpected bonus. Not many of his relatives were still alive. He took in the sea air and the sound of the waves against the ship and felt free: free to meet people, to engage in conversation or pray with individuals, or to arrange a worship service for the Sunday with the Captain of the ship. On these long sea journeys, it was not unusual for there to be Sunday worship service, if there was a willing member of the clergy among the passengers. A room was arranged and sometimes hymn books were available. The journey provided Ryer with time to read through the multitude of dates and events recorded in his Bible—so much for which to praise God. For Mum too there was a freedom from fear. Above all was the fellowship with Ryer after years of separation, and the happy anticipation of meeting her mother, her three brothers and her sister, Rie. All this was good.

On 25 August 1946, the ship entered familiar waters for Ryer when it docked in at Rotterdam. It was a thrill for Ryer and Jo to recognise familiar faces on the wharf.

On arrival, we moved in with one of Ryer's older sisters, Tante Greta, and her husband Dries, who were retirees. Tante is Dutch for Auntie and 'Greta' was an Anglicised version of her name. Their home had two bedrooms, one up and one down, and a small sitting room. The four of us lived upstairs in one bedroom. In this and other ways it seemed to us as if everything came in small measures in Holland.

Aunty Greta was a proverbial Dutch housewife. Her home was an almost fearful place for a child just recently out of a POW camp, where bare feet, simple clothes and few possessions were the norm. She turned the house inside out each day and cleaned it rigorously; the front doorstep and the footpath in front of the house were also included in the daily scrub. The brass doorstep was rubbed and polished daily and woe betide the one who put their feet on it! It had to shine! Everybody coming through the door would see it shine! Well, what does a brass doorstep mean to a six- or seven-year-old? I was in and out, in and out, playing down the street with children from the school nearby, and leaving marks behind as I went. Oh, dear me! What commotion this caused! Alone in our bedroom upstairs, Mum would remind me, 'Now, just jump over that step, otherwise Tante Greta will go outside to polish it again.'

Having a bath was also new experience. Bathrooms were a luxury in those days and bathing took place in the kitchen. Each member of the family had a bath on Saturday to be clean for the Sabbath day. With an additional four people in the house it became a regimented procedure. The door was shut and something in the shape of a very large baby bath made its appearance in the kitchen. I don't know where it was kept—probably in the shed outside. The kettle was boiled and the tub was filled. Whoever's turn it was had a bath in the tub or, in my case, a scrub by my mother. There were time limits to the weekly ritual; other family members needed that bath as well. Steam covered the tiny kitchen window, the walls and the well-scrubbed cooking pots on the shelf above. When we did this for the first time, it was really fun. Over time, though, it felt a bit restrictive. Sometimes a splash would make the floor wet. Oh, no! I can remember Mum always had a cloth to wipe the floor to avoid spills on the wet lino. Life was full of new experiences and expectations.

I still remember the tiny sitting room. It had a large window framed by two lace curtains which met in the centre, allowing just sufficient space to observe what was going on outside: Which neighbours went out? Who received mail that day? And, who was that young man talking to Mary from across the road? The focus of life was narrow. This was understandable. Here were two elderly Salvationists from the 'early Army' days of Vlaardingen Corps and they had rarely travelled beyond the boundaries of the town. This also affected the way they responded to Ryer. The emotional distance and the gap between their life experiences made it difficult for Ryer to find a commonality. After all those years away from the family he was still considered the 'baby brother', even though he had been the family's great adventurer, the only one who had stepped outside the boundaries of his own town and country. In the midst of these challenges, Ryer and Jo tried to focus on the importance of being with family. I was blissfully unaware of all that went on; I felt safe and secure.

School was a new experience. I hadn't attended school before, except perhaps for a couple of months in Healesville, of which I have very little memory. The lady who was the teacher of the first graders had been the young people's Sunday school teacher at The Salvation

Army when my mother attended the Vlaardingen Corps in her youth. She was another person who had not moved from the village and had continued to attend the same corps. She was a beautiful, gracious, elderly lady who was very understanding toward me during my time in grade one. I found it very difficult to sit still and adjust to so many children in one place. I doubt, however, if I was the only one; we were all children who had survived a war.

In contrast to school, it was fun to play on the street with the neighbours' children. The possibility of cars was unlikely. What fun to play hopscotch and ball games and to feel safe. I discovered, however, that there were very restrictive religious rules that were different from what I experienced at home. My parents had mellowed after many years on the mission field. I remember one Sunday after the morning service, playing with my ball just outside the front door. A ball was still a 'new' toy for me. I was bouncing it on the street and against the wall of the house and became aware of people looking at me in an unfriendly way. They didn't look very happy with me. I was told, 'No, no, not today, go inside! On the Lord's Day you do not play with a ball!' I did as I was told, but it all seemed very strange.

We experienced our first European winter in Vlaardingen. This was another adventure. In less than a year we travelled from the heat extremes of the east, including a mild Australian autumn and winter, to the extremes of the 1946–47 northern winter. It was an exceptionally harsh winter across Europe and England. The snow was unusually heavy and temperatures were very low. So soon after the war, people often struggled to stay warm. Retrospectively, it was amazing how quickly the European countries recovered and rebuilt their economies.

For us children, winter was a time to learn about snowballs and toboggans. There were several small dykes in our area, safeguarding the township from floods by the nearby river. In wintertime, when covered with a thick blanket of snow, the dyke became a playground for the local children. We would drag our toboggans all the way up to the top of the hill, and then launch ourselves downward, often with someone else, doing all we could in our descent to avoid the light pole at the bottom of the dyke. It was all new and exciting. It was also great exercise; if you wanted the toboggan at the top of the hill, you had to pull it up with you. Countless times we took the journey up the hill—dragging the toboggan—and then rapidly down the hill again. As children, we did not feel the cold; life was exciting and there was always food when we returned home.

To be out in this weather we also had to adjust to new clothing and boots. I remember a bonnet with a strap under the chin that seemed to be made of fur. It covered my ears and I could only just see through all the fuzz around my face to make my way to school. Gloves were essential, of course. I wore long pants to ward off the cold, and in those days girls didn't wear long pants except if they had a skirt over them, so I had a skirt over my pants as well. On the way to school from home the children began to roll a snowball. Gradually, other children would help to push it to the school yard where by that time it was big enough for us to make a snowman. Life was exciting! I had no sense of time, but who does when you are only six or seven years of age?

I remember visiting Tante Treijn, Dad's eldest sister. She was a big woman, best described as 'round' all over. She had thin, grey hair tightly pulled into a little bun, with little wisps not long enough to fit in the bun around her smiling face. Tante Treijn had a happy face and she gave me cuddles. In my child's mind, she was very different from Greta. Her twinkling eyes looked over her glasses at me. She said, 'Every year we have rabbit for Christmas.' These were rabbits people kept especially for Christmas dinner. This rabbit was very well looked after; it lived in a particular cage, kept spotless and he was well fed. He was enormous and very soft to touch—so different from the skinned rabbits we ate in Healesville! Even now I find it difficult to think that they fattened him up for almost a year and then ate him at Christmas. It seemed unbearable to me that you would do this to your pet, but every year a new rabbit arrived. This was one more new experience.

The one good thing my aunties had in common was that they were Salvationists—members of The Salvation Army. They attended the Vlaardingen Corps. Both aunties attended the service although they were very old. Auntie Treijn's son was a Captain in The Salvation Army. I remember the old corps as it was in my parents' days. That old Vlaardingen Corps building is no longer there. It was demolished to make room for a new housing estate. To get there from the main road we came through the narrow cobblestoned lane that ran along the right side of the hall to the back door, which was actually the main entrance. It was the place where my grandfather, Hermanus van Kapel, was saved and became a Salvationist. Readers will remember that he began the slow process of training men who had never held a brass instrument or read music, to make music to the glory of God. He became the corps' first bandmaster. It was the place where both my parents committed themselves to God, were married and received their call to Salvation Army officership.

On Sundays, during the cold months of winter there was a large red-hot stove just inside the hall. The fires had been burning in that stove for many hours prior to the 11am service. It was important on a winter Sunday morning when people had walked to the hall, often through thick snow, that they felt a warm welcome as they entered the house of the Lord. Vlaardingen was a well-established corps and on a Sunday morning the hall was filled with people for the Holiness meeting. It was a large, long building, although my child's perspective may have made it bigger. I wasn't used to brass bands. In fact, the whole experience of going to a Sunday meeting was new for me. When we lived in a POW camp we said our prayers on the bed and that was where Mum told us Bible stories. There was the holiness table which is, in my observation of visiting many countries, different from that in any other country except Indonesia. The holiness table in a Dutch Salvation Army corps is long and covered in a white cloth that reaches almost to the floor, and is bordered in crimson. I am not aware of where that design originated but perhaps it symbolises purity through the blood of Christ. We had similar traditions in Indonesia, no doubt because of the Dutch influence on the Army there. I had almost forgotten those early memories of the holiness table until I attended a Sunday meeting at Den Hague Corps with my cousin, Ben van Kapel, sometime during

2004–5. As I walked into the hall and saw the holiness table, I was deeply moved. There was an instant memory of a similar table in Vlaardingen in 1946.

My parents received a great welcome home on their first Sunday at the Vlaardingen Corps. It was an emotional experience for both of them as they renewed contacts with friends who were present at their farewell service 12 years ago. There were many prayers of thanksgiving for their safe return. Although we were only in Vlaardingen for a short time, I think it was very important for my parents to renew and re-establish these corps and family links.

During our stay in Vlaardingen we visited my maternal grandmother, Petronella van Kapel. She still lived in the province of Zeeland, on the Isle of Tholen in a village by the same name. Grandma was still a determined little lady, straight as a rod, with white hair. A lasting memory of that visit for me was the local breakfast favourite—large dark brown slices of rye bread. 'Gravelled sand' would have been a better name. It refused to go down my throat. Even a generous spread of butter with a glass of milk failed to wash it down, much to Grandma's ire. To this day, when I see neatly packed square slices of rye bread in the supermarket I am reminded of the visit to Grandma Petronella on the Isle of Tholen.

My parents also visited our mother's youngest brother Cor. As readers will remember, there was a three-year age difference between them, and Cor had retained a great fondness for Jo, who had been like a second mother to him after the death of their father, Hermanus. He was then a tiny six-year-old little boy, and he called her 'Yoey'. When Jo married and went overseas, the family almost fell apart because she had been the linchpin for the boys, and for baby Marijke who didn't know her father.

I have a letter Cor wrote to my mother on 26 August 1946 in which he describes his journey from Brabant (South Holland) with his young daughter Berta on the long train journey to Rotterdam to welcome our family—Jo, Ryer, Joan and me—when our ship arrived in Rotterdam.

Monday 26 August 1946 – Yesterday, the day of days, to see the arrival of the 'Bloemfontein' with at least 900 evacuees from Australia. At 6.00am I started the journey with Berta...and transferred at 7.45am...we arrived on time...a tram to Schiedam...at 8.30am in Rotterdam.[141]

Later that day the three brothers, Jan, Geer and Cor, and their wives met in Vlaardingen to celebrate the safe arrival of our family. Cor continues his story:

That afternoon was a real family celebration. The three brothers in particular were amazed by the change in Jo. Not only had her voice changed but she had become a free and confident woman of the world, able to express herself with conviction. It was wonderful! We were surprised![142]

Cor had trained as an engineer and his work involved operating sluices that were part of the lock system used in the management of the rise and fall of rivers in Holland. As much of Holland is below sea level, the management of rivers and waterways requires a carefully controlled system. Many of these lock systems were destroyed during WWII and so large strategic areas of Holland were flooded. Cor's work particularly involved the management of the Maas River (the Niewe Waterweg) as it flowed to the sea. It was one the first recovery projects the Dutch government set into motion after the war.

Cor and his wife, Janske, lived in the southern province of Holland known as Brabant. After the war they were among the first families provided with a brand-new and spacious house to fit their family of six children. The house was built for them on an island within the Maas River which was connected to the mainland by a footbridge. They named it 'The Pear Tree' in honour of the lone pear tree in their backyard.

We visited this enchanting spot during the unusually hot summer that followed the unusually cold winter. There was a section of the waterway where it was safe to swim as a family; there were also dykes around the island to be explored. The island itself was full of moles. These little round creatures dug holes everywhere. We could see the holes but never found moles. This did not stop us from spending endless days excavating alongside our nephews and nieces. Young as I was, it was obvious from our appearance that we were related to these cousins. The days were warm and we became tanned as we spent them in the open air. Life was full of fun and excitement. I have wonderful memories of this holiday. It was lovely for my parents to have time with family and in-laws and good for Joan and me to get to know cousins and experience family life.

Returning to Indonesia

For some time, from August 1946 to mid–1947, Ryer and Jo had been staying with family in Vlaardingen waiting for news from Headquarters in Bandung. Not one to sit around for small talk, Ryer was restless and concerned! He felt strongly that it was time they finished their furlough and returned to Indonesia, where the needs were great and workers few. When he inquired with Salvation Army Headquarters in Bandung about the possibility for a return to Indonesia, the place my parents considered home, he was advised that the civil war in central Java produced such political instability that it was not considered safe for women and children to return. Even European men were being advised that they returned at their own risk. Some Salvation Army appointments had been filled by new officers from Holland and this allowed some missionaries to return home for much-needed furlough. Ryer knew, however, that the imminent departure of Major and Mrs Muskee would leave the capital city of NEI without Salvation Army representatives. He was a visionary with a shepherd's heart. The ministry of The Salvation Army had to be re-established in the capital city. Ryer knew his way around Batavia and had a clear vision of what needed to be done. Jo knew, however, that without the assurance of accommodation and safety, she needed to remain in Holland with the children for the sake of their education. Somehow both Jo and Ryer had been reluctant to verbalise their thinking, fearing yet another separation.

Mum wondered, 'How long this time?' As on previous occasions, having considered the options, they again went on their knees and committed the matter to the Lord. The decision seemed so logical, but not without grief. Ryer would go ahead and, when the political situation stabilised in Batavia, Jo and the children would follow.

On 24 May 1947, Ryer departed from Rotterdam on MS *Ophir*. Major and Mrs Muskee departed for the Netherlands just prior to Ryer's arrival in Batavia. They were long-serving Dutch officers who were also interned during the war; it appears that after the war they were accommodated in a large non-Salvation Army property at Kramat 61 in connection with some social welfare-related work.

With Dad's departure, it seemed the logical thing for Jo to leave Vlaardingen. Jo's second brother, Geer, lived in The Hague. He was the headmaster of the local primary school and had a very good position there. Uncle Geer and his wife, Maya, with their two young sons, opened their 'upstairs' unit and fitted us in. Once again, our arrival meant that the family was tightly packed in. These gracious people gave us their bedroom for the six months we stayed with them. They lived on the first floor of a building, which was not uncommon in The Hague. This was a very different environment from Vlaardingen, both economically and socially. It was a much bigger city and close to universities. Family relationships were different as well. Mum was totally at home with them. Geer's wife, Maya, was a beautiful lady and we got on well with their young sons, Ben and Ed.

I can remember how cramped we were when it came to baths and washing arrangements for such a large family. I remember the tiny back verandah where the washing was dried. It must have been so difficult for them to have us there, but there was a wholesome relationship in the home and the children knew they were loved. We attended the primary school where Geer was headmaster. Joan had lost considerable time from school during the war, although our mother had endeavoured to maintain her education in the camp. Geer was able to bring Joan to the education level required for her age at primary school. This meant that she was able to fit into school when we returned to Indonesia. As I was so much younger, I didn't require this extra tuition.

These times spent with Geer and his family and with Cor and his family, were very precious and the memories of these periods together were very important to me when I returned to Holland as an adult. Those months gave us an opportunity to get to know each other and became a foundation for later visits.

Mum and Ryer kept in regular contact through weekly letters. Then came the letter Jo had been waiting for: 'I have secured a large, empty property at Kramat 55, a main road of Jakarta and an ideal position for a military home.' Jo's reply to Ryer's letter was what she said to her brother Geer, 'We're coming; I feel we've waited long enough. I can't be a burden to my relatives any longer and we need to be together again as a family. I feel the time is right now!' Jo was ready to make the move and contacted The Salvation Army Headquarters in Amsterdam, which arranged the required bookings on a ship going to Indonesia. No doubt they, in turn, would have contacted the Army's Headquarters in Bandung, Indonesia. Jo was a strong, determined woman, much like her mother and grandmother before her. She believed it was time to share the challenge of this new venture with Ryer. He needed her support and she was willing to take the risk. The warning of dangerous conditions due to the revolution was still valid for women and children, but Jo was confident that the Lord had led them this far and would continue to do so in the days ahead. Jo was also a woman of action. In her history of Kramat 55, she writes:

> On 29 October, we departed from Holland on a ship of the Dutch Merchant Navy [MS *Tarakan*] after having signed that I was prepared to travel on a ship that carried ammunition and the danger of hidden mines at sea. Among the passengers were teachers and men and women – in total, 27 passengers.[143]

Joan and I were the only children on board the MS *Tarakan*. On 4 November 1947, I had my 8th birthday on the ship. As I was the youngest passenger on the MS *Tarakan*, the chef made me a birthday cake and the passengers sang 'Happy Birthday, Sonja! It was a most memorable event in my young life.

CHAPTER 11

Indonesia after WWII 1946–1949

Bersiap Period (August 1945 to December 1947)

In November 1945, a parliamentary form of government was established in the Dutch East Indies and Sjahrir was appointed as Prime Minister. Initially the Dutch military was not present but they began to return to Indonesia in March and April 1946. By July 1946, the last Japanese were shipped out and all British troops were withdrawn by the end of the same year, leaving the Dutch military in charge with a still simmering Bersiap revolution.

The exact death toll from Bersiap ran into tens of thousands. More than 20,000 registered Indo-European civilians were abducted and were never found. Thousands of Indonesians also became the victims of war and violence driven by Bersiap. The merciless killing of thousands of innocent people shocked British commanders, moderate Indonesian leaders and the populace at large.[144] Indonesian leaders including Sukarno and Sjahrir tried to call for calm but were unable to prevent atrocities. These included the destruction of a small town, Depok, with a predominantly native Christian population, where many were tortured and killed. Other targets included Indonesian civil servants and the native elite, who under the Dutch and Japanese periods had been supporters of the ruling regime.

In an early reaction to the Bersiap atrocities, Indonesian independence leader and supporter of President Sukarno, Sutan

Sjahrir, issued this famous revolutionary pamphlet, 'Our Struggle.' He condemned the violence committed on fellow citizens as follows:

> Recent developments show our people's disarray... particularly the murder and cruelty aimed at Indos, Ambonese, and Menadonese who in any case are still our countrymen... This hatred towards Indos, Ambonese, Menadonese, can only be explained by a lack of national consciousness among the masses of our people... Hatred against minorities and foreigners are a hidden factor in any nationalist struggle...but a nationalist movement that lets itself be carried away by xenophobia will in the end find the whole world against itself...
>
> Only a nationalism that is founded in these feelings [of national consciousness] will take us further in world history.[145]

The anti-colonial conflict (August 1945–December 1946) came to an end during the final three months of 1946; however, pockets of hateful killings continued in Java beyond that date.[146] The country was now divided between two parties: the Dutch Army and the Indonesian Republican Army.

Homeless in Batavia

Given the political situation in Indonesia it was no surprise that in 1945–46 the Dutch government discouraged all women and children, and some men, from returning to Indonesia. The obvious exceptions would have been men and women employed by companies such as the BPM Oil Company, bankers, medical staff, other professional groups and the representatives of Christian churches.

As described in Chapter 10, Ryer departed from Holland on 24 May 1947 for Batavia NEI. His Officer Career Card records he arrived mid-June 1947 at Tanjung Priok, the harbour of Batavia. It also records an appointment to 'Batavia II Corps' from 14 June 1947 until 30 October 1947. This may have provided him with a temporary roof over his head.

I have no idea how he survived those initial weeks. No-one was at the harbour to meet him. He had no home and there was no Salvation Army address to which he could go to for a meal. One positive, however, was that he knew the city of Batavia. Somehow, he ended up at Kramat 61 where he acquired one large room; and managed to obtain for himself a bed, chair, table and small cupboard—nothing else. It became his 'centre' where he lived in dire poverty for some time.[147] I assume that The Salvation Army was in some way able to provide him with his salary and the expenses for his accommodation.

During these early days of rebuilding, good news came from THQ in Bandung. National officers who were advised by THQ to return to their home villages at the commencement of the war had begun to arrive at THQ in their uniforms indicating, 'We are here for service.' It was a time of great rejoicing and it warmed the hearts of Salvation Army leaders. There were celebrations of joy, reunions with friends, and tears for those lost during the conflict. It was not an easy journey to leave behind family, friends and the home village. It exhibited courage, a defiance of the impossible and a trust in the faithfulness of God who continued to remind his people of their calling to serve him. These officers returned after the war with the desire to fulfil that calling.

Batavia remained in a state of civil war and under NEI military control. Military personnel were visible everywhere. Civilian transportation, including bicycles, was limited to daylight hours only. After sunset, the predominant traffic in the city consisted of combat vehicles and trucks.

As a result of his service as a chaplain during the war, it did not take long for Ryer to be recognised by the military. Administrative changes took place at Kramat 61 not long after his arrival, however, and his temporary accommodation became the barracks of the Dutch military police. The commandant of the military police was in control of the city and Ryer was told he had to leave. He refused. He was told repeatedly that he had to leave. He always replied, 'You cannot do this to a world organisation such as The Salvation Army.' Even in these challenging circumstances, that protest was heard with tremendous respect.

The search for a suitable home

Ryer's objective was establishing a place of rest and relaxation for servicemen on leave, away from the military barracks. Replacement military personnel had arrived from the Netherlands, and many were young men. Instead of coming at the end of a war, they came at a time in which most civilians felt they were in a war that was worse than under the Japanese.

The challenge for Ryer was that The Salvation Army had no properties. Prior to the war, The Salvation Army did not own properties in Batavia, but rather rented them. When the Army was liquidated in May 1942, the children's home, corps buildings and other facilities were closed. During this first year, as Dutch military were returning, much of Batavia was still in disarray—many public and private buildings were empty and 'up for grabs'. Ryer investigated a number of empty properties in Batavia suitable for a Salvation Army military home. The war had ravaged the city and many traditional colonial homes were vacant and damaged. The size he looked for was the typical colonial home. Pre-war these homes were used not only by wealthy Europeans but also by many wealthy Asians. Ryer was particularly interested in a building with additional rooms behind the main building. Many of these homes originally belonged to people the Japanese targeted first: the men were interrogated by the Japanese Secret Police, the Kampei Tai, and were mostly not seen again. Their wives and children became prisoners of war. The Japanese removed the furniture and art from these estates, and transported such valuables to Japan by boat.

During that time The Salvation Army Chief Secretary, Brigadier Derek Ramaker, visited. He had heard about an empty house in the distant suburb of Djatinegara, previously known as 'Mr Cornelis'.[148] On inspection they found a derelict accommodation house with boarded-up windows, a legacy of the war. Ryer looked at the brigadier and said: 'I won't go in here! It's too far from the rest of the world. What type of work can I do here?' Ramaker was not happy and returned to the railway station for his journey back to Bandung.[149]

Reading Jo's notes, it would appear that the rush on buildings in Batavia was such that the police decided distribution of all large buildings would be managed by senior command. The military police had provided Ryer with a number of addresses of properties which were still available, including Kramat 55. A very short walk from the barracks of the military police, Kramat 55 caught Ryer's eye. A high bamboo fence at the end of the garden separated the property from a native village. In front of the fence stood a wide, extended room built using material from empty packing cases which had contained motor cars and spare parts. It was large enough to fit two rows of eight to 10 double bunks, with a walking space between. Ryer saw this as possible additional accommodation for visiting soldiers.

Ryer made an appointment to visit a Dutch civil servant who had the authority and responsibility to allocate buildings for special purposes, for example, to churches including The Salvation Army. He spoke with the secretaries, and he wrote letters, but was unable to obtain a personal interview with the relevant official. Each time Ryer came to see the official, he was either not in the office or not available. A day and an hour would be arranged for a meeting, but when Ryer came he got no further.[150] Ryer was aware that a number of civil servants were members of the Roman Catholic Church who were determined to take control of Kramat 55. It was located directly opposite a large Roman Catholic Franciscan monastery and school. In her account of this early period, Jo writes:

> In the meantime, a civil servant, representing the government in the Netherlands, had arrived in Batavia. The reason for his visit was to assist young men who were completing their military term in Indonesia to immigrate to New Zealand or Australia. There were many who wanted to take up this opportunity. Ryer knew this man.

> He too came from Vlaardingen. Before his conversion,
> Ryer was a member of the Dutch SDAP (Dutch Socialist
> Democratic Labour Party prior to WWII). In popular
> parlance, they were called 'the Reds' after the red flags
> they carried during their rallies. This friend had remained
> a 'Red' but was now a government civil servant. Ryer
> heard his name and decided to look him up. The 'Red'
> and the converted 'Red' talked things over![i]

The plan was now that Ryer should go once again to the official
to ask for Kramat 55. The result of this visit: the gentleman was not
there. The following day Ryer told the secretary that on his next
visit he would expect the keys to be given as requested on previous
occasions. He repeated again the purpose for the home. 'The building
is required for military men and for evangelical work.'

True to his word, Ryer was there again the following day. The
secretary was still murmuring something about the 'gentleman not
being in', but Ryer went to his door, knocked and went in. There
were no keys, but this time Ryer said: 'In an hour's time I'll be back
to fetch the keys. We've got a telegram ready for The Hague. I am in
contact with somebody here who is doing special work for the Dutch
government, and we need this building.'[151] Deep in his heart Ryer
knew he was going to win! He stood alone, but knew in Whom he
believed. An hour later Ryer knocked on the door again. The keys
lay on the table. Unbelievable! No pleasantries were exchanged![152]

All furniture, beds, tables, chairs—anything that was needed in
such a large institution, Ryer either bought or fetched from deserted
properties. Ryer was granted permission by the authorities of the
military police to clear empty properties for any furniture needed to
furnish the home. In 1947 Jakarta was still under military command.
There were no luxuries; cars were only for those with money; furniture
or building equipment was only available through military support.

While Batavia was still in a state of war, The Salvation Army's

---

[i] SDAP was The Dutch Socialist Democratic Labour Party prior to WW II. After
the war it became PVDA— The Party for the Workers, or Labour Party.

ownership of Kramat 55 was recognised by the Military Police. In due time Ryer notified the military barracks that there was a home where the 'boys' could spend their free time.

Scandinavian officer, Major Walo, was in charge of Batavia Corps II situated further down Jalan Kramat. Originally Batavia II was known as the Chinese Corps, but it was also attended by Indonesian people. The people of Chinese descent who attended the corps also spoke Bahasa. Major Walo was among the first officers to be given accommodation at Kramat 55. The Major was a tremendous support to Ryer during the early stages of setting up the Clubhouse prior to Jo's arrival. Being adept in the local language, the Major hired the first employees (servants), sharing out the work among them; she also dealt with the cook about the meals.

By mid-June 1947 the Batavia 1 (soon known as Jakarta 1) Corps, a Dutch language corps, was opened in the left pavilion of Kramat 55. The return of The Salvation Army stirred the heart of elderly Salvationists living in Batavia; they became faithful members of the corps. Melattie Brouwer mentioned that members of the home league 'kept contact with sister-members in their homes... For women who were not interned, the old comradeship had been a comfort and support. When members of Malang Home League came to Batavia, awaiting their migration to Holland, they joined the home league in Jakarta I Corps where their former corps officer, Mrs Major Van Kralingen was now the leader.'[153]

Fear of the Bersiap convinced many Indo-Europeans they would not be accepted in an independent Indonesia. After the transfer of sovereignty in December 1949, the large majority of Indo-Europeans left their 'home' country; however, from Melattie Brouwer's comments, it is evident that the migration of Indo-Europeans to Holland began well and truly before the official independence in 1949.

Dedication of the Open Door Military Clubhouse

Melattie Brouwer records, 'Military homes were opened in Medan (1.2.1947), Jakarta (30.10.1947). For the latter, a very suitable complex was rented at Kramat 55, where also Corps Jakarta I was established.'[154]

The following report, penned by an unknown writer, appeared in the NEI *Strijdkreet* (*War Cry*), December 1947 entitled 'The Opening of Batavia's Open Door Military Clubhouse'.

> '*Forward to the battle! Forward to the battle!*
> *The Salvation Army will continue to move forward to the* *battle'*.

These lines are most appropriate in the capital of Indonesia where, at 7.30 pm on 30 October, the opening took place of The Salvation Army Military Clubhouse situated at the centre for spiritual and social welfare at Kramat 55. Many officials, both military and civilian, including military chaplains Karsten and Brouwer, indicated their interest and support. We are also pleased with the return of our territorial leaders, Colonel and Mrs Lebbink, who had just arrived that morning on MS *Oranje*.

The ceremony was led by the Chief Secretary, Brigadier Ramaker. In his opening words he expressed the hope 'that the young men who come here will feel that this home is a "home away from home."'... With interest and great anticipation, we look forward to the arrival of the house-mother, Mrs Van Kralingen, who is currently on her way from Holland, on the SS *Tarakan*.' A number of speakers expressed their appreciation for the work the Army had done for the benefit of young military men and wished the house-father God's blessing.

A regular visitor, a Mr S.M.A. Kuperus, expressed his gratitude to Major Van Kralingen for all that he achieved in making this Clubhouse a reality.

The major himself spoke a few words and we were struck by the simple, gospel-rich testimony from this Salvation Army officer.[155]

In a separate report, but from the same *War Cry*, Brigadier Derek Ramaker wrote:

> For Major Van Kralingen it was a great occasion...and not only for the Major but we were all delighted. Much work was done to achieve this. We are indebted to the many people who supported this, in particular the Batavia Red Cross. We now regularly receive reports about the increasing popularity of this Clubhouse. Praise to God.[156]

Military clubhouses were approved and financially supported by the NEI government both pre- and post-war. It was an attempt by the government, with the support of the churches, to provide a 'home away from home' for military personnel on their free days in comfortable and wholesome settings. Specifically, this was to prevent men becoming infected by venereal diseases in the towns and villages while away from their barracks. Penicillin only became available in Indonesia in 1947–48. Readers will recall that a similar objective applied in Tarakan.

Salvation Army clubhouses were generally popular, with many military personnel visiting. Much of the popularity of these homes had to do with the high standards and compassionate availability of leadership. Not every person was comfortable in this type of work. Setting up a large institution such as a military clubhouse required careful planning and even a 'home away from home' requires its rules and behavioural expectations from the guests. All military homes had such rules and management needed to ensure these were followed. For instance:

- On arrival at the home every soldier had to give his name, rank and serial number; these were recorded. Every record had a number. All weapons, including hand grenades, were listed and locked in a designated cupboard. The soldiers were required to sign the register book and were given a copy of the record. Weapons were reclaimed on departure and the book was signed again.

- No alcohol was allowed on the premises. (This was not a big issue at that time.)
- Smoking was only permitted outside the building.
- No member of the opposite sex to the soldier was permitted on the property.

Sunday chapel services were open to all soldiers and counselling was available.

The dormitory roof

We arrived at Tanjung Priok, Batavia, on 29 November 1947, just before the start of the wet season. By the time our mother, Joan and I arrived, The Open Door was in full swing. Major Walo had been a tremendous support to Ryer in the interim and was pleased to hand over her job to Jo.

This appointment was one of the busiest and most demanding for my parents. As an example, one of my earliest memories from this time was seeing my father working on the roof of the dormitory. There was an important reason he was there. An increasing gathering of grey clouds with the occasional short burst of rain heralded the change of seasons to the summer monsoon of the southern hemisphere: a short burst of rain and the dormitory roof began to leak!

Ryer heard that the asphalt on the airfield runways was going to be removed; he was given permission to take it away. Day after day in the blazing heat of the sun he was there on the airfield by himself dragging the asphalt with big hooks while it was soft and pliable. The original layer of asphalt was too heavy for the roof and had to be split into three or four thinner layers. Back at Kramat 55, again in the midday heat, he began to unroll sections of asphalt and carried them piece by piece up the ladder, placing each section from the rooftop down to the guttering. He was badly sunburnt and had blisters on his hands from the hot asphalt. Just watching Ryer at work on the dormitory roof made Jo feel ill with worry. She knew he was at the end of his tether and it distressed her to see him so exhausted. He was losing weight and she was concerned about his health. The heaviness of the asphalt exhausted him and the relentless tropical weather drained his energy.

In many ways Ryer was a loner. He was used to doing things by himself from his youth. His wartime chaplaincy was a reflection of this—it was not his choice. Ryer would not have refused assistance, however. The full-time military person who had been assigned to the Clubhouse to assist Ryer refused to help him. From Ryer's perspective, the dormitory was needed and this task had to be done before the rains came, even if no-one else supported him. Eventually he covered the whole roof and made it waterproof. The remaining asphalt was used to level the ground where heavy vehicles parked and to preserve the ground in front of the dormitory. On completion of the work Ryer had a sense of 'mission accomplished'.

A home away from home

For Jo, Kramat 55 was the largest and most impractical abode in which she had lived (see photograph of front of the building in c. 1948, page 117). Nonetheless, she saw her task in making The Open Door a 'home away from home' for the men who came for a respite from a war zone. No-one worried about the external appearance of the property, complete with bullet holes in the solid walls. Instead of windows there were thick, prison-like bars; these were a reflection a longstanding pre-war method of securing one's property. Jo was, however, an expert homemaker and she set to work on the interior of the buildings. She spent many hours at her faithful treadle machine, which she had brought with her from the Netherlands, making curtains for the living quarters, and attractive ones for staff bedrooms and sitting room. Straight chairs on the verandah were replaced with comfortable rattan chairs and small coffee tables. The buildings were ready to serve the purpose for which they were intended.

There was nothing luxurious about the dormitory—it was

primitive. But the place was never empty! There was a typical Indonesian bathroom or *kamar mandi* with plenty of cold water. Everything was clean. Mattresses and pillows were covered with clean linen. Each bed had a folded, blue-striped, tropical flannelette blanket at the foot of the bed with a towel. Once a day the dormitory was sprayed with mosquito repellent and the door was then shut for some time.

The right pavilion had a long, wide verandah which was a real boon during the wet season when rain bucketed from the skies. It was possible to sit in a comfortable rattan chair and watch the rain without getting wet. Ryer allocated a room for travelling clergy or those needing a rest. He gave them a choice to be with their men or have privacy. It provided an opportunity for interviews or for personal recuperation.

The billiard table took the centre place in the building. Table tennis and board games were popular too, and Monopoly often held a crowd until late in the evening. It was usually Jo who would remind the group it was time for 'lights out' and 'Tomorrow is another day to continue the game!'

All vehicles had to pass my parents' bedroom window to park at the back of the property. Men who came from the war zone in the mountain areas of central Java usually travelled in closed trucks at night. Hardly an evening went by when Ryer did not have to point a driver to a bed where he could sleep. During the night, trucks or tanks were parked in the backyard, out of sight from the road. Although there was an enormous garden space across the front of the property, vehicles were not parked there for security reasons. It was not unusual for men returning to their military base from the civil war battlefield, at night, to come directly to The Open Door, often dirty and exhausted, in preference to going to the barracks further down the road. I was familiar with the heavy sound of combat vehicles and often heard the sound of a tank coming down Jalan Kramat on a quiet night. I knew it was coming to The Open Door when it slowed down on the main road and turned onto the narrower bicycle lane. From there it moved its caterpillar wheels across the bridge over the stormwater channel into the yard. There was the slow crunch over gravel and the vehicle would stop at my parents' window. A quiet voice would say, 'Stip...Stip, are you awake?' using Father's war-time nickname from when he held the rank of adjutant.

'Yes...I am.'

'Have you any spare beds?'

And my father would say: 'Yes! Yes, go through and I'll see you outside.'

Sometimes he would ask; 'Are you OK?' Or say, 'I'll see you in the morning,' after telling a 'known' driver to find a bed on the left or right side of the dormitory. And the vehicle would be driven slowly to the backyard.

Joan and I shared a room next to that of our parents. In the quietness of the night I could hear my father's brief conversation and I felt secure because he was there and I would go to sleep again.

The household

We were blessed with good and faithful servants, some of whom continued to work with The Salvation Army many years after we left Indonesia. Several became Christians.

I have a lasting memory from my childhood of the early morning aroma from freshly ground coffee wafting around the backyard. Most of our workers favoured a mug of *kopi tubruk* when they arrived for work in the morning. They would sit on the edge of the kitchen verandah and enjoy their coffee in silence. Some may not have had breakfast but they knew the strong coffee brew would take away hunger. Indonesia had coffee plantations in the mountain areas, and the locals, like our cook, knew how to roast the beans and grind them. Our workers liked it strong!

All our employees shared a daily rice meal. Some of the women day workers chose to take their meal home and share it with the family. They were all poor people. Food leftovers were shared out equally between day workers.

By 4pm most of the ironing was done and the women went home

to their families. The cook and the gardener/handyman lived on the premises, as did the senior houseboy who served as the go-between for Jo and the employees. Perhaps his most important task, aside from maintaining the cleanliness of the main building, was maintaining a fresh supply of filtered coffee and a good pot of tea for guests. He was honest and reliable and kept Jo informed on the physical welfare of the workers.

Despite the amount of perishable food used each day for meals at The Open Door, we did not have a refrigerator. What was a refrigerator? We had never heard of one! It was a non-available novelty just after the war. However, a generous surprise gift is always welcome. One day, Ryer came home with a white refrigerator. By today's standards it was small. It stood in the dining room. Everyone wanted to see it and touch it. Every day Jo polished the fingermarks off the door until the novelty wore off. Our houseboy was fascinated by the ice it produced and kept on opening the door to cool his hands on it. On one occasion Jo found the senior houseboy bent over with his face inside the fridge against the ice and the door partially closed. She called his name. With a sudden jerk he pulled his head out; a little patch on his cheek had frost on it. With his shaking hand, he touched the tender wet spot. 'What was your head doing in the fridge?' Jo asked. The answer was simple, 'I want to have a cool head!'

Wells

Kramat 55 had three strategically placed stone-walled wells. Wells in gardens were not unusual. Java had an abundance of groundwater. Generally, the water was clear and potable. After the war some people found skeletons in their wells. Our front well, between the left pavilion and Jalan Kramat, was filled with discarded weapons; we had no need to use this well. The second well was near the entrance of the right pavilion where our family lived after 1949. I would have been about 11 years of age by then. What fascinated me as a youngster was the occasional gentle tremor at the centre of the water indicating an active spring at the bottom of the well, which was very deep. The water always remained below ground level.

The third well was extremely well placed for multiple household purposes. It was near the kitchen at the back of the property. The daily laundry from the clubhouse was taken care of by three women. This well had a metal frame to which a rope and bucket were attached and, regardless of the amount of water used, the water would return to just below ground level at the end of washing day. In the early days after the war, the women were required for the daily washing of clothing, sheets and towels. Intense tropical heat dried the sheets of the first load pegged on the washing lines before the second load arrived. This laundry-well was closed on the public side, with a wide opening towards the kitchen. Eventually, the Chinese laundries opened up again before the monsoon rains commenced and they were pleased to take over the washing of bed linen.

Much later, when life in Batavia took on some form of normality again, Ryer had the water of the two wells checked annually by a pathologist. The tests were always clear. In an emergency, the well-water was safe to drink.

The life of a post-war child

> *When Mother, Joan and I were rescued from Banyu Biru in military trucks, I was told that the war was over. For some time that appeared to be true, when we were in Singapore and in Australia. Is it true though? Here we are back in Batavia and still in a 'state of war', with military trucks on the streets in Batavia and in our backyard.*

As I recall my post-war musings, a flood of memories stirs within me. On our return to Batavia, I was very lonely and the youngest child in a world of adults. Dad was busy and Mum was busy. Joan was busy getting ready for high school. The school year followed the European education system so by the end January we were halfway through the school year. Joan commenced high school and

I was still in primary school. Suddenly we were 'miles apart'. Joan soon had books and a little space adjacent to our room with a table on which to do her homework. She sometimes played Monopoly, but I was 'too young' to be involved in any game or activity at The Open Door. I discovered that it was not easy being a 'big' girl when you are the smallest in the family. I had about six to eight books on my bookshelf, all of which had been read. I had no toys, no friends of my age and did not play with dolls. I had nothing to do and the extreme heat every day zapped my energy. I was bored and got into mischief.

My parents realised I needed some activities. I loved animals, so my father asked one of the soldiers who was a carpenter by trade to make a Dutch rabbit warren on stilts to avoid white ants. It was brilliant! It had three sections, for father, mother and little ones! It had a drainage system and a feeding box. The gardener was enthralled with the fluffy animals and made sure they were well fed and that the box had a daily clean-out. After some time, there was a shortage of rabbit accommodation and eventually some of the big ones disappeared and came on a platter for Sunday dinner. I was so sad and refused my dinner. With the approach of the dry season and its extreme heat, however, green fodder was no longer available. Some special Sunday dinners decided the closure of the warren.

Working with military personnel and living at The Open Door was a good reason for expecting the unexpected! And so it was when one day a truck came in from the battlefront filled with seven or eight bleating goats. It took everyone by surprise. The houseboy and the gardener were laughing and even the cook came out of her kitchen to see if she had heard correctly. Ryer too, came out of his office, and seeing the two soldiers with grins on their faces, asked, 'Well what have we here?' The two soldiers explained that the animals were given to them by grateful villagers because the soldiers reclaimed their village for them. 'We thanked them for their kindness and explained that our barracks could not accommodate the animals, but they would not let us leave without their "gift". We thought, The Salvation Army usually knows how to deal with unusual situations.' Ryer laughed. 'Well, we're at the start of the "wet season" and early showers have given us grass at the moment, but when the dry season comes we'll have to find an alternative home for them.'

Ryer explained the situation to the houseboy, who in turn explained it to the gardener. Ryer suggested that the goats be kept in the backyard temporarily, and that the area behind the left pavilion, near the fence, be closed off with wire, to keep the goats there at night. The gardener, who was proud of the colourful gerberas he had planted along the driveway at the start of the wet season, despaired, for within one day all his hard work had been devoured by the goats. Any overhanging leafy branches of trees were soon disposed of and banana shoots required covers to protect new growth.

There were moments of delight, however. Within a couple of months two beautiful kid goats were born. We had some laughter too. One goat wandered in a 'forbidden' area near the washing-well where it caught one of its hind legs in the rope of the metal well-bucket, causing it to fall off the edge of the well. He soon became aware of the 'click-clack' sound of the handle hitting the bucket as he walked and the bucket bounced along the ground. Alarmed, he increased his walking speed. In so doing he increased the frequency of the 'click-clack, click-clack' sound, to which he reacted by running in circles, faster and faster, alarming all the other goats who then began to run in sympathy with him, bleating as they went. The sight and sound of bleating goats running away from a tangling bucket rope brought the workers from their rooms, laughing at the chaotic sight. The gardener did the brave thing. He stood on the rope; the click-clack stopped and the panting mob of exhausted goats quietened down, looking dizzy and bewildered. I still laugh when I think about it.

With the approach of the dry season, Ryer consulted with the houseboy and gardener regarding a suitable goat farmer. Their swift response was an indication for Ryer that the matter had already been discussed between them. This brought closure to the interesting experience of 'goat farming'.

A visit to Dr Van Buren

My first primary school days in Batavia find little space in my memory. I do remember one event, however. One morning, my father received a phone call from the school. He was told that I was not well and could someone take me home? When he arrived at the school the teacher told him that I had 'passed out' a couple of times when standing up and that my face was very white. This was very obvious to my father when he saw me. My parents were troubled and uncertain what to do. They decided to keep me home for a couple of days. The next morning, I followed my usual routine: I got out of bed and walked to my parents' room to wash my face and brush my teeth at their wash basin. While squeezing the toothpaste on the toothbrush I began to sway and I just heard Mum ask, 'What are you doing?' before I passed out again, toothbrush still in hand. Dad lifted me onto their bed and said: 'You and I are going the visit Dr Van Buren today.'

Dr Van Buren was a Jew and a man of big stature. He conducted a thorough check and showed me a drop of my blood on some white filter paper and he said: 'Your blood is pale pink and it should be red, like this' —and he showed me another paper with red on it. 'Every week after your iron injection we will see how the pink begins to change to red.' My blood test showed a severe iron deficiency and for this I received weekly iron injections for quite some time. Milk had not been available since before our return to Batavia. Supplies were beginning to arrive from the Netherlands through social welfare programmes. He advised my father that I needed at least one large glass of milk every day.

Dr Van Buren also recommended that my parents send me to the cooler climate of Bandung during the summer vacation. They agreed and on two successive summers I stayed at a senior citizens' retirement village owned by The Salvation Army. The manager was Major Geziena Smid who also had returned to the NEI after furlough in Holland. She treated me very kindly and I had such good food to eat. During my stay there I came to know some special 'grandmas'. One lady taught me about embroidery stitching, and cross stitching. She was called Moeske, an endearing word for 'grandmother', and that is how I still remember her. There was a Salvation Army corps in the village and I attended Sunday school and participated in a little drama. I was never homesick. I loved being there.

School life and more

I attended two different primary schools between grades two and four. Dutch-language schools were being closed in preference to the Indonesian language schools. Eventually my parents were successful in finding a third Dutch-language primary school for years five and six in the same street where Joan attended high school. This was a real answer to prayer. For my last two primary years, I travelled on the back of her bicycle— not without some concern from my parents. The Clubhouse had no car and my father did all his travelling either with the little buses in Jalan Kramat or by bicycle. They were Dutch-designed bicycles which had a passenger seat. Joan may not have been 18 years at the time, but it says something about her calm disposition and her steady nerves that she cycled from Kramat 55, along the bicycle track on the other side of the road, before eventually crossing Jalan Kramat, again without the aid of traffic lights, into another major road, Jalan Diponegoro. There she dropped me off at school and then cycled to her high school further up the road. After my last class for the day I walked up to her school and from there we began the return journey.

These journeys always had an element of risk and we were fortunate to survive an accident when I was in grade 6 (1951 or 1952). We were in the bicycle lane close to the crossing towards school, when a large military truck came towards us from the opposite direction, on my left side. I was sitting behind Joan with nothing to hold on to. Things happened rapidly. I looked up and on my left side I saw the face of an Indonesian military man through the truck's front windscreen before the vehicle hit us. The impact of the crash threw me in the air and onto the side of the truck. That was my last memory. The next thing I knew I was lying on the ground and I could hear the sound of an ambulance siren. Joan remembered the kind people who stayed with us until we were safely in the ambulance, which took us to the large Christian public hospital opposite the high school. Joan phoned our parents from the hospital. She had a little nick on her forehead which was sutured; it left no scar. I had a big gash on my left knee which was sutured; it could have been far worse. There were neither broken bones nor a damaged cartilage. God protected us. I was at home for a couple of days, but soon returned to school. We survived and no fuss was made.

There were elements of our school life that were distinctive to Indonesia, and reflective of the post-war situation. Most students at Dutch-speaking schools came from families who had lived in the NEI for many generations. They all spoke Dutch and Indonesian. In addition, some spoke another language at home, such as Chinese, Hindi, Javanese, Balinese or one of the 700 indigenous languages spoken on the NEI archipelago. We were used to this—it was the norm. Many young adults had lost years of their basic education during the war. At both primary school and high school this was evident by the number of students in their late teens who sat at the back of the classroom catching up on lost schooling.

Sometime during my first year of high school in 1952–53, we experienced a more disturbing reminder of the tensions beyond school. About eight or more young teenagers with heavy weapons came screaming through the school's verandahs, stopping at classrooms and directing their weapons at the teachers and students. I still remember the incident; it took place during a French class. The teacher was a no-nonsense person; he was cool and calm. He totally ignored what was taking place on the verandah, and continued the lesson. I was sitting in the front row nearest the door and saw the hatred in the eyes of the teenagers. It left me shaken. It was at times like this that I wondered, 'Is the war really over?'

Indonesian independence

By April 1949 the Dutch accepted they had to relinquish all claims on Indonesia. The hostility and warfare for Indonesian independence lasted until, under heavy political pressure of the United States and the United Nations, the Netherlands formally transferred sovereignty to Indonesia on 27 December 1949. Jakarta officially became the new name for Batavia on this date.

Jaap A. de Moor, in reviewing L. de Jong's *The Collapse of a Colonial Society: The Dutch in Indonesia during the Second World War*, wrote:

> In the first week of March 1942, the Japanese forces attacked and occupied the island of Java in the Dutch East Indies. Dutch colonial power rapidly collapsed under the Japanese onslaught and three-year occupation of the Indonesian archipelago began. This occupation ushered in the end of Dutch colonialism in Asia, although after the Japanese capitulation in 1945, the Dutch briefly returned to the Archipelago to fight the Indonesian freedom movement. This was to no avail, and by the end of 1949, Indonesia had become a free and independent republic.[157]

I suspect the Indonesian war of independence came to an end well before the official date of 27 December 1949. For my parents, it was the end of an era with the 'men in green uniforms'. The closure of The Open Door ministry for military personnel was an emotional period of loss for my parents, and for my father it remained a silent, rarely mentioned, grief. I clearly recall the occasion when, as a 10-year-old, I stood with my parents on the large front verandah when truck after truck with servicemen made their salute to my parents as they waved their green, blue or red berets, calling out, 'Thank you and goodbye' in Dutch, as they passed by Kramat 55 on their way to Tanjung Priok harbour for their return to Holland. Ryer and Jo waved their hands as tears rolled down their faces. They stood there each day until the last truck passed by. On one occasion, I heard Mum say: 'There goes our security!' The Dutch government had already commenced an evacuation process of thousands of civilian Europeans and Indo-Europeans to the Netherlands.

A change of direction

Salvation Army leadership in Bandung realised well in advance that with the imminent closure of The Open Door, Kramat 55 could become a wasted property. This was not to be; the organisation had planned ahead. Kramat 55 became the Training College for Salvation Army officers. The Salvation Army in Indonesia required committed and dedicated national officers who knew themselves called by God for a soul-saving ministry wherever they were needed.

The first post-war Salvation Army training session was run in Sulawesi. The name of the session was *Pembawa Damai*, meaning 'Bringers of Peace'—what an appropriate name! It commenced on 15 August 1948 with 12 cadets; a year later they were commissioned on 24–26 April 1949.[158] Training sessions around the world for each particular year share the same name on their sessional flag or pennant, but in the national language of the country. Prior to the war, Sulawesi division trained its own officers because of the language difference and distance from Java. Pre-war the Dutch-language Training College was in Bandung. From 1949 all cadets were trained in Jakarta at Kramat 55.

The new Training Principal was the previous Principal at Sulawesi, the Finnish officer, Major Elna Poutianen, who had served in Indonesia for many years. Both her husband and their little daughter died in the same year, while they were in Sulawesi. Medical facilities on that island were almost non-existent at that time. The major was a beautiful Christian, loved by all. I remember her well: tall, motherly and with white hair. The cadets called her *'Ibu'*, that is, 'Mother'.

CHAPTER 12

Indonesia after Independence 1950–1953

Territorial Public Relations

Ryer was at The Open Door from 30 October 1947 until 30 June 1950.
By the end of April 1950 Ryer was informed of his new appointment
as Secretary for the Public Relations Department; this took place on
1 July. Ryer was familiar with public relations work. His task was
to encourage companies and individuals to donate money in support
of The Salvation Army's multifaceted ministries and services. This
was a huge responsibility in Jakarta and its surrounds. To an extent,
he had already been doing much of this whilst at The Open Door.

It was Ryer's ability to present the organisation's needs, his quiet
demeanour, dry sense of humour, simplicity and honesty in business
endearing him to many people. He found a special friend in Will
Govaars who supported Ryer's work financially and always had
a vehicle available for transport. It surprised Ryer how during his
relatively short time back in Batavia (soon re-named Jakarta) he
continued to meet people who remembered him from their shared
war experiences and how pleased they always were to meet him
again. Ryer was also well known and appreciated by members of the
BPM in Batavia. Some of this stemmed back to his work as chaplain
and manager of the Tarakan Military Home in 1941; however, when
Tarakan surrendered to the Japanese, a number of oil company staff,
including the company's public relations officer, Gerrit van Geffen,

were also interned in Borneo camps. Not long after Ryer's arrival in Batavia the two men met up again. Van Geffen wasted no time introducing Ryer to the oil company's top man, who was not only delighted to meet Ryer again but also offered his full support for the work of The Salvation Army.

Ryer would also continue to oversight Jakarta I Corps with some support from Dutch-speaking Training College staff. For these appointments, he was granted a small motor scooter. Ryer was in his element. It did not take him long to obtain his licence.

Ryer's public relations work was successful beyond expectations. Whenever Ryer knocked at a door to raise funds, he was made welcome, usually because the manager knew him. The generosity of companies amazed him—even after Independence. Much of the money assisted the re-establishment of various Salvation Army social welfare ministries in Jakarta. One which Ryer commenced involved supporting Indo European families. Some had been associated with the KNIL and were now without work or income. Supplies such as tinned powdered milk had been provided by the NEI government prior to independence.

Ryer was on the road every day visiting clients and making friends. He was a meticulous accountant, and his own secretary. He worked from early morning to late evening keeping up with his correspondence. Jo made him a sleeveless 'security singlet' with pockets to hide money under his white uniform shirt when he went on his weekly visit to the bank. Trusted security staff were employed by most banks to safeguard their clients and their cars. Once inside the building there was a 'safe' room for those wishing to remove money from their clothing.

Jo had further reason to be concerned about Ryer's health. The downside of having the scooter was that he tried to do twice as much work because he did not have to walk, pedal a bicycle or take public transport. All this was good and he certainly covered more ground with his scooter, but he neglected himself physically. Exhaustion and a persistent dry cough eventually took Ryer to see Dr Van Buren who gave him a thorough check and sent him for an X-ray. The report showed shadows on his lungs. Dr Van Buren knew Ryer and held him in high regard, and I assume he advised him to reduce his working hours and take his afternoon rest.

Home life

The pavilion we moved into was the on the right side of the main building; a wide driveway separated the two buildings.[j] The pavilion had been empty for some months, and the interim period between April and July provided the necessary time for repairs to the roof and the building's electrical system. Our move in July allowed training staff maximum time to refurbish the main building. Our little family of four settled in quickly. Suddenly, everything changed. I saw much more of my parents; we had meals together like a family. I could talk about school or tell them about a funny story I had read. We had time for family prayers after meals with a reading from a modernised Dutch Bible for teenagers. This often led to interesting discussions.

The pavilion had a wide built-in verandah with windows all around from the back door to the front door. My bedroom was actually the end of the long passage made into a room, with windows looking out on the large front garden and beyond onto Jalan Kramat and its traffic. Joan and I had well-fitted, high mosquito nets, long enough to be tucked in on all sides of our beds at night. Joan's room was just outside our pavilion, next to the small kitchen where our new house help, Annie, created tasty rice meals for us. In no time at all the small pavilion felt like home again. My parents were very good at that. The sitting room became the work centre. Here Ryer kept his glass-door book cupboard for his precious Bible commentaries and other Christian literature. His desk fitted well against the wall of my bedroom. Ryer's open bookshelves for his remaining books were placed against the verandah wall facing the windows.

---

[j] Large family estates, like Kramat 55, were common both pre- and post-WWII and were usually associated with rich Chinese and Europeans. Pavilions were side-buildings, like the one we lived in; they suited a small family. The left pavilion, as viewed from Kramat, became a worship centre for The Salvation Army Jakarta I Corps.

Bread upon the waters

Our dining room was part of the glass-windowed extension of the pavilion. Schools began early and we were home for our 1.00pm rice meal. I can still 'see' myself on the right side of the table facing the main entrance into the property when a young Indonesian soldier wearing his green military outfit, without either beret or cap, came towards our unit. This was unusual. Somebody must have told him where we lived, because he made a beeline for the pavilion. By this time, we could all see him and we watched him curiously! Annie, our house helper, came out of the kitchen and spoke with him. He told her he wanted to speak to the '*Tuan*', the man of the house, to say thank you. In Bahasa Indonesia he explained to Annie who he was and told her of being in prison with his father in Batavia and how the Tuan took him out of prison and that he started school. Here, many years later, was the prisoner's son. He was now with the military, he had a good job and he wanted to say 'Thank you' to Dad and the missus for looking after him in 1937. My parents were taken aback with surprise and were obviously not sure how to respond. Dad went outside and had a few words with him at the door. As a little boy, he would have known Joan as a toddler; I was not born yet. As the expression says, so much water had gone under the bridge in those 13 years. Much to our surprise, Dad did not invite him inside. Joan and I asked: 'Why didn't you invite him in?' I think Dad was surprised or even overwhelmed by the visit and at a loss as to how to handle it.

His name was Siep

There were some happy moments which made a big change in my young life. Not long after our family moved to the pavilion, I was walking home from school with my friend, Yoke, who invited me to her house to see her new puppies. They were about six weeks old and all over the place.

'You can have one if you like.'

What a wonderful suggestion! How could I refuse such a kind

offer? Seeing my indecision, she asked me which one I liked the most. There was no hesitation as I had already seen the one I really liked.

'May I have this one? Oh, thank you, he is lovely.' Clutching the little bundle of energy against me with one hand, and my schoolbag with the other hand, I walked home. I wondered what my parents would say. What if I was told to return him? I crossed Jalan Kramat and walked on the footpath next to the bicycle path. I could see our home and walked very slowly.

Annie saw me first, *'Ah, anjing kecil'*, 'Ah, little dog'.

Mum saw me through the window. 'What have you got there? Where did you get him?'

'From my friend, Yoke. Can I keep him?'

Mum looked at me and I believe she read more in my facial expression than I realised. She smiled and said, 'Yes, but you will have to look after him.'

Looking after him was a labour of love. His name was Siep, pronounced 'Seep'. He had short, light-brown hair and an active tail. As he became bigger, Dad found a wide rattan chair for which Mum made a cushion with ties on the corners so it would not fall off the chair, which was placed near the front door and my bedroom. This was his bed. When he was bigger still, Dad bought him a collar. When there was a lot of lightning and thunder during the monsoon season, he often slept under my bed.

Siep had a 'wide' heritage. In Australia, we would describe him as a 'Heinz 57 varieties' dog, using the slogan of the American company that makes tinned and bottled food. Siep became an excellent watchdog; he was vicious to strange guests, but he had a great respect for 'uniform'. He would accept people in military greens and The Salvation Army white uniform as friends.

About the same time, Joan became the owner of an angora kitten which she called Mikkie. Joan's room was just outside our pavilion. It did not take long for Siep to 'sniff' the newcomer in Joan's bedroom. They were both still young, and quietly observed each other, but Siep's tail said it all: 'I like you'. He gently licked her tiny nose and the friendship was sealed. Soon they were eating from each other's plates.

Mikkie took a liking to Siep's tail and they would run in circles from one room to the next until they dropped exhausted near his chair where Mikkie curled up against Siep and they both fell asleep.

Mikkie had an angora pedigree and during our three years in the pavilion she was mated each year with a cat of a similar breed. Angora cats were much favoured by people within the local Chinese community, who were prepared to pay a high price for them. I was too young to know how it all worked, but each year Mikkie's kittens were successfully sold for a good price. The total amount of the money raised helped cover the cost of Joan's fares for her journey to Australia with the rest of the family in 1953. During the post-war days in Indonesia, The Salvation Army did not have the financial resources to support living expenses and travelling costs for children of officers over the age of 18 who were employed. Providentially, on completing her high school, Joan was accepted as a secretary at the Dutch Petroleum Company (BPM) in Jakarta. I can only see these two incidents as further provisions by God for our family.

After Ryer had used the motorbike for a couple weeks we discovered that, despite all the traffic noises of Jalan Kramat, Siep had learned the pitch of Ryer's scooter and knew Ryer was on his way home 10 minutes before he actually arrived. He became excited and restless and made funny sounds in anticipation of seeing Ryer until that moment when the motorbike was in sight and he started barking. Never was there a warmer welcome! While given the distance of time it may seem strange that I find myself shedding tears on writing this story about a faithful friend, I know that those who have had such a friend will understand.

The visit of General Albert Orsborn

In 1950, General Albert Orsborn visited Indonesia, becoming the first international leader of The Salvation Army to do so after WWII.[159] His eight-day visit had a tight schedule. As The Salvation Army's spiritual leader, the General's first and most important task was to meet in worship and thanksgiving with his officers and soldiers.

Salvationists and friends travelled from all over Java for this first Congress in Bandung after the war. They came in their pristine white uniforms to worship, to be encouraged and refreshed in spirit as they listened to the Word of God. It was a memorable event; many friendships were renewed.

It was sometime during this Congress when Ryer saw the familiar face of the now Captain Estafanus Simatupang. Their mutual regard for each other was evident in the warm handshake and the brief memories of Tarakan they shared together. Estafanus was proud to introduce his wife to Ryer. They had married after he left Tarakan and returned to his own tribal area on the east coast of Borneo. In his later years of officership Estafanus rose to the rank of Lieut-Colonel.

Although Ryer was the Public Relations Secretary in Jakarta, he had not been consulted by THQ concerning the General's visit in Jakarta or anywhere else in the archipelago. The Territorial Commander had expressed his desire to take charge of that himself. Very early in the General's visit, it was obvious that the planning for transportation had not been as satisfactory as it should have been. Some vehicles for the visit broke down and substitutes had to be improvised. General Orsborn also rightly expected that arrangements had been made for him to visit other Army centres within the period of the visit; however, this was not the case. The General wanted to see evangelical outreach in corps, social, medical and educational work and homes for children. He also hoped to meet officers and see the damage done during the war. 'I have to go from place to place,' he said. The General had a bare eight days to travel to distant areas of Java. Using a car or travel by train was impossible time-wise. As Public Relations Secretary, Ryer was present during these discussions and should have been informed about this part of the General's journey. However, the territory's senior leader was in control! The Chief Secretary, Brigadier Derek Ramaker, was uncomfortable. Listening to the translated conversation, Ryer sensed tension and the urgency of the situation. Looking at the Territorial Commander, Ryer said: 'Would you leave it to me, please? I'll see what I can do.' There was a firm 'Yes' from both the General and the Chief Secretary.

The Territorial Commander remained unconvinced that there was a possible way to take the General across Java.

Then, as before, it was evident that where The Salvation Army generally found an open door in various places, Ryer, because of his war service, found the door *very* wide open. He contacted Van Geffen and asked him to arrange an appointment for him with the Chief Executive of the Shell Oil Company, 'ASAP'. Van Geffen knew that asking for the company's plane could be like picking stars from the heavens, but he was willing to arrange an interview for Ryer with 'the boss'.[160] Ryer visited the Dutch Petroleum Company's Chief Executive and, because they knew each other, Ryer did not need to plead his cause. 'You can have my personal plane for as long as the General is here to go anywhere in Indonesia as long as the plane is back to base every night, ready to pick up the General again the next morning from wherever he had been overnight.' The success of Ryer's conversation is reflected in Albert Orsborn's book, *The House of My Pilgrimage*:

> I went to Djakarta for this interview [with President Sukarno] in a private plane belonging to a Dutch oil company. Had it not been for this kindness my party would not have seen much. The plane, usually used by the company directors, was an American 'Grumman': a very smart craft with eight comfortable armchairs.

Furthermore, the General's comments about the visit to the President were positive.

> My interview with President Sukarno gave me great satisfaction... In his large and cool office, the President, a man of middle age, received me cordially. I took an instant liking to him, and he came my way without hesitation as we spoke of our work.[161]

In this interview, the General records, he also learned some interesting things about President Sukarno and his contacts with The Salvation Army, long before he became the President.[162]

At the end of the General's visit to Indonesia, he and his party were in Jakarta saying their farewells to officers and Training College staff prior to their departure. Knowing the contribution Ryer had made to the success of his visit, General Orsborn walked over to Ryer and Jo with his interpreter. Looking at Ryer, he asked: 'And what can I do for you?' Ryer looked at him for a moment before he said: 'General, my wife and I with our two girls, had the privilege to spend some months in Australia to recover after the war and the people were so gracious. We have been discussing our future after we finish this term of service in July 1953. Rather than return to Holland, we would prefer to transfer to Melbourne, Australia. Although we have commenced English classes, we have not spoken to our leaders about this request.' The General looked at them both, 'Yes, I agree to that request. My secretary will take your personal details. When your time is getting close, write me a letter, privately! Do you understand what I am saying?' Ryer nodded, 'Yes, I do, thank you!'

For both Jo and Ryer, the visit from the General demonstrated strongly that Jakarta, the capital city of Indonesia and with the seat of government, was the very place where The Salvation Army Headquarters ought to have been situated. As time progressed after the war, many companies, including the BPM, Dutch Petroleum Company, had their corporate headquarters in Jakarta. From a business perspective, THQ would have been better placed in Jakarta, but this never eventuated.

Turning towards Australia

Early in 1953 my parents wrote their letter to General Albert Orsborn again expressing their desire to transfer to Melbourne, Australia, in preference to returning to Holland. Their six-year term of service in Indonesia would conclude during July or August that year.

Sadly, Ryer's health continued to decline and this was evident in his weight loss. Jo was most concerned. X-rays had recently been taken. One afternoon there was an unexpected home visit from Dr Van Buren in his big black car! I remember clearly what happened. The car stopped and the doctor opened the car window and called out loudly, 'Is that...so and so...dog of yours tied up?' I ran outside and said: 'Yes he is, Doctor.' I knew the doctor feared rabies, a contagious dog disease in Indonesia. Siep had been inoculated as a pup but the doctor knew he had to be cautious. I ran back inside and by this time my parents were there to greet the doctor, wondering why he had come. He had looked after the family for almost six years and never charged my parents a cent. Why was he here? He had brought the X-rays! The upshot was that the recent X-rays showed Ryer's lungs in a worsened condition than the previous photo. He held the two X-rays against the window for Ryer and pointed out the difference. They sat at the dining room table and Van Buren expressed his concern, telling Ryer that Australia had very strict laws against tuberculosis and the most recent X-ray could well prevent him entering the country. Ryer was to rest, catch up on extra sleep during the day and reduce the number of his work days. Three months could make a positive difference.

I do not know if Ryer obeyed the doctor's advice, but I'm certain that Jo would have encouraged him to take the matter seriously. The family was now counting the months to our transfer to Australia. Passports were being updated and medical examinations conducted plus certain inoculations which were required for entry into Australia. Ryer was used to making bookings for officers returning to their home territories for furlough. Now he was making bookings for himself and family to a new country; somehow this was surreal. They were not going 'home'—and yet they were. They were going to a 'new' home in a 'new' country. He felt excited about it.

August–September 1953

My parents were now in a packing mode. They were experienced travellers. Out came the huge wooden 'missionary trunks'. When it came to his books, Ryer was meticulous. I suspect my parents did most of their packing while Joan and I were at school. I was suddenly aware of a bare sitting room when I came home from school. The book cupboard was empty, and the photos and pictures had disappeared from the walls. Jo's sewing machine was gone.

Siep was unsettled; his tail was down. He would lie on the floor with his nose towards the sitting room. I knew there would be a day to say goodbye.

My parents were informed by the police that they would be interviewed by two navy blue-uniformed men. I do not know if they were members of the defence services or the police. My parents assumed it was in relation to their previous military work. Joan and I were present at this interview, but we were not involved in the discussions. Nothing came of it—or did it?

Three separate bookings were made by Ryer with ships destined for Sydney or Melbourne, over a period of weeks, and three times the bookings were cancelled by persons unknown about a week prior to the expected departure date. Someone was obviously watching the bookings on ships departing for Australia and wanted to delay our departure. These setbacks slowed our departure considerably. I give credit to my parents; they would obviously have been concerned and most frustrated with the delays. Ryer, who was so meticulous in everything he did and who arranged bookings for all officers, was especially frustrated. Neither of my parents talked about these matters, knowing it could distress us; however, Headquarters in Bandung was kept informed of the situation, as was the current Training Principal, Major Melattie Brouwer.

An Australian officer, Major Gladys Calliss, was due for her first homeland furlough and going to Melbourne. The Major first arrived in 1947 when Ryer welcomed her at Tanjung Priok harbour. Now she too was returning home, with the Van Kralingen family.

God's provision

On Monday 2 November 1953, Ryer made contact with a cargo ship docked at Jakarta. He knew most of these ships had a limited number of cabins for private clients. These boats are a little slower than normal passenger ships and more relaxed for those wishing for a quiet journey. Imagine Ryer's surprise when he was told: 'We have a cabin for two and a cabin for three people left; however, we are departing on Sunday 8 November.' Ryer was delighted! 'That will suit perfectly!' He discussed the relevant matters of finances, luggage and departure time.

Having arranged all this, Ryer contacted the Chief Secretary, Colonel Gerrit Ramaker, who immediately departed for Jakarta by train to conduct the farewell service on Friday 6 November. I had my 14th birthday on Wednesday 4 November. Major Gladys Calliss was staying at the College next door and was ready to join us.

I remember aspects of the farewell meeting and the crowd that fitted in the small corps building. People spoke so beautifully about my parents, including Colonel Ramaker, who regarded himself as a personal friend of Jo and Ryer. At the conclusion of the service and in true Salvation Army tradition, the Colonel asked for the Army's tricolour flag which was held over our family. He then committed Ryer, Jo, Joan and myself to God, after which we sang that well-known farewell song in Dutch:

> *God be with you till we meet again,*
> *By his counsels guide, uphold you,*
> *With his sheep securely fold you,*
> *God be with you till we meet again.*

> **Chorus**

> *Till we meet, till we meet,*
> *Till we meet at Jesus' feet;*
> *Till we meet, till we meet,*
> *God be with you till we meet again.*

> *God be with you till we meet again,*
> *'Neath his wings protecting hide you,*
> *Daily manna still provide you,*
> *God be with you till we meet again.*

God be with you till we meet again,
When life's perils thick confound you,
Put his arm unfailing round you;
God be with you till we meet again.

God be with you till we meet again,
Keep love's banner floating o'er you,
Smite death's threatening wave before you;
God be with you till we meet again.[163]

As we were singing there were tears on many faces including those of my parents. I could not sing—my tears were for Siep, my best friend! I wept more tears saying goodbye to Siep in 1953, when I left Indonesia as a 14-year-old, than for anything else. It took me a good six months living in Australia before I could say his name without tears. One great consolation for me was that Siep remained on the same compound and was adopted by Major Melattie Brouwer. Siep knew her well.

Two days later, early on the morning of Sunday 8 November, our family, together with Major Gladys Calliss, departed for Tanjung Priok. Captain Gijs Pattipeilohy, an officer from the Training College staff, accompanied us. He was a family friend and a gifted musician and artist. In the years that followed he reached the rank of Commissioner and eventually became the Territorial Commander in Indonesia. As we were saying goodbye that day, Dad took off his watch and placed it on the Captain's wrist. Captain Pattipeilohy did not have a watch and was deeply moved by this act of kindness and friendship.

As the ropes were released and the ship moved away from the moorings, the tugboats pulled the ship into deeper waters and our friends disappeared from sight. I had a sense of relief; we were off to an unknown future. Ryer had a smile on his face. He could feel the movement of the ship and he felt at home. 'We're on our way to Australia, thank God; we made it!' I heard our mother say to Ryer: 'I won't believe it until we are in international waters.' Ryer knew his Jo and put his arm around her as they walked together to their cabin.

It was a small ship with few passengers. Ryer celebrated his birthday on 17 November. Years later, Jo told Joan that for three weeks Ryer would sleep all night, get up in the morning, shave, have breakfast and go to bed again until she woke him for the evening meal. They would then walk around the deck or find comfortable chairs on which to sit and talk and breathe the fresh air. Gradually his body responded to the healing power of sleep. Then one morning he got up and was ready to face life again. He was a changed man—the man Jo knew from their early years as young officers in Indonesia. His smile, his Dutch humour and wit were still there. There was time to laugh. They were again on a journey together. Australia, here we come!

CHAPTER 13

A safe arrival

Unbeknown to Ryer and Jo, the Territorial Commander of the Australian Southern Territory, Commissioner John Evan Smith, was informed by The Salvation Army's IHQ that a Dutch officer-couple, Majors Ryer and Johanna van Kralingen, would be transferred from Indonesia to the Australian Southern Territory in November 1953.[164] These officers, with their two daughters, would require a 'homeland furlough' or extended leave, prior to receiving an appointment in the Southern Territory. Commissioner Evan Smith, a British officer, was to that time the longest serving Territorial Commander in Australia Southern Territory, spanning the period from October 1946–September 1953. Subsequently someone who worked at THQ told my parents that the Commissioner was most surprised and said, 'Australia is an English-speaking country! Can these officers speak English? There are no Dutch-speaking Salvationists in Australia.'

Up to 1953 the Australian Southern Territory had been an all-British 'branch' of The Salvation Army, although isolated due to distance from England and slow transport by sea. Air travel was still very limited. Australia had, however, been generous in sending out missionaries to Africa and eastern countries. Increasing migration into Australia, post-war and in the early 1950s, opened the door for the spread of the Gospel in many languages. Today, the Church in Australia works in many languages. Commissioner Evan Smith retired in September 1953.

His successor was another officer from Britain, Commissioner Charles Durman. However, Commissioner Durman was in a unique position both to welcome our family and the wave of post-WWII Dutch migrants arriving in Australia.

> As Territorial Commander for the Netherlands [1945 to 1950]…his task was the rebuilding of the Army's work halted by the occupying forces during the Second World War. His tireless reconstruction work was honoured by the Queen of Holland admitting him as an Officer of Orange Nassau.[165]

Appointed to the Australia Southern Territory by General Albert Osborn in 1953, Commissioner Charles Durman and Mrs Commissioner Jane Durman arrived in Melbourne in September 1953.

The next stage of our journey

On Sunday 22 November, a bright Australian spring day, our ship entered Port Jackson and we could see the famous Sydney Harbour Bridge. It was quite breathtaking to think that after only three weeks on the ship we were arriving in what looked like another world. Ryer was in his element and familiar with the procedures taking place down below; the ladder was lowered for the pilot to come on board to guide the ship into port. The ship would be there for a number of hours unloading goods, while some passengers disembarked. Those remaining on board, such as ourselves, were allowed to leave the ship after signing a register and had to be back on board at a given time. Looking down from the ship, my parents and Major Gladys Calliss were surprised to see a Salvation Army officer standing at the wharf. Not being in uniform, they waved their hands and he responded in a similar way. Major Alf Packer was an officer from the Australian Eastern Territory and his welcome made us feel instantly at home. It was good to have Major Calliss with us as a translator. Our English was still very limited.

This time it was a return to Melbourne by ship instead of a long train journey. Of course Ryer's first visit, just after the war, was by a direct flight from Borneo in 1945 on a military plane via Brisbane and on to Melbourne. As mentioned in Chapter 7, my mother, Joan and I departed sometime in March 1946 from Jakarta to Singapore. From there we travelled to Brisbane by boat, and then to Melbourne by train via Sydney. It all seemed a long time ago. Although my memories of 1953 are vague, I recall how pleased we were to have safely arrived in Australia.

Healesville and Cranbrook Lodge

The first entry on my parents' Officer Career Card for this period is: 'Arrived Australia for furlough 22.11.53–15.1.54'. After all the travelling of the past few weeks, returning to Healesville was like déjà vu—something like a homecoming. Our lives had radically changed since we left Jakarta. Every day was different. Finding ourselves back in this small country town where nothing much had changed in the last six years had a calming effect. The whole family needed recovery and rest. Major Stephen Berry greeted us at the station with a smile in his eyes and took us to Cranbrook Lodge, the new Salvation Army Rest Home, where he and his wife, Mrs Major Ruby Berry, were the managers. It was the end of the school year and I wondered if there would be anyone my age. Imagine my joy meeting Rhonda, the officers' daughter. I saw her sitting on the swing. She had beautiful long black hair in two plaits. We just looked at each other and smiled. I remember pointing at myself and saying, 'Sonja'. She took the hint and did the same thing, but better, 'I am Rhonda' and I repeated, 'I am Sonja'. We laughed together as I had my first lesson in English. Even though we did not speak each other's language we got on well together; I learned new words from her and we soon understood each other. Rhonda was my first friend in Australia and that moment was the beginning of a lifelong friendship. Even now, many years later, she occasionally reminds me of the strange words and expressions I used, much to our shared amusement.

The Lodge was an extensive property on a hill; it had a rose garden and a grassed area for family picnics. A wide gravel road circled around the Lodge, and its additional staff living quarters behind the building, to the main road. The front verandah of the Lodge with its comfortable chairs provided a panoramic view of Victoria's Great Dividing Range and its forested mountains. The Lodge may originally have been part of a family estate; it had numerous bedrooms, and a large kitchen and dining room. I recall the spacious and comfortable sitting room with the large open fire on cold evenings. Having just arrived from a tropical country, we sometimes found the evenings quite cold and the open fire made it very cosy! The sitting room also had a built-in cupboard with a variety of reading materials and indoor games, such as carpet bowls, Monopoly and puzzles for cold winter evenings. A garden stairway led to a deep second level of the property not visible from the verandah. It looked down on farmland with cows, sheep and some horses. For the first-time visitor, the sight of a well-trimmed grass croquet field, surrounded by high trees, would surely stir an instant desire to pick up a mallet and a wooden ball and hit the latter through a hoop! During the holiday season when every room at the Lodge was occupied, the croquet game was the drawcard. Age, grey hair, rank and status lost their significance in the battle with balls, hoops and mallets. For some players, it was a real effort to be gracious to the winning team!

Major Steve's vegetable gardens and fruit trees flourished. Ruby Berry and her support staff, Captains Dorothy Phillips and Isabel Ross—only ever known as 'Rossie'—not only produced jam and marmalade from home-grown fruit but were experts in producing nourishing roasts, and delectable cookies and cakes, including more sponge cakes, or strawberries and cream! It was all so different from the simple rice table we knew. Although our English was extremely limited, the expressions of love and care from the staff drew us into the fellowship. The brief morning devotional times in the sitting room united us in worship with other visitors. We sensed good humour and genuine Christian love and fellowship.

The Anchorage

The next entry on my parents' Officer Career Card reads: 'Transferred Australia Southern Territory 15.1.54'. Having completed their 'homeland furlough' my parents were now officially registered as transferred officers to the Australian Southern Territory. My parents were appointed to the Anchorage Men's Home in the suburb of Abbotsford, Melbourne. This was to be a short appointment to give them daily contact and conversational opportunities with residents and staff. Hopefully, it helped them to develop their fluency in English and give them an ear for the Australian accent. Most of the men who lived at the Anchorage had previous prison experiences. Allow me to give some insight on how The Salvation Army's prison work began and continued, as told by Barbara Bolton in her book, *Booth's Drum.*

> The Melbourne Home moved many times...until it found a permanent place in Abbotsford at the Anchorage in 1900. The goal of the home(s) was to provide what a hunted old man had asked for in 1883—another chance.[166]

The Anchorage dealt with second-hand goods donated by the public. The environment was alcohol-free and this provided opportunities for those with such an addiction to break away from it. This home also provided a second chance of employment for former prisoners. All the men were involved with the sorting of donated goods. Ryer worked with these men and they accepted him through simple conversation. Officers on the staff, like my parents, were available for spiritual counselling and to lead worship services on Sunday, which was a day of rest from the normal activities of sorting and selling at the shop associated with the Home. The shop was a precursor of the current Salvos Stores. When not leading worship services at the Anchorage, our family attended The Salvation Army Fairfield Corps—our first corps in Australia.

I was due to commence second-year high school. In Jakarta, the high school curriculum followed the Dutch Education system. In my first-year high school in Jakarta our subjects were Dutch, French, German (English was added in the second year) and the refined Bahasa Indonesia language. We were also taught algebra, mathematics, modern and ancient history and geography. We were informed that Collingwood Girls School was the only available school of a 'secondary' nature in our district but with a heavy domestic-science emphasis; the local council advised my parents that I should not attend a school outside the boundaries of the district. It seemed obvious to my parents that the Australian education system of the 1950s was not up to the standard of the Dutch curriculum in Indonesia and they would have benefited having someone to translate for them. The teachers at Collingwood Girls Secondary School were kindness itself and realised a high school with more academic subjects may have been more appropriate for me.

I was the only non-English-speaking girl in the school—the girls in my class considered me a novelty—however, within three months I spoke English. The teachers were encouraging and helpful. One teacher stands out in my memory: Ms Winifred Bisset was both my classroom teacher and the librarian. She checked my pronunciation of words and corrected 'bad' words I had picked up in the schoolyard. Every day I would rush through my sandwich lunch to get to the library. She started me on Enid Blyton's *The Famous Five* and I would take a book home and return it the following day, ready for the next book. The English was easy and it broadened my vocabulary. After form four (year 10), I transferred to MacRobertson Girls High School and obtained the qualifications to enter nursing. Many years later, in 1961, Ms Bisset attended my Nurses' Graduation in The Salvation Army City Temple at 69 Bourke Street, Melbourne.

New friends and a hope for greater things

News of my parents' arrival spread quickly among the Dutch people in Melbourne and beyond. This opened the door for Ryer and Jo to share with John and Nettie Berendsen, two Salvationists who had been officers for a short period in Holland. John and Nettie were most supportive of my parents and a friendship developed between the two couples. Eventually their conversation led to the influx of Dutch migrants to Box Hill Corps.

Commissioner Durman then appointed my parents to visit corps with migrants throughout the state of Victoria and to conduct Dutch worship services, using the local corps building. Sunday afternoon services for Dutch migrants always drew a large congregation, even in country corps. Many of these migrants would have been regular church attenders in Holland. Corps officers endeavoured to assist migrants to gain employment and accommodation. Many country corps benefited from the influx of migrants with a farming background. Contacts were made through pastoral visits to migrants on isolated farms in country areas and relationships developed with Salvationists from the Netherlands. These tokens of care and interest proved to be of great benefit as people integrated with The Salvation Army.

As early as May 1954, my parents received an invitation from Senior-Captain John Allan, Corps Officer of Box Hill Corps, to conduct an afternoon service for Dutch migrants. This would be my parents' first meeting for migrants. It was well received and at least 70 Dutch people from that area attended this first meeting. Senior-Captain Allan worked for several months with the Dutch comrades to provide fortnightly Sunday afternoon meetings for the 'New Australian Netherlanders'. As reported in *The War Cry* some months later,

> In May that year an excited Brother Kloprogge undertook to invite all the Dutch people in the district to a Sunday night meeting at Box Hill corps. It was arranged that Major and Mrs Van Kralingen, Dutch officers, who have also served as missionaries in Indonesia, now appointed in Melbourne, should lead the gathering partly in English and partly in Dutch. It was expected that a score might turn up but more than 70 gathered, and clamoured for such meetings. It was then arranged that a regular fortnightly gathering, for Dutch people only, should be held and conducted by Major and Mrs Van Kralingen.[167]

That year Commissioner Durman conducted the 45th anniversary of the Box Hill Corps.

> The afternoon meeting was doubly fortified when a crowd of Dutch Salvationists and friends swelled the number in the already packed citadel...to hear the Commissioner's illuminating, delightful, easy-to-listen-to talk of the Netherlands: a land of 'artistry and beauty—a land reclaimed from the sea by a bold, rugged and dauntless people, and a land where the Army is marching onward'. The Dutch comrades added colour and interest when under the leadership of Major Van Kralingen, they sang in rich, hearty tones in their native tongue.[168]

New Australian Centre in Port Melbourne

Nonja Peters, then Director of the Migration, Ethnicity, Refugees and Citizenship Research Unit, Curtin University of Technology, Western Australia, wrote:

> In the years following World War II, the Australian Government began to actively recruit European-born migrants to reverse population stagnation, overcome crucial labour shortages and maintain the war-boosted economy. Between 1951 and 1970, about 160,000 Dutch nationals migrated to Australia.[169]

In December 1954, my parents were appointed to the New Australian Centre in Port Melbourne, with accommodation in that suburb which brought the family closer to the harbour where ships with migrants arrived. The New Australian Centre, situated near the harbour, allowed members of the Dutch clergy opportunities to go on board migrant ships to make contact with church members. Australia was particularly open to receiving migrants from Europe during those years and the government was grateful to the churches in helping the assimilation process. As the then Minister for Immigration, Hubert Opperman M.P., wrote in an article published in *The War Cry,* 1965:

> From the moment they set foot on Australian soil, men, women and children from many lands find in their religious faith a source of strength and encouragement as they face the problems of adjustment to new surroundings... Churches of all denominations have extended to newcomers friendship, guidance and counsel. In an unfamiliar environment, familiar forms of worship and fellowship have provided a comforting link between the old and the new.
>
> The churches have also helped in meeting the material needs of migrants. There are significant numbers of people in Australia today whose smooth settlement into homes and jobs can be attributed to the sponsorship of membership of their faith...the churches have had an incalculable influence for good on the immigration programme.
>
> The task of showing warm friendship is never-ending, and the churches particularly can help. By preserving and strengthening the migrants' faith in God they provide the soundest of all foundations on which to build a new life. Let us rededicate ourselves to this purpose.[170]

Following the positive response from those who attended the meetings at the Box Hill Corps, requests for similar visits by my parents, Ryer and Jo, to other corps began to arrive throughout 1954 to August 1956. During those years my parents were involved in either visiting migrant families or conducting meetings. Ryer kept a careful record of all their activities and travelling expenses. Living in Port Melbourne simplified the travel plans to distant provincial cities like Ballarat and Bendigo and other smaller country centres. It also allowed Ryer and Jo to plan ahead.

On those Sundays when our parents were visiting migrants, Joan and I usually attended the South Melbourne Corps. Rob and 'Rossie' Hallett were most supportive with transport to and from the corps.

I was recently contacted by a retired Salvation Army officer, Major Betty Blackburn. She recalled how as newly commissioned officers in 1955, she and her husband were appointed to the Beechworth Corps in Northern Victoria. Arriving at the corps, they were surprised by the influx of Dutch migrants who requested that they invite the Majors Van Kralingen to conduct a Dutch service for them. The officers knew the corps did not have the financial resources for their salary, let alone the cost of inviting the Dutch officers! Being an enthusiastic new officer, and probably not fully aware of Army protocol, she decided to contact the Territorial Commander, Commissioner Durman, directly by phone!

'The corps does not have the money to pay for this visit. What can I do about that?' they asked. The Commissioner said: 'Send the bill to me!' Betty Blackburn never forgot that kindness from her leader. They had a wonderful meeting with the migrants.

I have no accurate memory of those days. However, I do recall that during one visit in the country my parents met with an elderly lady, mother of a large adult family, 'Moeke' Stolk. We came to know the family well and a few years later, in 1959, Joan married her youngest son, George.

Closer to home was the developing city of Dandenong, which was experiencing an enormous influx of Dutch migrants. While still a teenager, I accompanied my parents to a Dutch farm in the Dandenong Ranges for a Sunday afternoon house meeting. The time for the service was arranged between milking times. Neighbouring Dutch farmers had also been invited. It was a homely setting. The farmers came in their work clothes, some came in boots—these were left near the door—and several had their Bibles with them. There was a piano in the home to accompany the songs. I remember the enthusiastic singing and the earnest spirit of worship. It was a really special occasion!

During the early days, migrants were often disappointed and unsettled in their temporary accommodation. Some lived in old military barracks with leaking tin roofs. In the early 1950s attending church on a Sunday was still the norm; many were glad to get away from their accommodation to share in some good singing and listen to a good preacher. People wanted to hear the Gospel and, being Dutch, they also wanted to sing. Ryer was an evangelist at heart and his message was about being saved by Jesus. With his Dutch Reformed background, he had a good understanding of the beliefs of many of his listeners and people were saved.

During the 1954 Congress in the Melbourne Exhibition Building, Ryer was asked—at short notice—to have a group of migrants sing a 'company song' in Dutch. Uncertain as to what was meant, he taught them the chorus of a song by General Evangeline Booth in a back room of the building.

> *The world for God! The world for God!*
> *I give my heart! I'll do my part!*
> *The world for God! The world for God!*
> *I give my heart! I will do my part!* [171]

I recall two testimonies from this period. One woman in Dandenong said to Jo, 'Things have changed in my life since attending the services. I now attend church every Sunday, which I never used to do.' Another said, 'I attended the migrant service in Ballarat as a New Australian. We made that our home and decided to attend The Salvation Army church after hearing your husband. We've now been soldiers for many years.'

Dutch migrants settled quickly in Australia. Many of the younger generation spoke English as it is one of the compulsory languages in all high schools in the Netherlands. Although officially my parents were only given little more than a two-year appointment to work with Dutch migrants, there are now Salvationists with Dutch names of the third, and even the fourth, generation who no longer speak the language, and that does not include those who anglicised their names to simplify the pronunciation.

The late 1950s

From August 1956 till early 1960, Ryer served as the Assistant Special Efforts Secretary at THQ, while continuing with some weekend meetings amongst Dutch migrants. In January 1958, I left home to commence my general training for nursing at The Salvation Army Bethesda Hospital in Richmond, Melbourne, graduating in early 1961. One morning, during this period, I experienced an unwelcome reminder of hidden WWII memories. It was a beautiful spring day in November 1959. I was on an evening shift that day and had the morning off. The sun was warm and the trees were showing off their new green leaves. The city of Melbourne was just a short tram journey from the hospital. I was on my way to Little Bourke Street for a dual purpose. Buckley and Nunn was a department store known for its elegant clothing and footwear. I was interested in their latest embroidery designs which were usually on display at the back of the store. My second reason was that the neighbouring Myer department store had recently opened a coffee shop. This was not just ordinary coffee but 'cappuccino' with lots of 'fluff' on the top, and a vanilla slice. I walked down Collins Street, passing the Collins Street Independent Church (now St Michael's Uniting Church), and was about to cross Russell Street when the lights turned red. At that same moment, a small group—about four or five—young Japanese tourists arrived on the opposite side waiting for the light to change. They were a happy company, laughing and probably enjoying an overseas holiday. But something happened to me. It was the first time I had seen a Japanese person since I was a little girl during World War II. My whole body stiffened, I couldn't move, and my heart was pounding. Terror gripped me. I was unaware of traffic lights or the people who gathered around me waiting for the lights to change; when they did, the crowd rushed across Russell Street. Some must have wondered why I did not move. I stood paralysed, watching the Japanese tourists coming closer and chatting with each other as they walked towards me. But instead of coming onto the footpath where I was standing near the traffic light, they simply passed me by to wait for the green light to cross Collins Street. At that moment I heard a quiet Voice say, *'The war is over, the war is over.'* The tension drained out of me. My body began to relax. Of course! The war was over; I was safe! The traffic light was red again and gave me time to recover. I certainly needed some comfort food after that incident. What better than a cappuccino coffee and a vanilla slice?

CHAPTER 14

The onward journey

This side of heaven, perhaps all our safe arrivals are simply a time of rest before the onward journey. So it was for my family. Having settled in Australia, our journeys continued, as our parents approached retirement and Joan and I set out on adventures of our own.

The 1960s

Early in 1960 my parents were appointed to The Salvation Army Box Hill Boys Home and were resident members of staff. My father was the Financial Administrator for the Home.

My mother was one of a group of women who met once a week at the Boys Home to keep the boys in good clothing. The room had a sewing machine and all that one would expect in a sewing room: cottons, scissors, a box with buttons and a bag of clothing. During the winter months, someone made sure there was a burning log in the hearth when the women arrived. I suspect my father attended to that—it would have been typical of him: always caring for others. On the occasions when I had days off from nursing on that particular day of the week I frequently joined the women in the mending room. They would then give me shorts and shirts and the button box. I sometimes wondered if these lads played 'two-up' with their buttons! Sewing on buttons never came to an end.

I was a resident staff nurse at Bethesda Hospital, but went home on days off. Early in 1962 I commenced my midwifery training at Queen Victoria Women's Hospital and a year later I received my midwifery certificate. Halfway through that year I had the opportunity to do a four-month Infant Welfare nursing course at the small Queen Elizabeth Hospital for mothers and babies, then located in Parkville, close to the University of Melbourne. I found this to be an enjoyable and natural follow-up to midwifery.

An influx of migrants was attracted to the green and leafy eastern suburbs of Melbourne. Land was cleared, roads were made and inexpensive houses for families with low incomes began to shoot up like daisies. My parents were able to acquire a small house in a new housing area in Croydon, Victoria, in 1963. This provided a base for them to travel to their appointments and their involvement in The Salvation Army Ringwood Corps. I was able to live with them on days off from my nursing responsibilities. Joan and George had their own accommodation for their growing family and lived in the northern suburb of Heidelberg.

In March 1967, Joan and her husband, George Stolk, commenced work at the Box Hill Boys Home where they looked after 26 boys, aged from five until their teens. They were pleased to have had the experience of caring for such a large group of children. After three and a half years, however, when their own children were growing up and needing full-time care from both parents, it was time to hand over the boys in the Home to other carers.

Katherine in the Northern Territory

After completing the above-mentioned studies and some enjoyable holidays, I had a strong urge to 'spread my wings' away from the Melbourne scene. The Northern Territory was my choice of location. In the early 1960s this region was still under the jurisdiction of the Commonwealth Government in Canberra and I had to make my application to work at the Katherine Hospital through an assigned government health department office in

Melbourne. My application was accepted and in January 1964 I travelled by plane to Katherine.

I have wonderful memories of that year, and learned much. Television, computers and mobile phones were still in the future. There were 10 members of staff, and the matron, who I met in Melbourne during my infant welfare training course. I was delighted to make new friends. Most of the nurses were about my age and some were graduates from Melbourne hospitals.

Katherine Hospital was a 'bush' hospital; it was small and limited in medical facilities. One resident doctor was on call 24 hours a day. After-hours emergencies were few. Air conditioning was limited to the doctor's consulting rooms and the labour ward. One exception was the special room in the staff quarters reserved for the night nurse, to ensure she had a comfortable sleep during the day. Windows of both hospital and adjacent staff quarters were covered with fine wire, against mosquitoes, and had louvred glass slats allowing for ventilation. Ceiling fans were used throughout the hospital and staff quarters.

The large RAAF Air Base, Tindal, was being constructed near the Stuart Highway about 15 km south-east of Katherine while I was there. The Katherine civilian airport was near the hospital, a few kilometres away from the township.

It was not unusual for nurses to bring home an off-duty soldier after a movie or from a visit at a friend's place. Alcohol was not permitted on the nursing staff premises, but we had plenty of coffee and tea for visitors. One such afternoon occasion especially sticks in my memory. A couple of young servicemen came home with one of our nursing staff. We sat around the dining table and there was much conversation about the usual things: football, cricket and politics. There was a newcomer. He was quiet and very young; he also looked Dutch. I introduced myself as 'Sonja' and asked his name, and yes, he too had Dutch parents. He was 19 years of age and came to Australia as a small boy. We had something in common so I mentioned to him that my father had been in Tarakan with the Dutch troops when the Japanese made their first attack on the NEI. His sudden negative, almost abusive reply surprised me. It was obvious he misunderstood the situation in Tarakan during WWII. I was so incensed by this reaction that I wrote to my father to make sure I fully understood the situation. My father wrote back three tightly-typed pages dated 20 May 1964. Among other things, these pages provided a starting point for this book.

The hospital had a four-patient, air-conditioned ambulance and a full-time driver. There was always one staff member 'on call' for the whole day to accompany the ambulance driver when needed. It was usually our second day off. Katherine had no active X-ray department and lacked adequate surgical equipment. Extreme medical cases or severe injuries from road accidents on the Stuart Highway were transferred to Darwin. Flying Doctor services to outlying areas were required infrequently. The southern boundary for our ambulance was Daly Waters. Tennant Creek was linked with Alice Springs. Adelaide River was the northern boundary where Katherine transferred patients to the Darwin Ambulance.

The Stuart Highway is a long, straight road, and with the exception of an occasional traffic sign encouraging drivers to 'stop and have a little nap', there were kilometres of road without a sign of civilisation. It was not unusual for drivers to fall asleep behind the wheel and for their car or truck to run off the road into the bush without being seen by passing traffic. It was often only by 'bush telegraph' that the word of such accidents was passed on. Sometimes it was an observant driver seated in a high transport vehicle, with a wider vision to the left, who saw a car rolled over in the bush and notified the police who then contacted the hospital.

I was asked to commence a 'mother and baby' clinic in Katherine and another one in Pine Creek, about an hour north of Katherine. The hospital's station wagon was placed at my disposal for these long trips. I loved the contact with the mothers and their babies.

Katherine was the last town on the Stuart Highway in the Northern Territory to have a permanent river. Anything south from this township was considered desert. The Katherine River was at 'low level' for most of the year and on days off or after work it was a favourite place for us girls to cool off. The water was always clear. The flow of water was slow and safe for a swim. One thing that fascinated me was the number of active 'springs' in the river. These were visible when standing still in the water. The river was surrounded by large trees which were like a shade cloth against the sun. These trees added to the pleasure of being there. During the wet season many of these trees were completely covered by water.

The town had two small supermarkets and two chemists. It also had an old cinema with a leaky roof where faithful filmgoers—most of the population—gathered on Friday or Saturday evenings to see endless repetitions of old American Wild Western films. Of course, the Yankees won every conflict! If it rained, most people took an umbrella or a plastic raincoat to use in the cinema!

To my great joy there was also a small Salvation Army corps in Katherine where Majors (later Brigadiers) Victor Pedersen and his wife Olive were the corps officers. Olive looked after the corps during the week. Vic was the Army's Flying Padre to homesteads scattered all over the Northern Territory. He was away for much of the working week, but usually home for weekends when he conducted the Sunday service for a small congregation. The major and his wife were well known in Katherine. Their warm Christian witness went far beyond the small congregation that gathered on a Sunday morning. Their quarters became my second home.

Every day was a new experience. Territory climate was typically tropical—from the daily exhausting heat and humidity to the bucketing rains and floods of the monsoon season. Eventually the extreme heat was my physical undoing. The climate of the Northern Territory was similar to that in Jakarta and again I began to lose weight. Towards the end of my year in Katherine I was only 45 kg. I was, however, immensely grateful for the experience of that one year in Katherine, which indeed allowed me to 'spread my wings' professionally. I had considered a second year in the Territory, but had an ever-increasing sense within me saying, 'No, you must return to Melbourne.' Much later I realised this had been the prompting of God, the Holy Spirit. Looking back now, all those years later, I marvel at God's grace and guidance in my life. Returning to Melbourne was for a purpose yet to be confirmed. I knew God was in control for my next adventure!

At the end of February 1965, I arrived home in Croydon where my parents welcomed me with open arms. I was thin and exhausted. My mother decided on a 'feed Sonja' campaign. After four weeks of tender loving care and sleep I felt revived and ready to start work again. It was during these weeks at home that I began to do some regular walking with my father around the Croydon area. Ryer had turned 60 and now had less work among first-generation Dutch immigrants because of their rapid assimilation into Australia. The meetings for Dutch migrants gradually came to an end once people were settled in their homes and began to attend the local church of their choice. Ryer had not yet mastered English. When I arrived home, I noticed the 'sparkle' had gone from his eyes; he was withdrawn and quiet and there was little conversation between my parents. His hearing had deteriorated. He thought people were talking about him. Hearing aids 50 years ago were very visible and he refused to have one. We walked arm in arm and I loved his company. He was witty and we laughed together. He talked about his boyhood and some of his war experiences. Little did I realise then that these memories were laying a foundation for this book.

A car and an adventure

One of the first things I wanted to do when I arrived home from Katherine was to buy a car. I asked my brother-in-law, George, who was well informed about vehicles, to come with me. From the excellent salary I received in Katherine, of which I used very little personally, I was able to pay cash directly—less than $1,800! I drove home behind George, 'over the moon' with my new purchase. The letters 'JEM' on the number plate of my VW 1300 implied something beautiful and precious. In every sense of the word the little car was just that! My parents, who did not have a car, were perhaps somewhat overwhelmed by it all. One of my concerns for them was the distance they lived from both the Croydon railway station and the nearest

Salvation Army corps at Ringwood. Fortunately, a kind Salvationist living further along the Maroondah Highway was happy to pick them up for the Sunday morning meetings at the Ringwood Corps. At that time, I was an active member of the songster brigade of Box Hill Corps.

That same year I undertook an approximately six-month postgraduate course in eye and ear surgical nursing at the Royal Victorian Eye and Ear Hospital in Melbourne. Those attending the postgraduate course were considered as hospital staff. We had lectures early in the day and did practical work in the wards with staff support. I found this very helpful. Being a resident suited me well, as the accommodation was only a 15-minute walk to The Salvation Army City Temple Corps where I occasionally attended the Sunday morning service.

On completion of the course, there was a vacancy in one of the hospital's theatres and I was asked if I was interested to 'fill the gap'. I was delighted to accept this offer, but had planned to take an organised holiday after the course with my friend, 'Anna'. Fortunately, this delay was accepted and the appointment was confirmed. I think my parents were worried about the planned holiday. It was such a long journey and we were considered inexperienced travellers. They did not interfere, but gave tactful suggestions and warnings. As a parent of daughters, I can fully understand how they must have worried. Yet, I too had to learn that spreading my wings widened my horizons. I asked the Royal Automobile Club Victoria (RACV) to prepare a map for the journey by car to the still-under-construction Snowy Mountains Hydroelectric Scheme in New South Wales and a choice of some reasonably priced hotels in the towns in which we could stay overnight. The mapped-out journey was amazing even for beginners. As I was the driver, Anna was the navigator on the journey and she did well.

Anna and I had some laughs. We were obviously beginners when it came to camping. At the end of our first day we put up our little tent and brought in our airbeds to pump them up. We closed the tent 'door' and sprayed against the mosquitoes. After some food and drink, and a thank you prayer for a safe journey, we climbed into our airbeds. All was quiet. After a short sleep, I discovered my airbed was flat; all the air had escaped and I was literally lying on the ground. Although the door was shut, the mosquitoes found their way in. There must have been a legion of them. I switched on my torch to find the spray and used it liberally, but I think they were immune to it. Sleep eventually won the battle.

Walking around the Snowy Mountains Hydroelectric Scheme was an amazing experience. Anna and I were in a group with other tourists. The guide explained some of the mechanisms of water storage and power generation.

As we were about to commence our return journey to Melbourne from the Snowy Scheme, we had booked in at a relatively inexpensive hotel in a quiet town. It was an old place with narrow passages, but our room on the first floor was clean and the hotel appeared quiet. After the experiences of the last couple of days we had much to talk about as we went downstairs for our dinner. While we were having our meal the dividing doors of the dining room were pushed back, enlarging the room into a dance floor. Not long after we returned to our room, a crowd of local people began to arrive. Obviously, the hotel was known as an entertainment place; soon music reverberated through the corridors.

I was glad to be upstairs away from the music. However, Anna enjoyed an occasional twirl on the dance floor and went downstairs to check it out. I was ready for an early night when she returned to the room. Locking the door, she said; 'They are not my type!' For friendly Anna that was a strong statement, but I understood what she meant. I too felt uncomfortable about the place. Looking at her serious face, I began to laugh. 'Well, we've locked the door; the Lord will look after us! It's time to go to bed!'

Then there was a knock on the door. Anna looked at me. I said, 'Unlock the door and see who is there. I'll get my dressing gown.' Anna reported back that three well-dressed men with suits and ties were asking if they could have a lift with us the next day to a certain place in the direction we were travelling. I went to the door and saw

And the chorus, which was not used on that occasion, would have been totally applicable:

> *In the name, the precious name*
> *Of him who died for me,*
> *Through grace I'll win the promised crown,*
> *Whate'er my cross may be.*

Johanna van Kralingen (23 March 1909–9 June 1994)

My mother visited Holland in 1969 when Petronella was about 87 years of age and most unwell. Jo was there when Petronella passed away in February 1969. While also in the Netherlands, she was able to attend a reunion of those who had trained with her to become officers in 1930—including her war-time colleague and companion, the now Mrs Brigadier Marie Luitjes (see photograph on page 120).

On 2 December 1972 my mother married a long-time family friend, Colonel Garnet Samuel Palmer, a widower. Garnet's first wife had passed away sometime before Ryer. The wedding ceremony took place at The Salvation Army Ringwood Corps and was conducted by Commissioner Henry Warren from the Australia Eastern Territory. After her marriage to Garnet, Johanna sold her home in Croydon and lived with Garnet at the Inala Village from where they attended the Box Hill Corps. They were married for over 20 years. It was a happy marriage and their great enjoyment was having time to see their grandchildren. They even visited us in Zambia in 1974, where Garnet dedicated our third daughter, Cathy. Garnet was promoted to Glory on 29 January 1993. Jo remained in Inala and was transferred to a single unit, which was easier for her to manage.

In 1994, Ian and I were back in Melbourne, living not far from Inala Village and I contacted Jo most days. She was still doing her exercises and making friends in her new surroundings. On Thursday 9 June 1994, Ian and I were away for most of the day attending special meetings at Melbourne City Temple in Bourke Street, The Salvation Army's main meeting hall in the city. We arrived home later than expected. There was a telephone message from my mother; her voice was not clear, but I heard her say: 'I did not have good day today, talk tomorrow, bye!' It was late in the evening and she was in a safe place and probably asleep. I decided to visit her early the next morning and was there by 8.30 am. When I got to her room, I found she was in her night dress, sitting on her comfortable chair with her left arm stretched out and her hand just above the telephone. The Lord had called her Home just after that phone call. I notified Ian, who was already at Territorial Headquarters. My next calls were to Joan in Mooroolbark, then our three daughters, Sharon, Jenni and Cathy.

Johanna's funeral was conducted by Colonel Ronald Sketcher at Box Hill Corps. In his message for the funeral, the Territorial Commander, Commissioner John Clinch, wrote:

> The service of Mrs Colonel Palmer (Van Kralingen), reads like an extract from Hebrews chapter 11 where those biblical heroes of the faith are listed.
>
> What richness of experience was hers in the Netherlands, Indonesia and Australia.
>
> In Indonesia during the Second World War when occupation by the Japanese took place there was also hardship and deprivation, but her faith remained buoyant.
>
> I remember when Mrs Palmer with her first husband first came to soldier at my home corps of Fairfield and the impression made on me by the vibrant and positive expression of her Christian experience and Salvationism. As an officer, she was an excellent role model for an accepted candidate preparing for college...'[174]

The day following my mother's promotion to Glory, the daily reading was from Isaiah 43:1–3, a promise my parents and I found be true.

Fear not for I have redeemed you;
I have summoned you by name; you are mine
When you pass through the waters, I will help you
And when you pass through the rivers they will not sweep
over you...
For I am the Lord, your God...

Endnotes

Chapter 1 Ryer's Early Life

1 Jan van Kapel, letter to his sister, Johanna van Kralingen, 2 February 1971, translated by and in possession of Sonja I. Southwell.

2 Jan van Kapel, letter to his niece, Sonja Southwell, 13 June 1971, translated by and in possession of Sonja I. Southwell.

Chapter 2 Jo's background

3 Jan van Kapel, essay written in connection with the 75th anniversary (7 June 1906–1981) of The Salvation Army Vlaardingen Corps, 1981, translated by and in possession of Sonja I. Southwell.

4 ibid.

5 ibid.

6 ibid.

7 ibid.

8 ibid.

9 ibid.

10 ibid.

11 ibid.

12 C.H. Dunbar, 'We are out on the ocean sailing', Song 972, *The Song Book of The Salvation Army* (1930 edition), IHQ, London, UK.

13 Sidney Edward Cox, 'One golden dawning, one glorious morning', Chorus of Song 543, *The Song Book of The Salvation*

Army (2015 edition), © Copyright The General of The Salvation Army, IHQ, London, UK. Reproduced by permission.

Chapter 3 Time for decisions

14 Jan van Kapel, letter to his sister, Johanna, 2 February 1971, op. cit.
15 ibid.
16 ibid.
17 E.W. Blandly, Chorus 57, *The Song Book of The Salvation Army,* The General of The Salvation Army, London, UK 1986.

Chapter 4 Netherlands East Indies before the war

18 B. Hackett, Surabaya, Java Naval Base, Oil Facilities Under IJN Control, February 2013, p. 1, http://www.combinedfleet.com/JavaOil.htm, viewed 25/09/2013.
19 Johanna van Kralingen, 'Jo's Story', post-war essay, date unknown but possibly shortly after WW II and definitely before 1972, translated by and in possession of Sonja I. Southwell, p.1 of handwritten original.
20 Melattie Brouwer, *History of The Salvation Army in Indonesia, Volume 1, 1884–1949*, The Salvation Army, Hawthorn, Victoria, 1996, p. 112, section on Tarakan.

Chapter 5 Malang and De Wijk

21 Johanna van Kralingen, op. cit., p. 3 of handwritten original.
22 John 3:16–17, *The New English Bible*, 1961.
23 Johanna van Kralingen, op. cit., p. 1 in the handwritten original.
24 Edward Henry Joy, 'Is there a heart o'erbound by sorrow?', Chorus of Song 427, *The Song Book of The Salvation Army* (2015 edition), © Copyright The General of The Salvation Army, IHQ, London, UK. Reproduced by permission.
25 W. Cowper (1731–1800), Song 17, *The Song Book of The Salvation Army*, The General of The Salvation Army, 2015.
26 Johanna van Kralingen, op. cit.
27 ibid.

28 Melattie Brouwer, op. cit., p. 131.

29 Kennedy Hickman, *The Battle of the Java Sea—World War II*, https://www.thoughtco.com/battle-of-the-java-sea-2361432, updated 12 June 2017.

30 B. Hackett, op. cit.

31 Johanna van Kralingen, op.cit., p. 3.

32 *East Indies Camp Archives*, East Java Women's camps, https://www.indischekamparchieven.nl/en/general-information/per-island/java, viewed 29/05/2017.

33 Johanna van Kralingen, op. cit.

34 ibid.

35 ibid.

36 Sonja I. Southwell & Joan Stolk, recorded conversations, tapes and transcript in possession of Sonja I. Southwell, tape 1, side1, p. 2 of transcript. This conversation was recorded when Ian and Sonja Southwell visited Sonja's sister Joan, and her husband, George Stolk, in approximately 2003.

Chapter 6 Solo and Banyu Biru

37 Melattie Brouwer, op. cit., p. 150; for her service to prisoners of war the Netherlands Government awarded Brigadier Smid in 1949 the East Asia Star of Opposition, and in 1958 the Dutch Queen awarded her a Knight in the Order of Oranje Nassau. Later on, in the Netherlands she was awarded another 'Cross of Opposition, Remembrance'.

38 Sonja I. Southwell and Joan Stolk, op. cit., para 3 of transcript.

39 M. Brouwer, op. cit., p. 150.

40 Sonja I Southwell & Joan Stolk, op. cit., p. 6, para 2 of transcription.

41 J. van Dulm et al., *Geïllustreerde Atlas van de Japanse Kampen in Nederlands-Indië 1942–1945, Asia Maior*, Purmerend, 2000, pp. 150, 158, gives the transfer dates to Banyu as 30–31 May.

42 ibid., p. 145.

43 ibid., p. 150.

44 ibid., p. 133.

45 Shirley Fenton Huie, *The Forgotten Ones,* HarperCollins, Pymble NSW, 1992, p. 82.

46 E. van Kampen, 'Memories of the Dutch East Indies: From Plantation Society to Prisoner of Japan', *The Asia-Pacific Journal Japan Focus,* 2009, vol. 7, issue 1, no. 4, 'Pro-Independence Rally, August 1945', para. 6. http://apjjf.org/-Elizabeth-Van-Kampen/3002/article.html.

47 J. van Dulm et al., op. cit., p. 150.

48 E. van Kampen, op. cit., camp menu.

49 Administration in East Indies Camp Archives, http:www. indishekamparchieven.nl/en, viewed 12/09/2013.

50 Civilian camps in East Indies Camp Archives, http:www. indishekamparchieven.nl/en, viewed 10/09/2017.

51 Camp regulations in East Indies Camp Archives, http:www. indishekamparchieven.nl/en, viewed 12/09/2013.

52 J. van Dulm et al., op. cit., Camp Banyu Biru 11, p. 38.

53 Chris Tomlin, Ed Cash and Jesse Reeves, 'How great is our God', Song 64, *The Song Book of The Salvation Army* (2015 edition), IHQ, London, UK. © 2004 worshiptogether. com.songs, sixsteps Music (Admin. by kingswaysongs.com) Alletrop Music/Music Services (Admin. by Song Solutions www.songsolutions.org).

54 Types of camps in East Indies Camp Archives, http:www. indishekamparchieven.nl/en, viewed 12/09/2013.

Chapter 7 Freedom gained, lost, regained

55 Daily life in the camps in East Indies Camp Archives, http:www. indishekamparchieven.nl/en, viewed 12/09/2013.

56 Maikel Vrenken, 'A Common Approach? The British and Dutch in the Netherlands East Indies, 1945–1946', *The British Empire at War Research Group, Research Papers,* no. 5, 2014, p. 4, paras 1 and 2.

57 Jeffrey Hays, *Indonesia: Struggle for Independence,* 2008, updated June 2015, http://factsanddetails.com/indonesia/ History_and_Religion/sub6_1c/entry-3955.html.

58 Information supplied by Joost van Bodegom, drawn from 'Notes on the Banyu Biru Camps' by A.J.A.C. Nooteboom, a RAPWI-commandant, in charge of Banyu Biru XI Camp.

59 H.Th. Bussemaker, *Bersiap! Opstand in het Paradijs*, Zutphen, Netherlands, Walburg Pers, 2013, https://www.walburgpers.nl/winkel/geschiedenis/bersiap-indie-bussemaker, p. 172.

60 ibid., p. 173.

61 ibid., pp. 173, 174.

62 ibid., p.173, last para.

63 ibid.

64 Sonja I. Southwell and Joan Stolk, op. cit., tape 1, side 1, p. 6, para 2 of transcript.

Chapter 8 Ryer in Tarakan

65 Peter Stanley, *Tarakan. An Australian Tragedy,* Allen & Unwin, Sydney, Australia, 1997, p. 7.

66 Gavin Long, *The Final Campaigns, Australia in the War of 1939–1945, Series 1 – Army,* vol. VII, Australian War Memorial, Canberra, 1963, OCLC 1297619, 1963, pp. 406–408.

67 Ryer mentioned 1,550 men in Ryer L. van Kralingen, personal correspondence to Sonja I. van Kralingen (now Southwell), 20 May 1964, translated by and in possession of Sonja I. Southwell.

68 Melattie Brouwer, op. cit., p. 112.

69 G. van Geffen, 'Funeral tribute for Brigadier Van Kralingen', February 1971, in possession of Sonja I. Southwell. Van Geffen stated, 'The presence of women and children on the island had been prohibited for some time before Van Kralingen arrived in Tarakan.'

70 William Stolk, 'The Life and Ministry of Brigadier R.L. van Kralingen', page 2. An essay based on interviews with the Brigadier's widow, Mrs Johanna Palmer, and her daughter, Mrs Johanna (Joan) Stolk, 1986, in possession of Sonja I. Southwell.

71 G. van Geffen, op. cit.

72 ibid.

73 Melattie Brouwer, op. cit., p. 112.

74 This is confirmed by L. de Jong, *Het Koninkrijk der Nederlanden in de Tweede Wereldoorlog* [The Royal Netherlands in the Second World War], Deel IIa, [Section IIa], Nederlands-Indie I, tweede helft [second half], Gravenhage, Staatsuitgeverij, 1984, viewed in the electronic version, www.niod.nl/nl/koninkrijk, pp. 815–16; p. 793 in the original.

75 The Salvation Army, Australia Southern Territory, 'Netherlands East Indies Salvationists Courageously Remain at their Posts', *War Cry*, Australian edn, 4 April 1942, p. 5.

76 Ryer L. van Kralingen, 'Vermiste Personen te Tarakan "Borneo" oorlog met Japan 10–12 January 1942', personal war report to the Dutch Military on missing persons and burials on Tarakan (1942) and in Borneo (1942–45), date unknown but possibly 23 November 1945, when Van Kralingen made his official report. In possession of the Nederlands Institute voor Oorlog Documentatie (NIOD) – [Netherlands Institute of War Documentation], Amsterdam. The original copies of both this personal war report and his official war report are contained in file numbers 001922 and 067503, in possession of NIOD. NIOD provided the writer with copies. They include a cover page, a single typed page of Ryer's official war report, and then three typed pages of his personal war report, including missing persons and those he buried.

77 Ryer L. van Kralingen, personal correspondence, 1964, op. cit.

78 Ryer L. van Kralingen, personal correspondence, 1964; some documents give 1,300.

79 L. de Jong, p. 793 in the original and page 815 in the electronic version, para 1 and footnote.

80 Ryer L. van Kralingen, personal correspondence, 1964.

81 L. de Jong, op. cit., p. 815 and footnote; Algemeen Verloop van de Strijd in Indië XII, *The Japanese Operations in Netherlands Indië*, p. 794, paras 2, 3.

82 ibid.

83 J. van Dulm et al., op. cit., p. 189, left column, line 7.

84 Ryer L. van Kralingen, personal war report to the Dutch Military on missing persons and burials on Tarakan (1942) and in Borneo (1942–45), subsequently referred to as the 'personal war report'.

85 Ryer L. van Kralingen, 'Report on Interrogation. 23rd November, 1945, "R. L. van Kralingen"', official war report to the Dutch Military, 23 November 1945, before the ensign 'Meindersma Robert' in charge of the investigation concerning war criminals and collaborators in the NEI, in possession of the Nederlands Institute voor Oorlog Documentatie (NIOD) [Netherlands Institute of War Documentation], Amsterdam, subsequently referred to as the 'official war report'.

86 ibid., para 1.

87 J. van Dulm et. al., op. cit., Infanterie-kampement [A], last two lines in right column p. 188, and first six lines in left column p. 189, 12/01/1942.

88 ibid., p. 188, last 4 lines left column.

89 Psalm 73: 13–17, 23–28, *Holy Bible*, New International Version, 1984.

90 Psalm 73: 23–28, *Holy Bible*, New International Version, 1984.

91 J. van Dulm et al., op. cit., p. 189, lines 25–28.

92 L. de Jong, op. cit., pp. 796–797, 800.

93 ibid., p. 803.

Chapter 9 Ryer in Borneo

94 Ryer L. van Kralingen, personal correspondence, 1964.

95 Ryer L. van Kralingen, handwritten notes in Bible, in possession of Sonja I. Southwell.

96 J. van Dulm et al., op. cit., see footnote on p. 189, left column, line 14.

97 Ryer L. van Kralingen, official war report; seven men were in the group, only 1st Lieut. Lamers is mentioned, above.

98 Ryer L. van Kralingen, personal correspondence, 1964. The names of the officers in charge of these sections are mentioned in his official and personal war reports to Dutch Military but not included here.

99 Joshua 1: 9. NIV

100 Ryer L. van Kralingen, official war report, p. 2.

101 William Stolk, 1986.

102 Joshua 1: 9. NIV

103 Ryer L. van Kralingen, official war report, p. 4.

104 ibid.

105 Ryer L. van Kralingen, handwritten notes in Bible

106 Ryer L. van Kralingen, handwritten notes in Bible and also in war report, p. 2.

107 Ryer L. van Kralingen, official war report, p. 2.

108 J. van Dulm et al., op. cit., see footnote p. 191, left column, line 9.

109 Ryer L. van Kralingen, personal correspondence, op. cit.

110 Ryer L. van Kralingen, official war report.

111 Ryer L. van Kralingen, personal correspondence, op. cit..

112 Ryer L. van Kralingen, official war report.

113 ibid., p. 2, last 12 lines; Captain Brouwer was in charge of Samarinda 1 and 2.

114 Ryer L van Kralingen, personal correspondence, op. cit.

115 ibid.

116 See list of the deceased 'POWs in Borneo' along with 'List of deceased POWs in Tarakan' and 'Missing in Tarakan', found among the possessions of Ryer L. van Kralingen with a note indicating he received these while living at Kramat 61, early on his return to Jakarta in 1947, now in possession of Sonja I. Southwell. This list was probably created by the Dutch Military, but it is likely that Ryer's own lists contributed to its development. His list is hand-annotated.

117 Ryer L. van Kralingen, personal correspondence, op. cit.; as discussed above, this may have been a longer journey; they stopped twice to bury in the jungle beside the river the 12 men who died on the slow up-river journey—some of whom had been injured due to the American bombing. The other 18 died and were buried by Ryer at Puruk Cahu.

118 The funerals are recorded on the Puruk Cahu cemetery list below.

119 Ryer L van Kralingen, 'Poeroek-Tjahoe Kerkhof & Krygsgevangenen-Kerkhof' / 'Cemetery of Prisoners of War', scale 1 to 100, in possession of Sonja I. Southwell (see copy page 115). Years later, after Ryer's promotion to Glory, Jo found three foolscap pages with the names of the men Ryer had

buried. Included were carefully drawn maps by Ryer, showing the position of the Puruk Cahu Cemetery, morgue and grave sites where 18 soldiers were buried over a period of five weeks. Each grave had a number. On the left side of the page are written, with a fine pen and ink, the names of the 18 soldiers who were laid to rest there. Mr Van Geffen mentioned this document in his eulogy at Dad's funeral: 'A few days ago, Mrs Van Kralingen showed me a list...of names of men who died in the East Borneo POW camps. One can only guess the amount of work involved in contacting families to tell them in his own endearing way about a lost husband, father or son...'

120 Ryer L. van Kralingen, handwritten notes in Bible.
121 Max Fisher, https://www.theatlantic.com/international/archive/2012/08/the-emperors-speech-67-years-ago-hirohito-transformed-japan-forever/261166/.
122 Ryer L. van Kralingen, personal correspondence.
123 ibid.;
124 The Australian War Diaries (AWD) for the 2/31st Infantry Battalion, https://www.awm.gov.au/collection/C1368285, p. 184. NICA – Netherlands Indies Civil Administration.
125 Erik Wickberg (General), in his foreword to F. Coutts, *The History of The Salvation Army Volume VI, 1914–1946*, The Salvation Army, London, 1973, p. 5.
126 Melattie Brouwer, op. cit., p. 156, Officers Promoted to Glory 1942–1946.
127 William Parkinson, personal correspondence to Sonja I. Southwell, date unknown, in possession of Sonja I. Southwell.
128 William Stolk, 1986. Probably seven weeks rather than seven months. It was almost seven months after he wrote the letter before the family was re-united.

Chapter 10 After Liberation: In Australia and Holland

129 Ryer L. van Kralingen, personal war report, p. 2, gives October 1945 as the month Ryer arrived in Australia; the Netherlands East Indies Commission, initially based in Melbourne, formed

a government-in-exile in 1944. In September that year the administrative departments of that Commission, including KNIL HQ, the Netherlands East Indies Service (NEFIS), consulate offices and the NEI Red Cross, occupied a new headquarters at Camp Columbia, Wacol near Brisbane. https://www.awm.gov.au/visit/exhibitions/alliesinadversity/australia/columbia

130 Ryer L. van Kralingen, official war report.

131 As noted in Chapter 8, the original copies of Ryer's personal and official war reports are contained in file numbers 001922 and 067503, in possession of Nederlands Institute voor Oorlog Documentatie (NIOD) – [Netherlands Institute of War Documentation]. They include a cover page, a single typed page of Ryer's official war report, and then three typed pages of his personal war report, including missing persons and those he buried.

132 Johanna van Kralingen, handwritten notebook (c.1941–46).

133 Albert Kenyon, *Leonard Goes East,* Salvationist Publishing & Supplies, London, UK, 1952, the biography of Leonard Havergal Woodward.

134 Melattie Brouwer, op. cit., pp. 152–3.

135 Acts 2:3–4; and The Great Commission, Matthew 28:19–20.

136 Ryer L van Kralingen, personal war report; Ryer visited the Royal Australian Air Force HQ, Melbourne, in October 1945.

137 Ryer L. van Kralingen, personal correspondence, op. cit.

138 William Parkinson, op. cit.; Mangarra Girls High School is now Canterbury Girls High School.

139 Melattie Brouwer, op. cit., p. 149, paras 5–6. Brigadier Hendrick Loois died in Cimahi POW Camp 4, 25 July 1944. Mrs Loois died in Semarang POW Camp 11, July 1945.

140 William Parkinson, op. cit.

141 Cor van Kapel, letter to Johanna van Kralingen, 26 August 1946, translated by and in possession of Sonja I. Southwell.

142 ibid.

143 Johanna Palmer (formerly Johanna van Kralingen, nee Van Kapel), "'The beginning history of Kramat 55, Jakarta, in 1947" as told by Mrs Colonel J.F. Palmer Van Kralingen in

1980 to Lieut-Colonel Melattie Brouwer', translated by and in possession of Sonja I. Southwell, 1980.

Chapter 11 Indonesia after WWII 1946–1949

144 Bersiap in East Indies Camp Archives, https://www. indischekamparchieven.nl/en/general-information/bersiap.

145 Soetan Sjahrir, *Onze Strijd [Our Struggle]*, Vrij Nederland, Amsterdam, 1946, pp. 15–16.

146 Bersiap August 1945–December 1946 in East Indies Camp Archives WWII, http:www.indishekamparchieven.nl/en, viewed 13/08/2013.

147 Johanna Palmer, op. cit.

148 ibid.

149 ibid.

150 ibid.

151 ibid.

152 ibid.

153 Melattie Brouwer, op. cit., p. 163.

154 ibid., p. 162.

155 'Forward to the Battle', Song 468, *Liederen van het Leger des Heils* [Dutch *Salvation Army Song Book* – no names, no dates], Het Leger des Heils, Amsterdam, 1951, translated by Sonja I. Southwell; 'The Opening of Batavia's Open Door Military Clubhouse', NEI *Strijdkreet [War Cry]*, December 1947, translated by Sonja I. Southwell.

156 ibid.

157 J. de Moor, *The Journal of Military History*, vol. 69, no. 2, 2 April 2005, pp. 593–595; L. de Jong, *The Collapse of a Colonial Society: The Dutch in Indonesia during the Second World War*, KITLV Press, Leiden, The Netherlands, 2002, p. 570.

158 Melattie Brouwer, op. cit., pp. 164, 168, 169.

Chapter 12 Indonesia after Independence 1950–1953

159 Albert Orsborn, *The House of my Pilgrimage,* London, The Salvation Army, 1958, p. 266.

160 G. van Geffen, op. cit.

161 Albert Orsborn, op. cit.

162 ibid.

163 Jeremiah Eames Rankin, 'God be with you', Song 1027, *The Song Book of The Salvation Army* (2015 edition), © Copyright The General of The Salvation Army, IHQ, London, UK. Reproduced by permission.

Chapter 13 A safe arrival

164 The Australia Southern Territory then consisted of the states of Victoria, South Australia, Western Australia, Tasmania and the Northern Territory.

165 This quote was taken from an official obituary presented at Commissioner Durman's funeral, 25 April 1979. It was provided by The Salvation Army Heritage Office, Melbourne. No writer's name was given on the obituary.

166 Barbara Bolton, *Booth's Drum: The Salvation Army in Australia 1880–1980*, Hodder & Stoughton, Sydney, Auckland, London, Toronto, 1980, p. 111.

167 *War Cry*, Australian edn, October 1954, p. 1.

168 *War Cry*, 7 August 1954, p. 5.

169 Nonja Peters (Director of the Migration, Ethnicity, Refugees and Citizenship Research Unit, Curtin University of Technology, Western Australia). http://www.naa.gov.au/collection/publications/papers-and-podcasts/family-history/dutch-in-australia.aspx.

170 Hubert Opperman (Minister for Immigration), *War Cry*, Melbourne, Australia, 27 February 1965, pp. 5, 7.

171 E. Booth, 'The World for God', Chorus of Song 933, *The Song Book of The Salvation Army*, op. cit.

Chapter 14 The onward journey

172 Ian and Sonja Southwell, *Safely Led to Serve: A Joint Biography*, Balboa Press, Bloomington, Indiana, USA, 2017.

173 I. Watts, 'Am I a soldier of the cross' (verses), Song 947, *Song Book of The Salvation Army*, op. cit.

174 John Clinch (Commissioner), 'Written message in the program for the funeral of Colonel J Palmer', 14 June 1994, in possession of Sonja I. Southwell.

Glossary of Terms and Abbreviations

Bahasa Indonesia: The official language of Indonesia. 'Bahasa' alone means language.

Bataafse Petroleum Maatschappij (BPM): Dutch for Batavian Oil Company, a subsidiary of the Royal Dutch Shell oil company established in 1907, which extracted and refined oil in the Netherlands East Indies, now Indonesia.

Bersiap: The name given by the Dutch to a violent and chaotic phase of the Indonesian National Revolution following the end of World War II. The Indonesian word *bersiap* means 'get ready' or 'be prepared'.

Cadet: A Salvationist who is in training for officership.

Candidate: A soldier who has been accepted for officer training.

Chief Secretary (CS): The officer second-in-command of The Salvation Army in a territory.

Commission: A document presented publicly, authorising an officer, or local officer to fulfil a specified ministry.

Commissioning of Officers: The public ceremony during which cadets (see above) are ordained as ministers of religion and authorised to serve as officers within The Salvation Army.

Congress: Central gathering is often held annually and attended by most officers and many soldiers of the territory, command, region or division.

Corps: A Salvation Army unit established for the preaching of the gospel, worship, teaching and fellowship and to provide Christian-motivated service in the community. Corps is The Salvation Army term for a church or congregation.

Corps Cadet (CC): A young Salvationist who undertakes a course of study and practical training in a corps with a view to becoming effective in Salvation Army service.

Dedication Service: The public presentation of a building, program or person, for God's service and glory.

Fishing: A Salvation Army term describing the ministry of certain members of the congregation in a salvation meeting of moving around during the time of the appeal for decisions for Christ encouraging those who may be close to making that decision to actually do so. Based on Jesus' command to his fishermen disciples, 'Follow me and I will make you fishers of men' (Mark 1:17 *NIV*).

General: The officer elected to the supreme command of The Salvation Army throughout the world. All appointments are made and all regulations issued under the General's authority.

Het Leger des Heils: The Salvation Army in the Dutch language.

Home League (HL): Part of the women's ministries of The Salvation Army in which Christian influence is exerted and practical help given for the benefit of the individual, the family and the nation.

Ibu: Indonesian word for mother.

International Headquarters (IHQ): The offices in which the business connected with the command of the worldwide Salvation Army is transacted in London, UK.

International Secretary (IS): A position at IHQ with responsibility for the oversight and coordination of the work in a specific geographical zone or functional category and for advising the General on zonal and worldwide issues and policies.

Junior Soldier (JS): A boy or girl who, having accepted Jesus as their Saviour, has signed the Junior Soldier's Promise and become a Salvationist.

Kamar mandi: Indonesian bathroom. See Mandie/Mandi, below.

Koninklijk Nederlands Indisch Leger (KNIL): The Royal Netherlands East Indies Army.

Kopi/Koppi tubruk: Boiling water on roasted ground coffee, stirred and allowed to settle, before drinking.

Liederen van het Leger des Heils: Salvation Army Dutch Song Book.

Local Officer: A soldier appointed to a position of responsibility and authority in the corps; carrying out the duties of the appointment without being separated from regular employment or receiving remuneration from The Salvation Army.

Mandie/Mandi: A wash; as in, 'to have a wash'. See Kamar mandi, above.

Mercy Seat: A bench provided as a place where people can kneel to pray, seeking salvation or sanctification, or making a special consecration to God's will and service. The mercy seat is usually situated between the platform and main area of Salvation Army halls and is the focal point to remind all of God's reconciling and redeeming presence.

Netherlands East Indies (NEI): The Dutch colonial name for the islands of what became Indonesia in 1949.

Netherlands East Indies Forces Intelligence Services (NEFIS): A Dutch World War II era intelligence and special operations unit operating mainly in the Japanese-occupied Netherlands East Indies (now Indonesia).

Netherlands Indies Civil Administration (NICA): An organisation tasked with restoring civil administration and law of Dutch colonial rule after the surrender of the Japanese occupation forces in the NEI after World War II.

Nederlands Institute voor Oorlog Documentatie (NIOD): Netherlands Institute of War Documentation, Amsterdam.

Officer: A Salvationist who has been trained, commissioned and ordained to service and leadership in response to God's call. An officer is a recognised minister of religion.

Pastoral Care Council (PCC): Previously known as the Census Board, Established in each corps for the care of the soldiers etc, and maintenance of membership rolls.

Pemudas: Name given to Indonesian youth groups after WWII which were working for independence.

Promotion to Glory (pG): The Army's description of the death of Salvationists.

Ranks of Officers: Lieutenant, captain, major, lieut-colonel, colonel, commissioner, General. *Previous ranks* have included: ensign, adjutant, staff-captain, field-major, senior-captain, senior-major, brigadier and lieut-commissioner.

RAPWI: Recovery of Allied Prisoners of War and Internees.

Red Shield: A symbol saying 'The Salvation Army' in the local language, identifying personnel, buildings, equipment, mobile units, and emergency services.

Royal Automobile Club Victoria (RACV): A support organisation for motorists based in Victoria, Australia.

Salvation: The work of grace which God accomplishes in a repentant person whose trust is in Christ as Saviour, forgiving sin, giving new direction to life, and strength to live as God desires.

Salvationist: Full adult member of The Salvation Army; also known as a soldier (see below).

SDAP Netherlands: The Dutch Socialist Democratic Labour Party prior to WWII. After the war it became PVDA—Party for the Workers, or Labour Party

Sergeant: A Salvation Army soldier holding a warrant to serve in a non-commissioned position.

Soldier (Salvation Army): A converted person of at least 14 years of age who has, with the approval of the Senior Pastoral Care Council (see above), been enrolled as a member of The Salvation Army after signing the Soldier's Covenant.

Soldier's Covenant: The statement of beliefs and promises which every intending soldier is required to sign before enrolment. Previously called the 'Articles of War'.

Songsters: The Salvation Army description of a choir.

Tante: Dutch word for aunt.

Territorial Commander (TC): The officer in command of the Army in a Territory.

Territorial Headquarters (THQ): The offices in which the business connected with a Salvation Army territory is transacted.

Territory: A country, part of a country or several countries combined, in which Salvation Army work is organised under a Territorial Commander.

Training College: The name given to the theology and ministry training facility for Salvation Army officers in each territory.

Tuan: Indonesian word for the man of the house, 'Sir'. A form of address used as a mark of respect.

Young People's Sergeant-Major (YPSM): A local officer responsible for young people's work in a corps, under the commanding officer.

Note: Definitions of Salvation Army terms adapted from *The Salvation Army Year Book 2016* (London, UK; Salvation Books, The Salvation Army International Headquarters; 2015), pp. 18-20; also 12, 34-36 with permission of The General of The Salvation Army.

Bibliography

Published works

Algemeen Verloop van de Strijd in Indië XII, *The Japanese Operations in Netherlands Indië*, nd.

Australian War Memorial, 'Allies in Adversity, Australia and the Dutch in the Pacific War: The NEI government-in-exile', https://www.awm.gov.au/visit/exhibitions/alliesinadversity/australia/columbia.

Australian War Memorial, War Diaries, 2/31st Battalion, https://www.awm.gov.au/collection/U56074 https://www.awm.gov.au/collection/C1368285.

Bolton, Barbara, *Booth's Drum: The Salvation Army in Australia 1880–1980,* Hodder & Stoughton, Sydney, Auckland, London, Toronto, 1980.

Brouwer, Melattie, *History of The Salvation Army in Indonesia, Volume 1, 1884–1949*, The Salvation Army, Hawthorn, Victoria, 1996.

Bussemaker, H.Th., *Bersiap! Opstand in Paradijs. De Bersiap Periode of Java en Sumatra 1945–1946*, Zutphen, Netherlands, Walburg Pers, 2013, https://www.walburgpers.nl/winkel/geschiedenis/bersiap-indie-bussemaker.

Civilian Camp Archives, http://www.indishekamparchieven.nl/en, viewed 10/09/2017.

de Jong, Loe, *Het Koninkrijk der Nederlanden in de Tweede Wereldoorlog* [The Royal Netherlands in the Second World War], Deel IIa, [Section IIa], Nederlands-Indie I, tweede helft [second half], Nederlands Institute voor Oorlog Documentatie (NIOD) [Netherlands Institute of

War Documentation], Gravenhage, Staatsuitgeverij, 1984, viewed in the electronic version, www.niod.nl/nl/koninkrijk.

East Indies Camp Archives, 'East Java Women's Camps', https://www. indischekamparchieven.nl/en/general-information/per-island/java, viewed 29/05/2017.

East Indies Camp Archives, 'The Battle for Java 1942', https://www. indischekamparchieven.nl/en.

Encyclopedia Britannica, https://www.britannica.com/place/ Tarakan-Island.

Fisher, Max, https://www.theatlantic.com/international/archive/2012/08/ the-emperors-speech-67-years-ago-hirohito-transformed-japan-forever/261166/.

Hackett, B., *Surabaya, Java Naval Base, Oil Facilities Under IJN Control,* February 2013, http://www.combinedfleet.com/JavaOil.htm, viewed 25/09/2013.

Hays, Jeffrey, *Indonesia: Struggle for Independence,* 2008, updated June 2015, http://factsanddetails.com/indonesia/History_and_Religion/ sub6_1c/entry-3955.html.

Hickman, Kennedy, *The Battle of the Java Sea – World War II,* https:// www.thoughtco.com/battle-of-the-java-sea-2361432, updated 12 June 2017.

Holy Bible, New English Version, 1961, 1970.

Holy Bible, New International Version, 1984.

Huie, Shirley Fenton, *The Forgotten Ones,* HarperCollins, Pymble NSW, 1992.

Indonesian Camp Archives, 'Bersiap', https://www.indischekamparchieven. nl/en/general-information/bersiap; 'August 1945–December 1946 East Indies Camp Archives WWII'; also https://www. indischekamparchieven.nl/en, viewed 13/08/2013.

Kenyon, Albert, *Leonard Goes East,* Salvationist Publishing & Supplies, London, UK, 1952. The biography of Leonard Havergal Woodward.

Lewis, M. Paul, *Ethnologue: Languages of the World*, 16th edn, 2009, https://www.ethnologue.com/. SIL International, viewed, 17/11/ 2009.

Liederen van het Leger des Heils [Salvation Army Dutch Song Book], Het Leger des Heils, Amsterdam, 1951.

Long, Gavin, *The Final Campaigns, Australia in the War of 1939–1945, Series 1 – Army*, vol. VII, Australian War Memorial, Canberra, 1963, OCLC 1297619.

Moor, Jaap, *The Journey of Military History*, vol. 69, no. 2, April 2000.

Opperman, Hubert (Minister for Immigration), *War Cry*, Melbourne, Australia, 27 February 1965.

Orsborn, Albert, *The House of My Pilgrimage*, The Salvation Army, London, 1958.

Peters, Nonja (Director of the Migration, Ethnicity, Refugees and Citizenship Research Unit, Curtin University of Technology, Western Australia). http://www.naa.gov.au/collection/publications/papers-and-podcasts/family-history/dutch-in-australia.aspx.

Ricklefs, M.C., 'Timeline of the Indonesian National Revolution (1945–1950)', *A History of Modern Indonesia Since c. 1200*, 3rd edn, Palgrave Publisher, Basingstoke, United Kingdom, 2001.

Sjahrir, Soetan, *Onze Strijd [Our Struggle]*, Vrij Nederland, Amsterdam, 1946, pp.15–16, 27.

Southwell, Ian and Sonja, *Safely Led to Serve: A Joint Biography*, Balboa Press, Bloomington, Indiana, USA, 2017.

Stanley, Peter, *Tarakan. An Australian Tragedy*, Allen & Unwin, Sydney, Australia, 1997.

Strijdkreet (NEI War Cry), July 1947.

Strijdkreet (NEI War Cry), December 1947.

The Salvation Army, Australia Southern Territory, 'Netherlands East Indies Salvationists Courageously Remain at Their Posts', *War Cry*, Australian edn, 4 April 1942.

The Salvation Army, *War Cry*, Australian edn, 7 August 1954.

The Salvation Army, *War Cry*, Australian edn, October 1954.

The Salvation Army, *War Cry*, Australian edn, 27 February 1965.

The Salvation Army, *War Cry*, United Kingdom edn, obituaries, Commissioner Charles Durman's funeral, 25 April 1979.

The Song Book of The Salvation Army, The General of The Salvation Army, London, United Kingdom, 2015.

The Song Book of The Salvation Army, The General of The Salvation Army, London, United Kingdom, 1986.

Van Dulm, J.; Krijgsveld, W.J.; Legemaate, H.J.; Liesker, H.A.M.; Weijers, G.; and Braches, E.: *Geïllustreerde Atlas van de Japanse Kampen in Nederlands-Indië 1942–1945*, Asia Maior, Purmerend, 2000.

Van Kampen, E., 'Memories of the Dutch East indies: From Plantation Society to Prisoner of Japan', *The Asia-Pacific Journal Japan Focus*, http://apjjf.org/-Elizabeth-Van-Kampen/3002/article.html, 1 January 2009, vol. 7, issue 1, no. 4.

Vrenken, Maikel, 'A Common Approach? The British and Dutch in the Netherlands East Indies, 1945–1946', *The British Empire at War, Research Group, Research Papers*, no. 5, 2014, http://britishempireatwar.org, viewed 23/08/2016.

Unpublished works

John Clinch (Commissioner), 'Written message in the program for the funeral of Colonel J. Palmer', 14 June 1994, in possession of Sonja I. Southwell.

List of the deceased 'POWs in Borneo' along with 'List of deceased POWs in Tarakan' and 'Missing in Tarakan', found among the possessions of Ryer L. van Kralingen with a note indicating he received these while living at Kramat 61, early on his return to Jakarta in 1947, now in possession of Sonja I. Southwell. This list was probably created by the Dutch Military, but it is likely that Ryer's own lists contributed to its development. His list is hand-annotated.

A.J.A.C. Nooteboom, 'Notes on the Banyu Biru Camps' in a diary found by Joost van Bodegom in the Netherlands in the 1980s, and mentioned in personal correspondence to the author in December 2017. Van Bodegom, as a nine-year-old, served as one of Nooteboom's orderlies in Banyu Biru 11.

Obituary presented at Commissioner Charles Durman's funeral, 25 April 1979, no author given, in possession of The Salvation Army Heritage Office, Melbourne.

Johanna Palmer (formerly Johanna van Kralingen, nee van Kapel), '"The beginning history of Kramat 55, Jakarta, in 1947" as told by Mrs Colonel J.F. Palmer–van Kralingen in 1980 to Colonel Melattie Brouwer', 1980, translated by and in possession of Sonja I Southwell.

William Parkinson, personal correspondence to Sonja I. Southwell, date unknown, in possession of Sonja I Southwell.

Sonja I. Southwell and Joan Stolk, recorded conversations, tapes and transcript in possession of Sonja I. Southwell. This conversation was recorded when Ian and Sonja Southwell visited Sonja's sister Joan, and her husband, George Stolk, in approximately 2003.

William Stolk, 'The Life and Ministry of Brigadier R.L. van Kralingen', an essay based on interviews with the Brigadier's widow, Mrs Johanna Palmer and her daughter, Mrs Johanna (Joan) Stolk, 1986, in possession of Sonja I. Southwell.

G. van Geffen, 'Funeral tribute for Brigadier Van Kralingen', February 1971, in possession of Sonja I. Southwell, Melbourne, Australia.

Cor van Kapel, letter to Johanna van Kralingen, 26 August 1946, translated by and in possession of Sonja I. Southwell.

Jan van Kapel, letter to his sister, Johanna van Kralingen, 2 February 1971, translated by and in possession of Sonja I. Southwell.

Jan van Kapel, letter to his niece, Sonja Southwell, 13 June 1971, translated by and in possession of Sonja I Southwell.

Jan van Kapel, essay written in connection with the 75th anniversary (7 June 1906–1981) of The Salvation Army Vlaardingen Corps, 1981, translated by and in possession of Sonja I. Southwell.

Johanna van Kralingen, 'Jo's Story', post-war essay, date unknown but possibly shortly after WWII and definitely before 1972, translated by and in possession of Sonja I. Southwell.

Johanna van Kralingen, handwritten notebook (c.1941–46).

Ryer L. van Kralingen, handwritten notes in Bible, in possession of Sonja I. Southwell.

Ryer L. van Kralingen, personal correspondence to Sonja I. van Kralingen (now Southwell), 20 May 1964, translated by and in possession of Sonja I. Southwell.

Ryer L. van Kralingen, 'Vermiste Personen te Tarakan "Borneo" oorlog met Japan 10–12 January 1942', personal war report to the Dutch Military on missing persons and burials on Tarakan (1942) and in Borneo (1942–45), date unknown but possibly 23 November 1945, when Van Kralingen made his official report. In possession of the Nederlands Institute voor Oorlog Documentatie (NIOD) – Netherlands Institute of War Documentation, Amsterdam, file number 001922.

Ryer L. van Kralingen, 'Report on Interrogation. 23rd November, 1945, "R.L. van Kralingen"', official war report to the Dutch Military, 23 November 1945, before the ensign 'Meindersma Robert' in charge of the investigation concerning war criminals and collaborators in the NEI, in possession of the Nederlands Institute voor Oorlog Documentatie (NIOD) [Netherlands Institute of War Documentation], Amsterdam, file number 067503.

Ryer L. van Kralingen, 'Poeroek-Tjahoe Kerkhof & Krygsgevangenen-Kerkhof' / 'Cemetery of Prisoners of War', scale 1 to 100, in possession of Sonja I. Southwell.

About The Author

Lieut-Colonel Sonja Southwell is the daughter of Dutch Salvation Army officer-missionaries and was born in Indonesia just prior to World War II before eventually moving with her parents to Australia in 1953. Prior to marriage to her husband, Ian, in 1967, she was a fully qualified nurse, midwife and infant welfare sister.

Subsequent to training as a Salvation Army officer herself, she served from 1969 till 2007 in pastoral, medical, officer training, administrative, women's ministries and leader development appointments in Zambia, the Philippines, Australia, Korea, China, the United Kingdom and some 19 other countries.

She has three adult daughters and three grandchildren. Following retirement in 2007, she is still involved in pastoral care, interchurch and other ministries on behalf of The Salvation Army in Melbourne, Australia.

Sonja is the co-author with Ian of a companion volume outlining their shared ministries around the world entitled *Safely Led to Serve: A Joint Biography* (Balboa Press, 2017).

A Safe Arrival

www.facebook.com/asafearrivalbook/